Play
Acoustic

Edited by

Dave Hunter

Play Acoustic

Edited by
Dave Hunter

A BACKBEAT BOOK
First edition 2005
Published by Backbeat Books
600 Harrison Street,
San Francisco, CA94107, US
www.backbeatbooks.com

An imprint of The Music Player Network United
Entertainment Media Inc.

Published for Backbeat Books by Outline Press Ltd,
2a Union Court, 20-22 Union Road, London, SW4 6JP, England.
www.backbeatuk.com

ISBN 0-87930-853-2

ART DIRECTOR: Nigel Osborne
EDITORIAL DIRECTOR: Tony Bacon
EDITOR: John Morrish
DESIGN: Paul Cooper Design

Origination by Solidity Graphics Ltd and printed by Colorprint Offset (Hong Kong)

05 06 07 08 09 5 4 3 2 1

Acoustic Guitar History

INTRODUCTION

From its distant roots as the unrespected accompaniment of travelling showmen, minstrels, gypsies, and troubadours, the guitar has grown to be the most played instrument in the world. And despite its death knell being sounded by electronic music just 25 years ago, the acoustic guitar in particular is enjoying an unprecedented boom in popularity. Players today are enjoying a renaissance in both musical styles and types of instrument, and better examples of both are available than ever before. The bulk of this book points you toward a range of playing styles that every fan of acoustic music will want to master, but it's also worth taking a detailed look at how the instrument itself came to be the versatile, emotive means of expression that we know it to be today.

The evolution of the acoustic guitar as most players know it is largely a tale of European craftsmanship transplanted to the New World, and influenced by the musical diversity of the great melting-pot. The instrument arrived fitted out for the needs of an antique music, and down the winding road of its next 150 years was adapted for the needs of everything from Civil War rally songs to slave spirituals, cowboy camp songs to dancehall jazz, and unplugged rock to fingerstyle virtuosity. Today's top instruments are certainly recognizable in the petite, hourglass-bodied, fiddlehead flat-top of the 1850s, but the guitar has come a long, long way, and is a better instrument today – and available in a far broader and more affordable range of makes and styles – than ever before in its history.

For many years, and for the vast majority of players, the guitar of yearning and desire could be summed up in a single word: Martin. A small handful of other makes helped to fill the short list of acoustic brands to aspire to, headed by Gibson and followed, in the early part of the century, by the likes of Washburn/Lyon & Healy and the Larson Brothers, or, later, by Guild or Ovation. In truth, the upmarket selections have always comprised a pretty narrow field (for archtop, this list has always begun with Gibson, running to Epiphone, Gretsch, D'Angelico and Stromberg in the classic years of the jazz box). The reality, however, was always that nine out of ten players would take home something from one of the 'budget' brands: a Harmony, Kay, or Regal in the old days, or a Yamaha, Aria, or Asian-made Washburn in the past few decades… while the Martins, Gibsons and Guilds remained the stuff of dreams.

Today there is both far more to dream about, and far more to get your hands on. While some players and collectors yearn for great vintage acoustics of German herringbone inlay and Brazilian rosewood, better guitars are being made than ever before, and for less money. The luthier's skill has been elevated in the achievements of a surprising number of top-notch artisan guitar-makers, and Martin and Gibson have had to make room for the likes of Santa Cruz, Bourgeois, Collings, Gallagher, Froggy Bottom and a dozen more builders of impressive breadth and talent. The likes of Taylor and Tacoma stride an impressive middle ground that blends handcrafted standards with mass-production efficiency and pricing. At the same time, and really since the early 1970s, a number of Asian imports have shown a maturity and consistency that let them rival much of what the USA and Europe has to offer. Brands like Takamine and Alvarez Yairi have proved themselves in both tonal achievements and professional endorsements.

Sure, the players still dream, but more frequently than ever reality lets them get their hands on an instrument that plays and sounds like nothing their fathers or grandfathers could have afforded. These are high times in the acoustic cafes, for sure,

MARTIN

Nevertheless, it all started with the small-bodied, gut-strung, flat-topped instruments of a German immigrant, Christian Friedrich Martin, who was building guitars almost from the time he arrived in New York in 1833. Aged 37, a skilled luthier who had completed a long apprenticeship at one of Europe's most respected guitar-makers – Stauffer, in Vienna – C.F. Martin came to the new world to escape the restrictive trade laws of his hometown of Markneukirchen, Saxony (now Germany, though formerly East Germany). He was hell-bent on making his mark on the young country's stringed instrument trade. He did that, and more. By the 1850s Martin was selling guitars designed along new lines that would revolutionise the performance of the instrument, and which are still echoed in the constructional details of the vast majority of flat-tops available today.

In the late 1830s, Martin had moved his family and his business to Cherry Hill, Pennsylvania, and eventually to nearby Nazareth, which has been Martin's famous address ever since (despite the relocation, however, guitars were still labelled as being made in New York until the end of the 1800s). From this time onwards, the maker's guitars came to look more like the great flat-tops they would eventually spawn, and less like the old-world minstrels' instruments that early 18th century European guitars may appear to us today to resemble. Martin simplified his styling considerably, dropping the superfluous ornamental woodwork and elaborate inlays on all but the occasional display or custom-order model, while inside he evolved constructional details that would pave the way for the modern instrument.

The move from rudimentary ladder bracing to the fanned bracing of Spanish 'classical' guitars of the time (about the only Spanish guitars, really) made his smaller instruments more toneful than most of anything else that was available, while the evolution of his X-braced tops on the larger guitars had a more complex impact on these models' capabilities. Although the full potential of the design would become fully realised only gradually, the sturdy crossed bracing format allowed both the braces and the guitar's top to be thinner and lighter, which in turn yielded more resonance and volume on the gut-strung guitars of the day. When Martin would evolve to predominantly steel-string production early in the next century, this X-bracing would be ready to take the strain without necessitating any tone-dampening thickening of the vibrating top or widening of the internal braces. This really was a design for the future, and one of the many ingredients that made Martin guitars, for many years, one of the most forward-looking makers in existence.

When we talk about the 'larger guitars' of the period, these are still small-bodied acoustics by today's standards. Martin's largest guitar of the 1850s was the 12¾"-wide Size 1, a width that most players today would expect to see in a little parlour guitar. Before the end of the decade, however, body sizes and decorative styles still in use today were being established. The larger Size 0 – one of the smallest standard Martins available today – was introduced and would remain the company's largest 'concert' guitar until the arrival of the 00 some 20 years later. Most models were available in a range of styles from 17 to 42, numbers that indicated their

OPPOSITE PAGE **In the beginning: a five-course guitar of about 1590, probably Portuguese.** TOP **A Stauffer-style guitar by C.F. Martin, from 1830.** BELOW **The early Martin family home and workshop in Cherry Hill, near Nazareth, Pennsylvania.**

wholesale prices at the time the system was established. They ranged from plain guitars with simple binding and few or no inlays, to guitars with fancier abalone purfling, position markers and rosettes, and included models with basic but elegant herringbone trim and snowflake inlays in between. Even at the upper level, however, Martin guitars were mostly simpler and more austere in decoration than some of the pearl-packed showpieces of other makers. The emphasis was always on sound and build quality, and C.F. Martin apparently saw excessively ornate decoration as potentially getting in the way of these more important goals (as do many of today's top makers of both flat-tops and archtops, it is worth noting). Once in place, the look of these numbered styles would see few changes for the following 90-odd years, until the impact of World War II eventually forced some changes of its own.

In the early part of the following century the notion of stringing guitars with steel started gaining popularity, but Martin was relatively slow to take up the trend. Before 1916 Martin manufactured the occasional custom-order guitar to take steel strings, but its first

such consistent production models came in the form of the 'K' series guitars (named for their koa wood construction) designed to be played in the lap-steel position, as used for the popular Hawaiian music of the time. In this way, the format that would become Martin's stock in trade grew from the fringes of the market – though a popular 'fringe' in the day – and in fact it would rise upward from the bottom, too. By the early 1920s Martin was offering steel strings on the lowliest of its standard 'Spanish' style guitars, the mahogany-bodied 2-17, and by the end of the decade steel strings had spread throughout the line as the standard dress.

For Martin, it was probably an easier conversion than for others, the sturdy X-bracing of the larger models being already primed to take the greater strain that the tension of steel strings would put on the guitars' tops and bridges – although certainly a considerable degree of adaptation was still required to make the new designs secure. Even so, on plenty of old guitars you can see the strain of the application of steel strings to a design that still had its

OPPOSITE PAGE LEFT TO RIGHT **Three early Martins: a 1-28 from c1820; a 0-42 from c1898; and a mahogany 2-17 from c1930, the first Martin to be offered with steel strings.**
LEFT **The Mound City Blues Blowers, featuring Eddie Lang on a Martin guitar.**

roots in the gentler pull of gut, in the form of a subtle arching, or 'bellying', around the area of the top just behind the bridge. Many newer guitars will exhibit the same symptoms, especially those with particularly thin tops and light bracing – but it's not necessarily a cause for concern. As Norman Blake put it, "Never trust a guitar without a belly." And while those steel strings may appear to test a guitar's structural integrity, they also get it wailing with a far throatier voice than anything gut could ever manage, and can particularly help those thin-topped, lightly-braced flat-tops sing sweetly indeed.

Having weathered both the mandolin and ukulele booms of the early part of the century, and in fact seen extra bursts of business in each craze that allowed the company to expand, Martin was entering its heyday in the 1930s with the guitar firmly at the centre of its business. While the financial pinch of the depression upon musicians unsurprisingly meant the lower-end models would remain the core of the business, the era saw a continually wider acceptance of the guitar as an instrument, while Martin itself honed both new and existing models into guitars that would become respected for all time.

Martin guitars were now settling into certain constructional and decorative standards that have remained famous among aficionados. While the most affordable models remained all-mahogany guitars, the next rung up now had a mahogany back and sides, mahogany neck, rosewood fingerboard and bridge, and a spruce top. Spruce was the standard throughout the range for this tonally crucial part of the instrument, but mid-range and upper models generally were made with rosewood back and sides partnered with an ebony bridge and fingerboard.

In addition to establishing certain standards, Martin also began to push the boundaries in crucial ways. For a time the 000 – just a mid-sized guitar by today's standards – had been the company's largest 'concert' model. Initially at the request of guitarist and banjo player Perry Bechtel, this was adapted at the end of the 1920s to carry a neck that joined the body at the 14th fret rather than at the 12th, as was previously the standard, which resulted in the 'Orchestra Model' or OM design. Over the next few years, this longer neck would become standard on most Martin models.

This evolution had also brought to life the largest yet of the Martins, although a 'non-Martin Martin' of significantly greater dimensions had existed for a few years already. In 1916 Martin had made a line of unusually large, thick-waisted, somewhat pear-shaped guitars at the request of instrument retailer the Oliver Ditson Company. These guitars, which approached 16″ across the lower bout, were dubbed 'Dreadnoughts' for their resemblance to the profile of the large British warships of the same name. While they were no raging success, orders were steady enough to prove the idea had some merit. In the late 1920s the Ditson company changed hands and ceased to order guitars from Martin, so Martin took up the flag itself, and by 1931 was offering D-1 and D-2 Dreadnoughts under its own name. At around the same time, country music was becoming big stuff both on radio and in large dancehalls across the country, and these large instruments were near-instant successes with many pros seeking the volume required to belt out this new music. Dreadnoughts quickly set the standard for both booming country rhythm guitar and speedy bluegrass flatpicking, and the body style grew to become the most popular acoustic shape of all.

Having proved their place in the market, these models finally appeared in the Martin catalogue in 1935, in the full standard range of Styles 18 to 42. In 1938 they were joined by the D-45 as a production model, a guitar nearly as elaborate as the abalone-encrusted 12-fret version of the same made for singing cowboy star Gene Autry five years before, minus the fancy engraved fingerboard. While these pearl wonders would become many a collector's greatest ambition, it was the humble D-18 that always achieved the greatest sales, and in fact the more workmanlike styles throughout the range have usually proved the most popular.

At the height of the big-band era of the 1930s and early 1940s, Martin flirted with archtops, which were proving so successful for Gibson, Epiphone, Gretsch and others. It seems the Martin company just never quite got the hang of the style, however, and models of the day look more like halfhearted adaptations of the flat-tops it was already doing so well with. When America entered World War II in 1942, the archtops were dropped, hand in hand with plenty of other changes.

This marks the end of the real glory days. Martin would not only survive the universal clampdowns that the war meant for American guitar-makers, but would thrive and remain the most respected acoustic brand the world over. The company would build some great guitars again after the war, too, but no model would again quite reach the epitome of its form – arguably until the historical reissues of the modern era sought to reproduce vintage models in precise detail.

Wartime restrictions in various forms hit Martin, and other makers, hard: steel could no longer be used for neck reinforcement, so the long-abandoned ebony reinforcement strips were reinstated; for the same reasons, only inferior tuners could be sourced; and abalone could no longer be obtained in the quantities needed for the elaborate trim required by Style 42 and 45 guitars. Also, Martin had obtained its delicate herringbone trim from Germany since at least the middle of the previous century, but once stocks had dried up it could no longer obtain further supplies from the fallen European nation after the war. And in a constructional change, a trend for using heavy gauge steel strings like those fitted to big archtops forced Martin to stop scalloping its tops' support braces in 1944, leaving them thicker and better able to support the strain of a whopping .014″ or .015″ set. With the heavy strings these were still loud guitars – when hit hard enough to get the entire shebang moving, that is – and the thicker braces did at least prevent excessive bellying and top distortion under tension. When many players returned to medium strings, however (which have become the more popular gauge for larger flat-tops over time), they found the post-war Martins didn't quite have the life, sparkle and resonance of their forebears.

OPPOSITE PAGE **A Martin deadnought of 1924, built for the retailer Ditson.** BELOW **Elvis Presley was a prominent Martin enthusiast.**

Although its roster was significantly reined in from that great design boom of the 1928-42 period, Martin continued to fare well with musicians once it – and the country – had recovered from the more immediate effects of the war years. A great number of country & western artists continued to set the pace on Martin Dreadnoughts, and the model's position as rhythm guitar mainstay carried over into rock'n'roll throughout the 1950s, thanks in no small part to Elvis Presley's early use of a D-18 and D-28. The folk boom of the late 1950s and early 1960s further boosted the sales of America's pre-eminent acoustic guitar-maker, and the increased business helped Martin to experiment once again with introducing new models.

Part of the folk ethos of the 1960s was a general embracing of simpler things – times, musical styles, guitars, what have you – and while Martin was the foremost brand of the movement, it was its models of 40 or 50 years or more earlier that were really the target of the folkies' longing. On the back of this craze, the company successfully introduced the austere 0-16NY and then 00-21NY (NY for 'New York', indicating guitars styled after the simple instruments produced under Martin's New York label in the 1800s), and reintroduced a number of other 12-fret models, not precise reissues as we know the term today, but guitars that captured some of the image of models of the 1920s and 1930s. Models such as the D-18S and D-28S, and other 00, 000 and OM types found favour with more than a few leaders of the folk scene – including the likes of Pete Yarrow and Tom Paxton – and the demand for these retro designs was secured. The mid-1960s also saw the

RIGHT **A Martin D-35 from 1968.** CENTRE **Tom Paxton, with his Dreadnought, epitomised the mid-1960s folk boom.** OPPOSITE PAGE **David Crosby and Graham Nash, shown in the Crosby Stills & Nash era, favoured a pair of D-45s.**

introduction of the D-35, with a return to lighter bracing and a three-piece rosewood back conceived as a way of combating a shortage of Brazilian rosewood planks wide enough for the making of traditional two-piece backs. Martin's grandest dreadnought even returned to the scene in 1968 with the relaunch of the D-45.

Having sold more than 22,000 guitars in 1971, Martin moved only around 8,000 units in 1978. A workers' strike of more than eight months in 1977 was no doubt partly responsible for this big dent in the company's production levels, but the acoustic market was certainly slowing. More pertinent for today's players – and guitar buyers – is the fact that it is universally agreed that the company's build quality was slipping throughout these years. Fans of the brand note this as one of the lowest ebbs in Martin's overall impressive achievement. At the start of the decade, Martin had added a rosewood plate beneath new guitars' bridges, and also increased the thickness of the ends of the top braces, all in an apparent bid to add further stability to the instruments' tops. The changes made 1970s Martins even more resistant to the problems of bridges pulling upward and tops distorting under the tension of heavier string gauges, but they also clamped their voices considerably, and plenty of players noticed a certain constipated sound and feel in new examples of the day.

Another factor, one that Martin could do nothing about, drew a line under the collectability of guitars from 1970 onward in many people's eyes. An embargo imposed upon exports of whole logs of Brazilian rosewood in 1969 found most makers, Martin included, turning to Indian rosewood for their guitar backs, sides and fingerboards. Few players would have noted it at the time – and in fact relatively few at any time could realistically identify any great sonic difference between the two types – but Brazilian rosewood has become another indication of collectability in a vintage guitar.

Amid this general decline, Martin did at least one thing right. In 1976, for the first time in 30 years, players could once again lay their hands on a gorgeous herringbone-trimmed Martin in the form of the HD-28. Its instant

success showed that many players were more interested in looking backward than forward when it came to acoustic design and trim, and – after a few years of readjustment and recovery – the reissues programme would be one of the company's more successful business strategies.

Not to say Martin got there all at once, and the recovery was indeed pretty tough going for a few years. In 1982 the company shipped only around 3,000 guitars, less than 15 per cent of its achievement of just 11 years previous. This was pretty much the bottom; there was nowhere to go but up, and fortunately this is where Martin was gradually headed. The rest of the decade offered more hard times, but there were also lessons learned that eventually saw a stronger Martin entering the 1990s.

The company had experimented with new styles in 1981 in the form of a series of cutaway flat-tops, which a number of competitors had offered for years, and although these didn't catch on terribly well, they opened the door for more contemporary Martin designs to come. Also, a Custom Shop programme, started in 1979, further reinforced the thinking that more players were interested in old Martins than in new ones, with orders coming fast and thick for guitars made with features that had been abandoned for many decades. These were just a trickle compared to the standard production models, but once again they indicated a way forward. Along with homing in on two strands of thinking – a pursuit of the new, bounded by a retrieval of the old – a reorganisation of the executive ranks helped position Martin to compete with the synthesiser revolution. Frank Herbert Martin departed as president but his father, C.F. Martin III, remained as chairman of the board, and his son, C.F. Martin IV (known as Chris), was soon voted in as vice president. In the hands of a fifth generation Martin, the company was pulling itself together to move on.

Martin's fortunes had improved by the early 1990s, thanks to both the combined successes of some new standard and limited edition Custom Shop models, and to the surprising uptake of the Mexican-made Martin Backpacker travel guitars introduced at the start of the decade. But there was more competition in the wings, too. While acoustic guitars were enjoying a renewed popularity, large bites of that cherry were being taken by more affordable but still high-quality guitars from the likes of Taylor, Takamine, and others. The plain 16 Series guitar offered a Martin at the lower end

ABOVE **Chris Martin of Coldplay with a cutaway acoustic-electric Martin in mahogany.** OPPOSITE PAGE **A Gibson Style O from 1905.**

of the upscale market, but that still meant a high-end price tag as far as many players' budgets were concerned. Martin's reply to the price war came in 1993 in the form of the D-1, a simple but elegant-looking Dreadnought. It saved costs by employing laminated sides – though with a solid spruce top and mahogany back – and less labour-intensive catalysed finish and mortise and tenon neck joint, in contrast to the traditional Martins' nitrocellulose lacquer finish and dovetail neck joint. The differences in both construction and materials knocked a big chunk off even the D-16's price tag, and players took up the new, more affordable Martin in their droves.

A year later Martin homed in on a new twist on the reissues game, by marketing vintage-styled or custom-designed models under famous artists' names and calling them 'Signature Edition' guitars. The new angle provided limited runs of what were often extremely precise and sometimes also custom-modded upmarket Martin reissues, and used the star player associations to nudge pricing up a notch or two further than even a standard reissue might command. The line began with an elaborate Gene Autry D-45, and progressed to include an Eric Clapton 000-42 EC, a Marty Stuart HD-40MS, Jimmie Rodgers 000-45JR, Joan Baez 0-45JB, Martin Carthy 000-18MC, two Paul Simon models (the OM-42PS and more affordable PS2), and many, many more – with new Signature artists announced twice yearly to this day.

The perpetual interest in old Martins was further consolidated in 1996, when the sporadic 'vintage reissue' type models offered through the years were given an official line as the Vintage Series. Over the next few years pre-war features such as vintage style tuners, V-shaped necks, aged-look lacquer, and – where appropriate – herringbone trim appeared on models such as the HD-28V, OM-28V, 000-28VS and HD-28VS (both with 12-fret necks), D-18V, OM-18V, 00-18V, and 000-28EC (a less fancy Eric Clapton model, this time a production Vintage Series guitar rather than a limited Signature Edition). Others would follow through the years, and the series would become hugely popular with players, and an enormous success for Martin.

As the end of the century approached, Martin expanded at both low and high ends. A broader range of both 1 and 16 Series guitars was offered, joined by the spartan Road Series guitars with laminated sides and backs, the all-mahogany 15 Series, and eventually the even less expensive X Series models built with tops of composite wood fibre. Meanwhile, further Vintage Series and Signature Edition guitars were added, joined by the acclaimed Golden Era vintage-precise models, which included not only tops made of long-scarce Adirondack spruce, but Brazilian rosewood backs and sides on models in Style 28 and 45 – the first time such could be found on a Martin in any numbers for some 27 years.

Having filled only around 3,000 orders in 1982, and not many more per year through the middle part of that decade, Martin built more than 280,000 guitars through the course of the 1990s. In the new millennium, the company's success appears to be continuing apace, and – while the competition in both high-end and well-made student level guitars is fiercer than ever – this 168-year-old company finally seems comfortable and confident at nearly every level of the market. Players in their thousands still dream of one day strumming a Martin guitar – and more of them are able to achieve that dream today than ever before.

GIBSON

Where Martin has continually failed to electrify, Gibson has become even better known for its classic electric guitars than for its acoustics. But this fellow survivor from the 19th century has occasionally rivalled Martin in the flat-top business, and entirely dominated the acoustic archtop market during the years of that instrument's heyday. No surprise, really, when you consider that founder Orville Gibson actually invented the archtop guitar, and the company that carried on his name brought the format to its zenith in designs of the 1920s and 1930s.

Despite its substantial legacy, Gibson is a couple of generations younger than Martin. Orville Gibson was born in Chateaugay, New York, in 1856 when C.F. Martin was already setting the pace for the X-braced flat-tops of the future in his New York City and then Pennsylvania workshops. After moving to Kalamazoo, Michigan, in the 1880s, however, Gibson pursued an entirely different course of acoustic instrument design, one far more influenced by the great violinmakers than by the new directions in large fretted instruments that were already proving successful with the makers that would become his rivals.

Gibson hand-carved his mandolin and guitar tops and backs into an arched shape from two centre-joined planks of solid wood – spruce for the tops, usually walnut for the backs and sides. The carved arch formed an inherently strong structure for these

ABOVE **Big Bill Broonzy with a later Style O, now featuring a cutaway, effectively the first of its kind.** OPPOSITE PAGE TOP **Eddie Lang and his Gibson L5, with Seger Ellis and his Embassy Orchestra.** OPPOSITE PAGE RIGHT **A Gibson L Artist model from 1906.**

soundboards, so that bracing could be kept to a minimum and not overly impede acoustic vibrations. In another crucial difference from the flat-tops of the day, these archtop guitars were also fitted right from the start with steel strings such as Gibson was using on his mandolins (far and away the most popular fretted instruments of the day, as they would remain for a couple of decades more). These Gibson guitars carried round or oval holes, so from the front weren't radically different looking instruments, but on close examination their design and construction differed from popular flat-tops in almost every detail.

The archtop guitars exhibited a slightly darker and warmer but more precise voice than the bright, lively, but potentially boomy flat-tops, but when taken to the size of many of Gibson's early creations – which reached some 18″ across the lower bout, nearly 4″ broader than almost anything from Martin, Washburn, or other significant makers – they became impressively loud instruments for their day. The steel strings, body dimensions and resultant volume of 'The Gibson' guitars set the standards for professional instruments that needed to be heard amid a crowded bandstand in the days before amplification, and this carried through into the jazz era, when Gibson archtops entered their golden age. Together, these factors gave Gibson a prominent lead in a corner of the guitar market that was barely threatened by another maker for a good four or five decades.

Not long after attaining his first significant success as a maker, Orville Gibson parted ways with the company that would carry his name on into the future. In 1902, with Gibson himself unable to meet the demand for his instruments, a consortium of music store owners and lawyers bought up the rights to his name and formed the Gibson Mandolin-Guitar Manufacturing Company Ltd, retaining Orville merely as a consultant. This relationship was short-lived, and he soon parted ways with the new operation. He retained a shareholding in the company until his death in 1918, but had no further hands-on influence on the guitars that bore his name.

The new company ramped up production, offering two lines of guitars in three sizes and a range of decorative styles, the round-holed Style O and oval-holed Style L. Tops continued to be carved from solid spruce – the most popular wood for both quality archtop and flat-top guitars to this day – and the backs and sides were still of walnut (though, oddly, this was publicised as being maple). Gibson soon changed to backs and sides of birch, and finally settled on actual maple in the late 1920s, and this remains the pre-eminent wood for the backs and sides of archtop guitars. While the carved, arched spruce top exhibits an inherently warm, rounded tonality, maple's voice is tighter, brighter, and more defined. Together, they offer a full, rich sound with good note definition, which – partnered with the impressive volume of the larger Gibsons – proved just the qualities that many professional musicians were seeking.

Although Orville Gibson had invented the archtop guitar, he hadn't come close to perfecting it. His own designs incorporated an integral bridge with strings anchored behind the saddle piece in the same wooden plate, as on traditional flat-tops, and a fairly shallow neck pitch to allow an acceptably low string height over the length of the fingerboard. Having taking his carved-arch designs from the world of violin-making, it is surprising

upon consideration that he didn't follow this format further, employing the separate bridge and tailpiece arrangement of those instruments, coupled to a more sharply back-angled neck to achieve the necessary break angle of strings over bridge. Soon, his successors were doing just that, and thanks to the increased downward pressure of the strings on the bridge, and thus the top – a pressure required to really get a sturdy arched top moving – Gibsons were becoming even louder and more toneful guitars, even though most of the largest models settled in at around 16″ rather than the massive 18″ of some of Orville Gibson's early creations.

While the mandolin was still Gibson's most popular product, the company quickly realised many advances in guitar design that wouldn't be fully appreciated until many years later. Partnering what might be seen as an elaborately superfluous decorative element, a carved scroll-like 'horn' at the upper bass bout of some fancy Style O guitars of 1908 and after, was an extremely practical, even ingenious recession of the treble bout at the other side of the neck end. This was the first commonly seen 'cutaway' design – allowing players an unprecedented reach up to the 15th fret. Production cutaway designs wouldn't reappear until later in the 1930s. But in 1912, just a few years after this Style O, another Gibson design, the L-4, introduced a look that is echoed far more in archtops down the years than anything previously produced by Gibson (although it still carried the oval hole of the day rather than f-holes – this despite its L Series tag alongside the round-holed models). This 16″ guitar had a more symmetrical body shape and a plainer dress, and appealed to players who were coming to appreciate the functional over the fanciful.

The first Gibson-made flat-top guitar arrived in the late 1910s, in the form of the cheap and basic 'Army Navy' model, which was aimed primarily at servicemen stationed on duty at the close of World War I. But these are a mere footnote in the company's

A custom-built Gibson 'Nick Lucas', with 'Florentine' decoration, from 1928. Lucas was a popular crooner and guitarist of the day, famous for 'Tip-Toe Through The Tulips'.

history today; a far more significant development of around the same time was Gibson managers' hiring of mandolin virtuoso and design dabbler Lloyd Loar in a bid to revive the fading mandolin craze. Loar went some way toward doing that with his refined creations (his F-5 mandolin is widely considered the finest such instrument ever made), but this little eight-stringed instrument's era was still on the wane. More significant to any history of the acoustic guitar is Loar's development of the L-5 guitar of 1922, originally conceived as the largest member of the new mandolin line, but soon put forward as a Gibson flagship in its own right.

By employing a pair of f-holes in place of the L-4's oval soundhole, the L-5 took the archtop guitar yet another step towards the violin that had inspired Orville Gibson nearly 40 years before, and it incorporated other refinements besides. A new tone-bar bracing system, featuring two parallel braces running under the top from body end to neck joint, offered a livelier response; a floating, height-adjustable bridge allowed players to determine both string length and height, for optimum (well, nearly) intonation and action; and a radical new adjustable truss-rod allowed, for the first time, player adjustment of neck bow. These new Gibsons were the most fine-tunable, precision-adjustable guitars ever made, and in the new gently graduated 'Cremona brown' sunburst finish, they looked the business, too.

Pros like Eddie Lang and Fred Guy were already playing L-4s, and these and many others took up the advanced new L-5 in droves. While Gibson was fast establishing itself as the brand of choice in the jazz world, the guitar as an instrument still didn't have enough popularity to keep the company afloat, so mandolins, Hawaiian guitars, and banjos (never a Gibson strong suit) also helped to pay the bills.

As its archtops settled in as the market leader, Gibson bowed to another burgeoning market and released its first 'proper' flat-top guitar in 1926 in the form of the simple, now arch-less L-1. The company still clearly didn't believe in the virtue of the flat-top as a serious instrument – as the L-1's rigid cross bracing and lack of a truss-rod make clear – but servicemen, college students, blues belters, and even a few country and cowboy singers were playing these flat-tops, so Gibson must have thought it had better jump on the bandwagon. Just two years later Gibson accepted that a quality flat-top was a viable product, and signed up Nick Lucas, the first recorded guitar star, as a signature artist. The Nick Lucas model debuted with the same body size and shape as the L-1, but was significantly deeper, so produced a rich, loud sound for its size. This guitar reached its epitome in 1933, with a slightly larger and still quite deep body, a 14-fret neck, and back and sides of solid rosewood.

Although the company was struggling, like so many other guitar-makers, merely to survive the Great Depression – and achieving this partly by making ultra-cheap Kalamazoo-branded guitars and even wooden toys – the early to mid-1930s proved a time of major development, in design terms at least. In 1934, no doubt partly in response to competition from newcomer Epiphone, Gibson boldly 'advanced' the bodies of the four largest of its six-strong archtop range from 16″ to 17″. This made the cutting maple-bodied archtops even louder and better able to compete in the volume wars on the bandstand.

For a time the two companies chased each other: Epiphone 'advanced' its body sizes, and Gibson pushed the envelope even further by returning to the mammoth 18″ body size occasionally seen way back in the 1890s, and introduced the superb, high-end Super 400. So it went… until Gibson trumped the bid once and for all with its Premier models of 1939: L-5 and Super 400 guitars

18

with rounded cutaways, and available in an optional natural (blonde) finish. In 1957 Gibson would win this battle hands down by purchasing Epiphone, but for now the company had maintained its position as leading archtop-maker by virtue of design and quality.

Meanwhile, Gibson's most serious and long-lasting foray into the flat-top market had come in 1934 with the introduction of the round-shouldered dreadnought shaped Jumbo, with a 16″ lower bout. This one model was replaced by two in 1936, the J-35 and the Advanced Jumbo. Each carried the same body shape and 16″ width, but the latter featured rosewood back and sides for the first time on any Gibson, making it as rich as it was loud. All the while, the company was having reasonable success with its smaller L-1, L-0 and L-00 flat-tops, but its most striking model of the breed came in 1937 in the form of a custom instrument originally made for singing cowboy Ray Whitley (no doubt a response to Martin's coup with the Gene Autry D-45). This 17″ flat-top had rounded bouts that made it more curvaceous than the thick-wasted Dreadnought look, and was a striking instrument on stage. Production models were introduced as the Super Jumbo, later Super Jumbo 200 or merely SJ-200. Made with rosewood back and sides before the war, and maple after, this guitar proved the only real rival to Martin's D-45 as the instrument that declared a country singer had made it. Through the years the two rivals would seek to outdo each other in pearl trim and fancy script fingerboard name inlays as the custom orders rolled in from one country & western star or another.

World War II slowed Gibson's production, but didn't halt it entirely as it did that of some other makers. Steel shortages required guitars to be built without truss-rods, but Gibson introduced several new models nonetheless, notably the J-45, J-50, and Southern Jumbo. With guitar amplification now firmly entrenched as the gigging guitarist's saviour, the era of the great acoustic archtops was over (no such beast would ever surpass the whopping Super 400 in the company's catalogue), and Gibson's own examples of the breed were emerging more and more often as factory-spec electric models carrying one or two built-in or floating pickups. The company had segued relatively smoothly into flat-top production, and its position as a market leader rarely seemed in any great danger. In 1944 Gibson was taken over by the huge Chicago Musical Instruments corporation (CMI), but this did little to disrupt the flow.

 Post-war introductions came only in dribbles, and included the J-185, in appearance very much a smaller 16″ version of the SJ-200 (which was now simply the J-200), the CJ-100 with pointed cutaway and optional pickup, and J-160 with standard pickup – a lame performer as an acoustic, but made famous for its use by The Beatles on many early recordings. A maple-bodied Dreadnought called the Dove arrived in the early 1960s, followed by the Hummingbird, and an Everly Brothers signature model with the rounded contours of a J-185. Sales of Gibson's Jumbos and smaller L Series flat-tops (now 'LG' for 'little guitar') ticked along nicely, but just when Martin was capitalizing on the folk boom of the late 1950s and early 1960s, Gibson executives decided to 'upgrade' many models in ways that would ultimately only make them less desirable both to players and collectors. This seemingly pointless decline in design integrity persisted through much of the next three decades.

It is worth noting that Gibson archtops were made to a range of scale-lengths, some to what is commonly considered the 'full length' 25½″ of the Martin standard (some even a little longer), and some quite a bit shorter. For its flat-tops, however, the company settled in on a 24⅝″ scale-length (not quite the 24¾″ that is usually quoted), which offers a slightly easier playing feel than the longer string length of Martin and many others, but with a little less power and volume, all else being equal, and sometimes a touch less harmonic sparkle as well.

A height-adjustable bridge fitted to many flat-tops in 1957 served mainly just to deaden

these instruments' tonal response, while other efforts to strengthen tops further choked off acoustic resonance. In a strange parallel to Martin's ill-advised introduction of heavier bracing and a reinforcing rosewood bridge plate in 1970, Gibson – under new owners Ecuadorian Company Ltd (ECL), soon renamed Norlin – began doubling its X-bracing in 1971 to create sturdier, but tonally dead soundboards. Quality declined rapidly in the late 1960s and 1970s, along with the company's reputation as an acoustic maker. Noble but misguided efforts to redesign the Gibson flat-top in 1977 in the form of the Mark Series fizzled. Certainly the quality of Gibson electrics suffered too under Norlin in the 1970s and early 1980s, but the regime nearly snuffed out the company's great acoustic legacy entirely.

Norlin had opened offices in Nashville, Tennessee, in 1970, followed by some manufacturing facilities in 1974. In 1984 Gibson production left the Kalamazoo plant entirely. By this time, however, Norlin was running into difficulties, and Gibson soon went the way of other musical instrument divisions the company had been selling off. Rather than heralding the death of the 100-year-old brand, the change probably spared Gibson acoustics. A team of friends who had met at Harvard Business School applied their studies to the ailing company, trimmed and refined it, and were soon seeing a profit. In 1987 they bought the Flatiron mandolin company in Belgrade, Montana, and transplanted many of its skilled makers to a new Gibson acoustic guitar plant opened in nearby Bozeman soon after that. Bozeman, Montana, was even further from Kalamazoo than Nashville, but the opening of this facility marked the salvation of Gibson acoustics, and soon the finest such instruments in 30 or 40 years were coming out of the new western workshops.

In the early 1990s innovative Star and Starburst cutaway models in fully acoustic and electro-acoustic variations showed that Gibson could indeed apply its name to technologically advanced acoustic guitars, while a rosewood-bodied J-60 Dreadnought and the affordable Working Man series offered competition at both ends of the 'quality' price bracket. Meanwhile, the greatest renewed interest in 'new' Gibson acoustics was offered to precisely detailed reissues along the lines of the J-45, J-200, Blues King (a revised L-00), Nick Lucas and a stream of others. This revision of past glories even grew confident enough to include the return of two models of a type many players probably thought they'd never see again: fully acoustic archtops. In 1995, the Nashville Custom Shop brought out a reissue of the 1934 L-5, which was followed in 2003 by an L-7 cutaway from the Bozeman factory.

Gibson's renewed success in the acoustic market is nothing like Martin's rejuvenation at the end of the last century, but has brought a number of great models back from the brink, and offered some good-sounding new designs besides. And of course the acoustic branch is only a portion of the efforts of a company that has increasingly concentrated on the electric market since the dawn of amplification, and certainly since the arrival of the first Les Paul model in 1952. Even so, if the quality continues to reach the standards achieved in Bozeman over the past 10 years, Gibson acoustics should be here to stay.

OPPOSITE PAGE LEFT **An SJ-200 Custom model, built in 1937 for country artist Ray Whitley.** OPPOSITE PAGE TOP **The Everly Brothers in 1963, with a pair of J-200s.** BELOW **Sheryl Crow with her prized 1962 Country Western.**

THE CHICAGO MAKERS

Even with Martin located in Nazareth, Pennsylvania, and Gibson in Kalamazoo, Michigan, the centre of the American guitar industry in the early to mid-1900s was Chicago, Illinois, in mass manufacturing terms at least. And although no detailed records exist to back up such a claim, it's a fair bet to say that more guitars were made in Chicago between around 1890 and 1960 than in the rest of the country combined – if not the rest of the world. Some of the names will not sound familiar to players of today who haven't yet dabbled in the history of the instrument, but giants like Harmony, Kay, Washburn and parent company Lyon & Healy, the Larson Brothers, and Regal combined to make the Windy City a veritable clearing house for the burgeoning six-string. During this great midwestern city's boom years there might still have been more cattle in Chicago than guitars, but it wasn't for want of trying.

Washburn is known today as a quality Asian-made brand, but from the 1880s to the 1920s guitars bearing the George Washburn label and other brands of the Lyon & Healy company formed Martin's biggest rival in the quality flat-top market. They also provided many more affordable instruments to buyers with shallower pockets. The company was founded by former Ditson reps George Washburn Lyon and Patrick Healy in the late 1860s, initially to retail instruments bought in from other makers, but by the early 1880s was offering guitars and other items manufactured at its own new facility.

Washburns were never as well made as Martins; they were extremely late with most models in moving from cross-bracing (also known as 'ladder' bracing) to the strong yet musical X-bracing pattern, and made a virtue of their factory-built origins versus Martin's hand craftsmanship. But they were better guitars than many others of the day, and they came in a range of current shapes and decorative styles that could equally lure any player who wasn't aware of the fine points of acoustic construction.

Outwardly, most early Washburns bore a resemblance to the popular Martins, too, which were clearly seen as design leaders even 120 years ago. They were mainly small-bodied instruments with rounded lower bouts, narrow waists, and proportionally narrow shoulders of the styles ranging from what we would today consider 'parlour guitars' to 00 or smaller 'concert'-sized guitars, and were often made from good stocks of solid spruce and Brazilian rosewood. Some collectors today get excited about highly decorative early Washburns such as the Grand Concert model 309, with elaborate fingerboard inlays of pearl and silver, but the vast majority of the maker's instruments were simpler affairs that could be sold across the country in general stores, music shops, teaching studios and via catalogue houses for far less than the 309's lofty $155 retail price.

Models in familiar plainer styles and small to medium sizes were Washburn's stock in trade through the brand's first era, and were also the main offerings of other Lyon & Healy brands such as College Line, Jupiter, Lakeside and American Conservatory, although a few forward-looking larger instruments were occasionally offered, such as the 15″ wide Washburn Contra Bass of 1889 (with a 27½″ scale-length), or the jumbo-sized Lakeside Bass Guitar of 1912, which beat the Martin/Ditson Dreadnought to the market by four years, and was a little larger besides. These were fringe efforts, however, and never caught on in any numbers.

Washburn's model offerings were trimmed down after World War I, and were generally less elaborate besides, but the quality of these guitars increased if anything, thanks largely to a wider employment of the X-bracing that had been a Martin standard for more than 50 years by then, a move which also made them easily adaptable to the newly popular steel strings. Players and collectors alike are occasionally thrilled to discover a top Washburn model of the 1920s that easily rivals a Martin 0-18 or 00-28 for sound, construction quality and materials, but sells for a fraction of the price.

In the late 1920s the Washburn brand underwent a number of ownership and managerial changes, and this generally marks the end of the great first era of the American-made guitars. J.R. Stewart bought Lyon & Healy's manufacturing facility in 1928. Although L&H continued for a time to market the guitars, it sold off its entire distribution business to Chicago's Tonk Brothers just a year later. Tonk marketed J.R. Stewart-built Washburns until the onset of the Great Depression sent that manufacturer out of business, then farmed out guitar production to the rather more downmarket Regal. Regal was founded in Indianapolis in 1896 and moved to Chicago in 1904, after which it was purchased by an expanding Lyon & Healy. Through the years that followed, however, it maintained a line totally separate to L&H's Washburn guitars, and Regal was again a separate entity from that rapidly dissolving company by the time it took on the building of Washburn-branded guitars for Tonk Brothers.

Regal guitars were marketed under a wide range of other names (including many other Tonk Brothers brands, Bacon & Day, Slingerland, Recording King and others), and were mostly workmanlike but well-built instruments. Even prior to 1930 they rarely stretched to the quality of the better Washburns – nor certainly anything like what Martin was turning out – but were nevertheless solid, playable, good value guitars made with all solid woods, and popular with a wide range of students and shallow-pocketed professionals alike.

Regal-built Washburns weren't bad guitars as such, but were generally lesser instruments than they had been throughout most of the make's preceding history. Having swelled to massive proportions by the late 1930s, Regal suffered badly during the war years and emerged mainly offering downmarket flat-tops and archtops. Washburn-branded guitars had continued to slip down the quality scales and vanished in all but name at the outset of WWII, while their manufacturer of some ten years didn't survive much past it.

In 1974 Beckman Musical Industries of Los Angeles purchased the rights to the Washburn name and applied it to a range of basic Japanese imports. But the brand was soon passed back to Chicago, and in the hands of a small company called Fretted Instruments (later Washburn International) began to ascend the quality scales once again, with better and better imports coming in from Japan through the 1980s and into the 1990s and beyond. Guitars in the Festival Series, Native American Series, and the wide-ranging D series of Dreadnoughts have contained respected models, including the likes of the D-61 'Wildwood' with a solid spruce top, all solid rosewood back and sides, and ebony bridge and fingerboard.

Harmony was founded in Chicago in 1892 by yet another German immigrant, Wilhelm J.F. Schultz, and soon after that began the association with the growing Sears catalogue and

OPPOSITE PAGE **A Lyon & Healy Washburn Style 108 from 1892.**
BELOW **A Harmony Monterey from 1948** BOTTOM **Harmony's catalogue from 1959.**

department store company that enabled it to grow into the world's largest manufacturer of guitars. The build quality of Harmony instruments rarely matched those of Gibson or Martin, or even of Washburn's more elevated models, but they were generally much better than their later reputation might lead you to believe today. Harmony was building guitars for steel strings as early as 1899; Gene Autry, Roy Smeck, and Bradley Kinkaid numbered among its endorsement artists; and until the passing of the brand in the mid-1970s to a 'rebadging' importer selling Korean-made instruments, all its American-made acoustics were constructed of all solid woods. On top of all this, Harmony had the pricing that enabled it to land guitars in the hands of players that Gibson or Martin just couldn't reach.

The Hawaiian music craze of the 1910s and 1920s provided one of Harmony's first big sales booms, and the Supertone brand name – acquired by Harmony in 1916 – was a mainstay of budget and mid-range instruments in that genre for years. All-koa and all-mahogany Hawaiian guitars appeared under the Supertone brand, and the name shifted to a range of other Harmony models over the years. Other popular Harmony trademarks would include the Vagabond and Patrician flat-tops and Cremona archtops of the early 1930s, the Vogue, Monterey and Marquise lines of the late 1930s, the budget Stellas of the late 1930s and early 1940s, and the unusual aluminium-trimmed Holiday Colorama series of the 1950s. And in an unusual lateral shift, the seemingly ubiquitous Sovereign Dreadnoughts of Harmony's later years had acquired their name from a series of resonator guitars of the 1930s. Increasingly cheap and well-made Japanese imports of the early 1970s offered competition that Harmony just couldn't fight. Sales fell away, and in 1976 the name was sold off. It has changed hands a few times since, only to appear on various ranges of Asian import, never with any lasting success in the market.

The Stella name had, along with the Sovereign brand, been a standby of the Oscar Schmidt company of Jersey City, New Jersey, which was also a Sears supplier from the early 1900s until the sale of its guitar factory in 1935, which resulted in the names being acquired by Harmony in 1938. Oscar Schmidt was a respected maker, much in the Washburn-Harmony range, that had been manufacturing stringed instruments since 1879. Some of the company's parlour guitars of the early 20th century were decent enough instruments, but never attained the fame of the generally less well-built – but larger, and louder – Stella models such as the 12-string guitar famously played by Huddie 'Leadbelly' Ledbetter, and the six- and 12-strings played by Blind Willie McTell, Charlie Patton, Blind Blake and many others. None of the Oscar Schmidt-made guitars have achieved A-list (or even B-list, perhaps) status with players or collectors, but these Stellas have risen above the crowd – C-list at least – thanks to their classic acoustic blues associations.

For decades, Kay was slugging it out nearly blow for blow with Chicago budget rival Harmony, and never achieved quite the same sales numbers, but made a mighty dent in the market nonetheless. If anything, though, the brand probably achieved a slightly better reputation for quality during much of its 80-plus-year run as an American instrument-maker, although from as early as the 1920s construction of some of the company's guitars often included the use of durable laminates rather than the solid woods that Harmony universally employed. The Kay name itself, however, only came about in the 1920s when Henry Kay Kuhrmeyer joined the Stromberg-Voisinet Company, which had evolved out of the Groeshl company founded in Chicago in 1890. (Note that that Stromberg-Voisinet was a completely different company from the Stromberg that made high-end archtop guitars.)

A range of jumbo flat-tops appeared around 1926 under the Kay Kraft name, and by the early 1930s the success of the brand had inspired a company name change to Kay Musical Instrument Company. By the late 1930s Kay was well established as a brand name in itself. Despite the depression, the 1930s were a big time for Kay in a number of ways: the company offered everything from high-end archtops with carved spruce tops to budget-line Hawaiian and Spanish guitars for the Oahu company. Between the war years and the early 1960s, Kay archtops were often the next choice down from top-range makes like Gibson, Epiphone, Stromberg or Gretsch, while a range of flat-tops continued to fill student and novice needs. In 1967 Kay was sold to Valco, the large electric guitar, amplifier and resonator manufacturer and together these great Chicago manufacturers folded in 1968.

THE NEW YORKERS

Through the middle 60 years of the 20th century, another pair of American guitar manufacturers managed occasionally to knock on Gibson's and Martin's doors in terms of quality and reputation and steal more than a few customers from both of these great makers. These manufacturers succeeded each other in the same factory. From the 1930s to the mid-1950s, Epiphone proved a rival mainly to Gibson, excelling in quality archtops in particular; in 1953, a fledgling guitar company named Guild took over Epiphone's former New York factory, and achieved surprising success with each of the three very different popular types of acoustics: classical, archtop and flat-top.

The Epiphone company's roots stretch back to Anastasios Stathopoulo's fiddle and lute

The Five Spirits of Rhythm, featuring Teddy Bunn on the Epiphone Deluxe Masterbilt guitar.

workshop in 1870s Turkey. He brought the business to New York in 1903, and his son Epaminondas – known as 'Epi' – took over upon his death in 1915. In 1928 the House Of Stathopoulo changed its name to the Epiphone Banjo Company on the back of its success in that market following World War I, but it soon grew to be a top maker of acoustic and eventually electric archtop guitars – and remained so through the years when this instrument was king of the six-strings.

Epiphone seemed to be almost eternally following Gibson, and its designs were usually not far off those of the inventor and acknowledged premier maker of such instruments. But the New York company's growing list of star players soon indicated that many were willing to choose an Epi over a Gibson. Over the years, Epiphone archtops would be played, mostly in their electric form, by Al Caiola, Joe Pass, George Van Eps, Tony Mottola, Harry Volpe and many others.

When Epiphone moved from banjos to guitars, the assault on Gibson's dominance came in a big way. The Masterbilt line of 1931 carried seven models, all with carved arched top and back, and the largest – the Deluxe, Triumph and Spartan – were nearly half an inch bigger than Gibson's largest model of the day, with lesser models such as the Blackstone offering midpriced options further down the market. As described in the Gibson section above, the companies slugged it out throughout the decade. In 1936 Epiphone introduced the impressive 18½″ wide Emperor, which soon became a popular top-notch pros' choice, and by the next year had upped the size on its next three biggies by another inch. Epiphone's famous Frequensator tailpiece arrived in 1939, and many models became available in blonde in 1940-41. All of the upper-range models of this period were made to very high standards.

Early period Epi flat-tops aren't remembered as well as are the archtops, but the company made some fine models. The FT Deluxe of 1939-42 and FT210 Deluxe Cutaway of the early 1950s are excellent large flat-tops made in roughly 'jumbo' and 'super-jumbo' styles respectively, although the Frontier and Texan of the 1940s and early 1950s – while perfectly decent guitars – aren't nearly as sought-after by players or collectors. Epiphone's 'golden era' really mirrored that of the archtop itself, and when these guitars' popularity waned, so did Epiphones' fortunes.

The company had success with some electric versions of its acoustic archtops, but labour disputes and the inability of a new owner to overcome them (or to offer any further competition to Gibson and the others) finally did in the name as an independent entity. C.G. Conn purchased Epiphone in 1953, and transferred production to Philadelphia until 1955 (when the Stathopoulos took over again) to get away from troubles with the New York workforce. In 1957, Gibson parent company CMI purchased Epiphone and moved production to Kalamazoo, where the brand appeared mainly on more affordable variations of existing Gibson acoustic and electric designs, which did remain US-built until 1969. Today, the name resides somewhat further downmarket, gracing 'budget' Asian-made versions of Gibson models, which have served to give players who might never afford the originals a form of access to a few classic Gibson flat-top models, as well as to some newer designs. Meanwhile, however, Epiphone's abandoned New York factory had given birth to another great American guitar name.

Polish immigrant Al Dronge was the man behind Guild, and he guided the company very ably from its founding until his death in a plane crash in 1972, after which former vice president Leon Tell took the helm.

In 1956, Guild changed locations from New York City to Hoboken, New Jersey, and then in 1969 it moved again to Westerly, Rhode Island. Meanwhile, in 1966, ownership passed to Avnet, Inc, (with Dronge staying on as as president), then to a group of investors in 1986, then to the FAAS Corporation in 1989, and finally to Fender Musical Instruments in 1995 – which signalled the closure of the Westerly plant and a shift of production to Fender's factory in Corona, California. But despite all the upheavals, Guild never underwent the appreciable dip in quality that its two larger competitors are well documented as having weathered.

Guild's very first offerings comprised a range of flat-tops, from the large 17″ Navarre F-50 that ably rivalled Gibson's J-200 for many years, to the jumbo-sized F-40, the 000-sized F-30 and the small-bodied F-20. Their spruce tops and maple sides were of solid wood, but their backs were made from laminated maple pressed into an arched shape, which therefore had enough structural rigidity to make back braces unnecessary. While some people may consider the use of laminated woods to be a 'downmarket' constructional technique, Guild was definitely using it for advanced design purposes and not for any appreciable savings in materials or labour. In terms of sound, performance, and stability, the technique proved a success. These were soon joined by the Stuart A-550 archtop with a carved spruce top (soon joined by a similar Johnny Smith Award acoustic-electric archtop when that top jazz player's endorsement was secured). These and others took hold with players immediately, and Guild's reputation spread quickly. Many players found Guild offered a 'best of both worlds' alternative, straddling desirable Gibson and Martin features: they carried Martin's longer 25½″ scale length and more musical bracing, Gibson's adjustable truss-rod and slimmer neck, and the more frequent option of rosewood, a more Martin-like feature.

Guild's Mark Series of classical guitars arrived in 1961, and further important models were added to the line in 1963, including the D-40 and D-50 Dreadnoughts and the F-212 and F-312 12-string flat-tops, which were joined a few years later by the big 17″ 12-string models that would become the most popular of their type on the market. G Series Dreadnoughts arrived in the 1970s, while the acoustic archtops disappeared in a declining market for that breed. Lines expanded and then contracted over the years, and Guild suffered along with many acoustic makers in the electronic music boom of the late 1970s and early 1980s, and wasn't aided by the swift ownership changes that followed. Under Fender, production and quality seem to have stabilised again, and the Guild brand now provides that historic electric instruments company with its own rival to Gibson and Martin acoustics, something it could never manage with its own efforts. Acoustic archtops are even back at the top of the market – albeit mostly with floating magnetic pickups – in the form of a number of Guild-branded models designed by the great contemporary archtop-maker Robert Benedetto, and other actual Benedetto models hand-built in the Guild Custom Shop under close supervision from their namesake.

A third New York maker, which would eventually make its biggest impression with electric hollow-bodies in the rock'n'roll years, seemed for a time to be able to run with the two leading American archtop makers. Gretsch had been making drums and banjos in New York City since 1883, and in the early 1930s the company began manufacturing archtop and flat-top guitars when these appeared to be taking the limelight from the banjo. Models like the big 18″-wide Synchromatic of the early 1940s, with its cat's-eye soundholes, stairstep bridge and deluxe binding and position markers, had the power and grace of any of the big Gibsons or Epiphones, and became the choice of Count Basie guitarist Freddie Green for one. But the Gretsches were never as well made as the archtops of the 'big two', nor those of Stromberg, D'Angelico, or a handful of other big builders in the genre. They are impressive guitars, certainly, and possess all the right ingredients, but relatively

OPPOSITE PAGE **A 1949 Epiphone Emperor.** BELOW **A Guild F-50R-NT flat-top from 1975.**

few have survived in great playing condition. Gretsch flat-tops didn't fare much better in the quality stakes, though some have become collectible for aesthetic or historic reasons, such as the G-branded Rancher of the 1950s.

GYPSY JAZZ GUITARS

The continuing, even booming popularity of guitarist Django Reinhardt and the sprightly, melodic 'Gypsy jazz' style of which he long formed the centre, has spawned a perhaps surprising cottage industry building a type of guitar that has only really excelled at this single style of playing. Rob Aylward, John Le Voi, Maurice Dupont and Shelly Parks all offer instruments in the approximate Selmer-Maccaferri design, as pioneered more than 75 years ago, and taken up by Reinhardt almost immediately after its arrival on the scene.

Maccaferri was an Italian-born luthier and concert (classical) guitarist, whose relatively radical design ideas were taken up by London music store manager Ben Davis and promoted to Henri Selmer, head of the enormous French saxophone maker, as a sound basis for a guitar of the same brand. The Selmer factory in France began limited production of the instruments in late 1931, and the first models arrived for sale in London in 1932. They were taken up mostly by jazz players, although Maccaferri himself favoured the gut-string variants, as did a few other classical players of the day. But the steel-string models were unlike anything the majority of jazzers were strumming at the time. They were – and remain – a different breed of guitar entirely.

Selmer-Maccaferri instruments are large-bodied, flat-top guitars, often with a D-shaped or round soundhole placed under the strings and a deep, 'flattened' looking cutaway. Many models were originally built with circular wooden 'resonators' mounted under their tops, intended to aid projection and volume. If anything, these usually damaged the tone of the guitars to which they were fitted, and players simply removed them, or custom-ordered new Selmers without resonators. The steel-string Orchestre is the real classic of the early years of the Selmer-Maccaferris, but others existed, such as the cutaway-less Hawaien, and gut-string models such as the Concert (with the cutaway), Espagnol, and Classique. All – both steel and gut models – were made with laminated back and sides, not as a cost cutting exercise, but for well-defined tonal considerations researched by Maccaferri.

In 1933, only shortly before the instrument's most famous endorser took up the brand, Maccaferri parted ways with Selmer after a contract dispute. He returned briefly to his playing career, which itself was cut short after he fractured his wrist in a swimming accident. For a time he took up the manufacture of reeds for musical instruments, and dabbled in other types of guitar design, before being hooked by the possibilities of injection-moulded plastic instruments. Experiments with plastics led to his founding of Mastro Industries, which introduced a plastic ukulele in 1949, and the famous Maccaferri plastic guitars in the early 1950s. Despite their appearance and their general perception today, instruments such as the Maccaferri G-30 flat-top and G-40 archtop – moulded from a material called Dow Styron – were presented as serious instruments, and were even taken up by a number of pros in their day.

The plastic image could never quite cut it credibility-wise, however, and Maccaferri gave up applying the process to 'serious' instruments just a few years into the effort. Mastro continued to offer a number of downscaled plastic guitars through the 1960s, but these were no longer intended as professional-grade players' instruments. In the 1970s and 1980s Mario Maccaferri occasionally returned to lutherie, and even produced his Selmer-style wooden Gypsy jazz guitars again, first as the CSL Gypsy (in partnership with Englishman Maurice Summerfield, and manufactured in Japan at the Hoshino factory, where Ibanez guitars were made), and later in collaboration with high-end New York maker John Monteleone. Maccaferri died in 1993 at the age of 92.

OPPOSITE PAGE **Freddie Green, guitarist with Count Basie, pictured in 1968 with his Gretsch Synchromatic 400.** ABOVE **A plastic Maccaferri Romancer from 1960 and a 1955 advertisement for the revolutionary instrument.**

ABOVE **A 1932 example of the Selmer-Maccaferri Modèle Orchestre.** ABOVE RIGHT **The Rosenberg trio epitomise the Gypsy jazz style on their original Selmer instruments.** OPPOSITE PAGE TOP **Julian Cope with a 12-string Ovation Adamas.** OPPOSITE PAGE RIGHT **Kazuo Yairi produces fine guitars like this AR300 from his workshop.** OPPOSITE PAGE BOTTOM **Alvarez Yairi, endorsed by Ani DiFranco, is a factory line produced in association with him.**

Meanwhile, Selmer had continued not only to manufacture guitars to the style initiated by Maccaferri, but in fact make impressive progress in perfecting the breed. The company's remaining luthiers did away with the internal resonator, changed the soundhole from D-shaped to round and finally to oval, and swapped the 12-fret neck for 14. The model was newly dubbed the Modèle Jazz, and with this shape and name the Selmer jazz guitar achieved its ultimate form – a thing actually quite distinct from anything that ever graced the drawing board of its 'originator', whose name was of course by now removed from it anyway. Selmer closed its guitar works in 1952, by which time only around 900 guitars had been produced, a good half of them the Modèle Jazz.

A BOWL-BACKED WONDER

Ovation's revolutionary bowl-backed shape was born in 1965 when helicopter company owner Charles H. Kaman returned to his first love, the guitar, and struck upon a favourable design for a fibreglass composite body structure. For such a radical departure from traditional design, the prototypes received a surprisingly enthusiastic response from the pro players Kaman who saw them, and the production models that rolled out from 1966 also gained a swift and wide acceptance. Charlie Byrd, Larry Coryell, Jerry Reed, Al Di Meola and Adrian Legg have all played Ovations through much of their careers, but Glen Campbell's early endorsement of a shallow-bowled model in 1968 – since dubbed the Balladeer – and his use of the instrument on his popular TV show, gave the brand its biggest early boost.

The lively sound and smooth performance of models such as the Classic, Legend, Custom Legend, Pacemaker 12-string, and nylon-string Country Artist rivalled even that of Martin and Gibson in the early to mid-1970s, when the quality of those guitars was declining and many players were clearly willing to try something new. They were probably helped along in doing so by these Ovations' mid-level price tags, too. In 1973 Ovation introduced the more affordable Applause line, in an effort to pre-empt the Asian copyists who were plaguing other big brands, and was soon reaching the entry and lower-mid level players as well. The company ascended to the other end of the scale in 1976 with the Adamas line. Disproving the general rule that anything less than fully solid-wood construction means a downmarket result, the Adamas guitars carried tops made from a thin carbon-graphite/birch

laminate, with 22 small soundholes of various sizes located around the upper bass bout. These also found their mark, and soon became both the choice of many pros, and a model for enthusiastic amateurs to aspire to.

While some players found the sound of these guitars a little 'synthetic', the Elites that followed in 1982 carried solid spruce tops for a warmer, more traditional tone, but still displayed the Adamas's multi-soundholed look. At around the same time, the Collector's Series gave the company something to promote to guitar collectors who had traditionally pursued the vintage-associated brands, and helped further establish Ovation as a maker that was here to stay.

In addition to their space-aged shape and construction, Ovation guitars also revolutionised the notion of electrification of an acoustic instrument. They were the first mass production models to come from the factory in a number of electro-acoustic options, and became many players' first road to plugged-in acoustic guitar playing. Having weathered the general acoustic slump of the early 1980s, Ovation expanded both in sales and model selection in the years that followed. Today it remains one of the larger-selling US makes, and a strong alternative brand that plenty of players continue to favour.

THE FAR-EASTERN COMPETITION

While the acoustic guitar market was declining in the late 1970s and early 1980s, many improving Japanese imports were offering competition to long-standing American brands. Ibanez is best known for its broad range of electric guitars, which first came to prominence as quality 'copies' of many American designs in the early 1970s, but the company has been making acoustics since the 1930s. Ibanez flat-tops first became known in the US mainly as decent 'copies' of Gibson and Martin designs that shadowed the company's electrics of that time. But more original recent lines, such as the all solid-woods Naturalwoods, acoustic-

Ani DiFranco
One Righteous Babe.

The Alvarez Yairi WY1
One Righteous Guitar.

Check it out
at a retailer
near you.

Alvarez

electric AE, Ragtime, and solid-topped Artwood series of the 1980s, or the innovative MASA or Talman models of today, offer good alternatives to players looking for something different. Most Ibanez production shifted from Japan to Korea in 1992, and has remained there since.

Alvarez and the upmarket Alvarez Yairi have long histories in Japan, and have produced a range of quality entry and mid-level acoustics for many years – topped by some high-end, all solid-woods models made to totally original designs by AY that rival almost anything produced in the USA or Europe. Another Japanese maker, Takamine, has provided yet another quality alternative that has even lured many pros away from classic American brands. Regardless of sales numbers, or any arguments about copies v originals, Yamaha has probably forged a more solid and long-lasting place for itself in western markets than any of the other Japanese makers.

ABOVE **Bruce Springsteen pictured in 1993 with his Yamaha in an unusual black finish.** OPPOSITE PAGE **A Taylor 315CE from 2002.**

Yamaha began making pedal organs in Japan in 1887, and was manufacturing pianos by 1900. It was making its own guitars by 1946, but didn't become well known in the USA until the mid-1960s when its good-value classicals and, a little later, steel-string flat-tops made inroads into the student, amateur folkie and campfire scene. By the 1970s these steel-string FGs and classical Gs were among the better 'lower mid-level' guitars available, and were finding a place for themselves largely on the strength of original design rather than being the copies that most Japanese makers were still offering. Hand-made L Series and luxuriously ornate N Series models followed, and the brand quickly earned the respect among many more accomplished amateurs and some professionals that it had enjoyed with student and novice players for ten years.

The company's guitar lines have both expanded and advanced over the years, without their popularity ever having waned. Over the past decade and a half, lines such as the thinline electro-acoustic APXs, solid-topped GD classicals and DW Dreadnoughts, decorative and versatile CPX Compass Series, and CSF parlour guitars have won lots of fans. Meanwhile, Korean maker Samick has put guitars in almost as many players' hands as any of its Japanese rivals, though frequently under other names, such as Hondo.

While the quality eastern imports that have been pervasive since the 1970s seemed destined to wipe out US-made entry level acoustics, plenty of home-grown alternatives have pitched solid competition for any upmarket model that Gibson, Guild or Martin can produce, in terms of sound and build quality, if not in numbers.

WESTERN PROMISE

Even for production volume, however, one US maker has put up an astounding fight in the upper mid-range bracket since the mid-1980s. Born out of an easy-going artisans' scene of the early 1970s, centred around a cooperative Southern California lutherie workshop, Taylor Guitars has grown into an amazingly efficient and prolific maker, turning out around 270 instruments per day by the early 21st century, which rivals any current American guitar manufacturer. Taylor's success with labour-saving production techniques such as the use of computer numeric control (CNC) cutting and routing machines and bolt-on neck joints has also dragged other large, long-established makers into modern manufactory by dint of their need to compete.

Bob Taylor and Kurt Listug, two of the original three Taylor founders, have forged their success largely through a combination of Taylor's design sense and Listug's business acumen, but the pair certainly traced a strenuous learning curve to get from the company's birth in 1974 to where they are today. Through the course of the early 1980s the company evolved from building rather standard jumbo and Dreadnought style guitars to producing a range of sizes in original new shapes devised mainly by Bob Taylor himself. The first of these appeared in the form of a grand concert-shaped, small-bodied Size 2 model, two of which were displayed at the 1984 NAMM show in the form of a mahogany-bodied 512 and rosewood-bodied 812. By this time Taylor's numerical naming system was well established, denoting wood types, body size and shape, and styling, but variations and changes over the years make it difficult to offer a quick, easy guide to all of these.

By the early 1990s Taylor had a growing list of endorsees, one of whom was Leo Kottke, whose Signature Model 12-string – with 'flattened', Selmer-like cutaway and a design intended to maximised dropped tunings – rapidly earned a lot of respect in that genre. A few years later in 1996 Taylor made further waves by introducing the 400 series, the most affordable American-made all solid-woods guitar at that time. By now, you'd better believe that Martin and plenty of other makers were taking notice. In the late 1990s and early in the following decade Taylor offered a number of special issue lines that were fancier than almost anything the maker had produced previously. The 25th Anniversary XXV-DR Dreadnought and XXV-GA grand auditorium of 1999, and the Commemorative Series guitars that followed were made with deluxe wood choices (including Taylor's use of some Brazilian rosewood for the first time since 1977) and exotic inlays. Following these, the Gallery Series extended the inlay themes to a range of underwater designs.

At the other end of the market, Taylor's affordable three-quarter size Baby guitar has been a major hit with everyone from young players to travelling guitarists and slack-key stylists, and is one of the main models to have helped spark a far-reaching craze for small-bodied and travel-sized acoustics. At the time of writing, Taylor's staff of nearly 400 turn out close to 50,000 guitars a year, making the company one of the acknowledged leaders in the quality acoustic market.

After Taylor and Martin, the Tacoma company, founded in Seattle, Washington, in 1997 can already lay claim to being the third largest guitar manufacturer in the USA. The company's roots stem just a little bit further back than this, as the Tacoma facility was established as a wood processor and occasional maker of contracted-out acoustics for other brands, primarily Washburn. Two of Tacoma's first offerings, the medium-bodied C1C Chief and travel-sized P1 Papoose, gained immediate attention for their offset, teardrop-shaped soundholes positioned at the bass-side upper bout, their plain attire, and their impressive sound and build quality at the price. Tacoma also offers many more traditional designs, and has since unveiled an impressively wide range, including the florentine-cutaway EM16 and EM10, the Laurence Juber-designed E Series, the EBZ24 with Brazilian rosewood back and sides, and many more, totalling more than 70 instruments in the range. Since 1998 Tacoma has also offered the foreign-made Olympia by Tacoma line of more affordable guitars built to the US maker's designs.

Other independent quality North American makers bloomed mainly in workshops offering Martin-style guitars in wood options, appointments, and build standards that many players felt Martin itself couldn't deliver at the time. Many of these have moved on to produce more original designs, but most are still paying homage to

that granddaddy of the American flat-top, and often topping it, as their reviews and star endorsement lists continually prove. Companies like Mossman, Gurian, Traugott, Bourgeois, Froggy Bottom, Collings, Gallagher and Santa Cruz were all born of this ethos – although, to be fair, many have moved on to include (or even started out including) more original designs. And the last of these can certainly no longer be filed under 'small maker.'

Richard Hoover, Bruce Ross, and William Davis formed the Santa Cruz Guitar Company in – yep – Santa Cruz, California, in 1976, and quickly built up a steady roster of clients from the local acoustic scene who were looking for a little more than the traditional brands were offering. Early koa-bodied Santa Cruz D Style Dreadnoughts became popular with fingerpickers on the scene in particular, thanks in part to their wider than standard 1¹³⁄₁₆″ fingerboard width at the nut. Other models had subtly innovative twists on classic designs that made them just that extra bit more appealing to serious players: the small but deep-bodied 13-fret H, the FTC with its flat top but carved arched back, the Tony Rice model based on a Martin Dreadnought with enlarged soundhole, the FS model aimed at fingerstyle players, and many others. Not all were great successes in sales terms – and in fact the classic Martin/Gibson-style models that followed would prove Santa Cruz's real bread'n'butter – but they showed what this maker could do, and caught the attention of more than a few name players. And by offering beautifully-made guitars like the 00, 000 and Dreadnought models, with slot headstocks and 12 frets clear of the body, or the beautifully appointed, prewar-styled Vintage D, Santa Cruz (now solely owned by Richard Hoover) is once again providing a breed of vintage acoustic that can't easily be obtained elsewhere.

None of these independent makers is a 'budget' option, of course, and some – the smaller workshops in particular, where each guitar is likely to receive some attention from the company founder – wear price tags that are higher than all but the most elaborate of limited edition Martins. But more and more players have come to appreciate that there's plenty of worth to be had in a well-made, hand-crafted acoustic instrument, and that the realm of justifiable 'expensive guitars' extends to more than just vintage Martins and Gibsons. If nothing else, the list of star players who have sold off their 'M' or 'G' branded acoustics to play something from the above list of makers attests to the success of these smaller luthiers.

CANADIANS & EUROPEANS

Our space here is limited, and we have stuck mainly with the major historical American makers, the modern upstarts, and their Asian rivals. But great guitars have been coming out of Canada for decades, and of course many of the founders of the American art of stringed instrument-making brought their craft from Europe in the first place, and many fine instruments are still being built there.

Between the makes of Robert Godin's LaSiDo company, which covers the lower to mid-range price brackets (which includes La Patrie classical guitars, and Seagull, Norman, and Simon & Patrick Luthier flat-tops), and the mid- to high-end instruments of Jean Larrivée's self-named company, the major Canadian builders have got the market well covered. Since founding his Harmony Lab custom guitar workshop in Montreal in 1968, Godin has been responsible for launching an impressive number of different brands and designs, mainly with the aim of providing good sounding and playing guitars to beginners and students – or just anyone who doesn't have a lot to spend, but seeks an instrument that outperforms its price tag. The results have paid off, and each of the makes under the LaSiDo umbrella provides outstanding value for the money.

Larrivée is an equally independent-minded guitar-maker, who also founded his company in 1968 – in Toronto this time – to manufacture only classical guitars at the start. Local demand for quality steel-string guitars led him into that realm in 1971, but his nylon beginnings left an impression on his design sense, and his first and still most popular L Style appears to be very much a classical guitar adapted for steel-string playing. Which is not to say they are half-baked conversion jobs; the early versions of these were upmarket, custom-made instruments that performed stunningly, and the production models that have followed are still impressive performers, with a snappy response and full voice. The company also offers Dreadnoughts, jumbos, 00 models with 12 frets to the body, and a petite parlour model that has won a lot of admirers. The 03 Series of 1997 became the most affordable all solid-wood flat-top made in North America at the time of its introduction, and further good value models have followed, all aligned with the Larrivée design ethos and the good sound and performance that goes with it.

The ever-decreasing cost of good entry-level guitars manufactured in North America and of course the constant competition – and ever increasing quality – of the Asian imports means that importing guitars from Europe to the US and Canada has rarely been an appealing proposition. But plenty of guitars from across the water are deserving of respect.

Continental makers such as Höfner, Levin, Goya, Eko, Framus and Hagström provided European and British players with the full range of acoustic types for decades, though they are little seen outside Europe. Germany's Lakewood, Finland's Landola and the Czech Republic's Furch are larger builders worthy of a lot of respect today, but among the mid- to high-end makes, Northern Ireland's Lowden probably has the best reputation.

Over the course of its 30-year history, Lowden has grown steadily into a recognised brand in the acoustic world, and gathered a number of pro endorsements along the way, including players like Richard Thompson, Pierre Bensusan, Jan Akkerman, Jacques Stotzem, Michael Hedges, David Gray and others. After a number of custom-built efforts, George Lowden got running as a production maker in the proper sense in the late 1970s. In 1985, after some years in which the guitars were built in Japan, George started a factory in Bangor, Northern Ireland. Unfortunately, it ran into money trouble after only three years and changed hands. George gave the new company a license to build his designs. But in 2003 that agreement came to an end. At the start of 2004, what had been the Lowden Guitar Company changed its name to Avalon Guitars. Avalon has now dropped the Lowden designs, including his distinctive bracing, and started again with a new range.

George Lowden, meanwhile, is once again producing his own designs in a small, six-person atelier under his own direct supervision. He also hand-builds custom instruments himself. George's role in producing the guitars that bear his name has varied over the years, but most Lowden instruments are along the lines of a number of his original designs. Never one to follow tradition, Lowden has steered away from the classic Martin X-bracing since

Ed Robertson of The Barenaked Ladies with his Canadian-built Larrivée.

1976, using instead his own modified A-bracing system that, for one thing, helps to prevent boominess in Dreadnoughts and other large-bodied guitars. His original O Series (also 'Original Series Jumbo'), a rounded, medium-large-bodied shape, continues to be the company's most popular range. The F Series 'Midi Jumbo' and S Series 'Small Bodied' are also popular, while the D Series comes as close as anything the company does to the original Martin Dreadnought shape.

The high quality of a number of great British luthiers working today warrants greater coverage than space here allows. The craft has really blossomed in the UK in recent years, and with guitars from the likes of Manson, Brook, Fylde, Dave King, Tom Mates, Moon and others available on a homegrown basis, without shipping costs or import duties added to their cost, more and more British players are finding they don't have to turn to North America to hunt down a first-class, high-end acoustic guitar.

BELOW **A National Style 0 square-neck resonator guitar from 1935.**
OPPOSITE PAGE **Son House, master of Delta blues, with his trademark National.**

RESONATORS

Before guitarists were broadcasting their playing through a paper speaker cone coupled to an electronic amplifier, they were pumping it out through the spun-aluminium speaker cones of National guitars' unique built-in acoustic amplification system. The principle is just the same, in acoustic terms: a moving cone that enlarges the vibrational energy transferred into it, and thereby amplifies a sound. A simple thing, but in the days of drowned out flat-tops and archtops on increasingly louder bandstands, this self-projecting design was a revelation.

Born out of an idea devised by Hawaiian-style player George Beauchamp, and made a reality by Los Angeles inventor John Dopyera, the first production resonator guitar was released in 1927 by Dopyera's own National company, which had been founded just a year before to build banjos. In fact the success of National's tri-cone resonator guitar, and the single-cone designs that would soon follow from Dopyera's breakaway company Dobro, would serve to put more than a few banjos into storage, thanks to the incredible improvements in volume that they offered over traditional guitars. Of course by only the middle of the next decade the increasing prevalence of electric amplification for guitars would equally put plenty of resonator guitars into storage... but that haunting, metallic, reverberant sound would survive down the years, and is more popular today than ever before.

The first resos had bodies of 'German silver', which is actually a nickel alloy (others would soon also be made of bell brass), and carried three thin spun-aluminium cones that opened toward the inside back of the body, with their apexes resting on a three-point bridge piece for transference of string vibrations. National's original Silver Hawaiian came in four styles of increasing decoration, numbered from Style 1's plain body to Style 4's elaborate floral engravings, and each was available in round or square neck, the latter far more popular in the days when most were played lap-style with a steel slide. The original Dobros, on the other hand, had wooden bodies and a single, larger spun-aluminium cone that opened outward. Both were aimed at roughly the same target market in the late 1920s and early 1930s, but down the years the steel-bodied Nationals have evolved to become the Delta blues players' favourite, while the Dobro has generally been the bluegrass slide player's guitar of choice. In the face of this wood-bodied rivalry, National quickly stepped in to make its own more affordable single-cone models in both wood and metal – as well as many more decorative versions of the type – and over the years there has been no end of confusion between the two makes among players less than totally immersed in the details of their parallel histories.

National offered resonator guitars until 1941, but during the war years the company evolved into the wider-reaching Valco of Chicago, which concentrated more heavily on the electric guitar market. The Dobro name has cropped up under a range of owners in the intervening years, but these resos have been made by the Original Musical Instrument company since 1970. Meanwhile, both wood- and metal-bodied tri-cone and single-cone resos in many original National types are again being made to a high standard by the National Reso-Phonic company, founded in San Luis Obispo, California, in 1989. A range of smaller makers are also currently producing similar designs, while budget versions of both metal and wood resonator guitars are available from Asian import brands like Ozark and Vintage. All can take a little practice to get the hang of, but the better of them will sound gorgeous with the right touch and technique – and still offer the loudest acoustic performance of the unplugged world.

Notation & Tablature

Over the past decade and a half, acoustic guitar has exploded out of all recognition. Not only is the instrument at the centre of a musical genre of its own, thanks to the boom in folk and 'unplugged' music in recent years, it has also regained a prominent place in pop, rock and jazz. Acoustic-only players are no longer chained to the campfire – and we're doing far more than just strumming. Given the number of styles in which the acoustic instrument is paramount, the modern player needs to master a wide range of techniques in order to become a complete musician. Hold on tight – this book gets you there.

Most players will always want to specialise to some extent in one type of music or another, however eclectic their understanding of the bigger picture. But the degree of cross-fertilisation between genres today is immense. As a guitarist you stand to benefit enormously from the inspiration offered by previously unfamiliar forms. Jazz can influence blues, country can influence rock, Latin can influence pop, African can influence jazz… and on it goes, in a near-infinite variety of combinations.

The following chapters offer a grounding in 11 of the most crucial forms of guitar playing today, with the aim of helping you to hone your skills in your chosen style while broadening your ability to encompass a whole range of musical moods. Newcomers to guitar playing will have a chance to make a start with some of the more basic lessons in the 'Getting Started' chapter that opens the book; it is the only one aimed at the absolute beginner. Otherwise, each chapter carries a range of lessons suited to players ranging from novice to advanced. Even the most skilled pro should be able to take away a few new tricks and useful licks from these pages.

Given the space allowed, none of these chapters pretends to be 'the final word' on a style, either, although each offers the skills needed to make you confident in the genre. If one – or a number – of the new styles really grabs you, you will be well equipped to begin deeper study. Or you can just take a few new klezmer and Celtic licks to your next blues gig, and blow your own boundaries.

GUIDE TO NOTATION SYMBOLS

If you're not familiar with the symbols used in standard music notation and tablature (tab), this section provides an introduction to most of what you will encounter. As the range of musical symbols is vast, this primer won't be exhaustive, but it will give you enough to get you through the following chapters. You'll find further guidance on any new symbols or instructions you encounter – particularly in more advanced notation – within the explanatory text accompanying the exercises themselves.

All exercises, other than those of pure rhythm notation, will be represented in both standard notation and tab; while some symbols are common to both systems, others are used only on one or the other. While many exercises will include suggested chords for accompaniment below the bottom tab line, chord boxes will not always be given, unless the chords themselves are the point of the study, or the author feels it would be particularly helpful to provide some guidance about unfamiliar chords. Note also that indications of rhythm will be given only in the standard notation, through the use of traditional note values.

READING TABLATURE

A complete course in reading music in standard notation would take more space than is available here. But tablature – tab, for short – is easily explained.

Tab is essentially a method of showing finger placements that correspond to the notes shown on the stave of music directly above it. It enables guitarists with no traditional music-reading skills to play exercises regardless. If you're new to tab, the key points to note are that it uses no traditional 'notes' as such but carries numbers in their place, that it is made up of six horizontal lines instead of five and that it carries no clef or key signature. Each of the six horizontal lines represents a string on the guitar – beginning with the lowest line, representing the low E-string. To help you remember which way is up, the notes of the open strings are written alongside the tab lines (see figure 1, top). For exercises in 'alternate' tunings, the altered string-note values will be given instead, as in the exercise in DADGAD tuning (figure 1, bottom). Numbers on the lines indicate the fret at which to hold down that string, while a zero (0) indicates that an open string is to be played.

Figure 1

The majority of notation symbols are used to instruct you in the nuances of finger movement required to play a piece with the correct 'feel'.

The notation – or string/fret number combinations in the tab – tells you which notes to sound, but without the symbols it would be nearly impossible to determine the subtleties of playing technique that make a particular style of riff recognisable.

Bends String bends are indicated by a starting note to be played before the bend occurs, and a small 'arch' symbol linking it to a second note (sometimes in parentheses), which is the note achieved at the peak of the bend. In tab, the arch links the starting note to the fret number which equates to the second note, even though the bending finger stays at the same fret.

'BU' instructs you to 'bend up' (figure 1). Bend releases are signified in the reverse, 'BD' telling you to 'bend down' (figure 2).

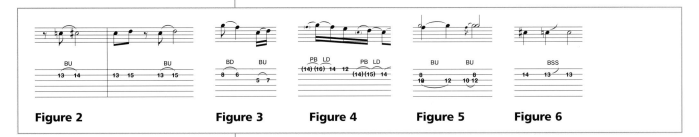

Figure 2   **Figure 3**   **Figure 4**   **Figure 5**   **Figure 6**

When the pre-bend note is not to be sounded but merely provides a starting fret position to bend from, it will be in parentheses, with 'PB' for 'pre-bend' (below-right). 'LD' means 'let down' (figure 4). You will also see an upside-down arch below notes where the symbol would otherwise clash with an un-bent note on a higher string (figure 5). Where an up-bend is intended as more of an inflection, without a concluding note a full tone higher, you will see the initials 'BSS' for 'bend semitone sharp' (figure 6).

Fingerings Some exercises offer fingering guidance in the form of small numerals alongside the notes in the stave, telling you which finger to use for fretting that note, where 1 = index (figure 7). If a riff is repeated, these fingerings will generally only be given for the first example to avoid cluttering the stave.

Gliss Gliss is short for 'glissando', the term used in classical music to indicate a steady slide between notes. In more contemporary forms the technique is often referred to as a 'slide' or 'finger slide', but still indicated as 'gliss' in the notation. A gliss can go up or down (figures 8 and 8a).

With a gliss from one note to another, an arch symbol – similar to that used to indicate a bend – appears in the stave, with an arch or adjoining line in the tab. The technique involves simply playing the first note, then sliding along the required number of frets to reach the second note. A gliss symbol placed before or after a single note (figures 9 and 9a) tells you to slide to or from an unspecified pitch, but to land on the note given.

Hammer-ons and Pull-offs Notes generated by hammering on or pulling off a string at a particular fret are indicated with a linking arch and the absence of a picking symbol. Other runs are generated with a picked note to start, with those following hammered or pulled.

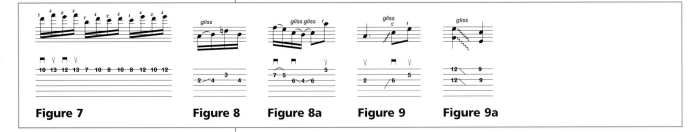

Figure 7   **Figure 8**   **Figure 8a**   **Figure 9**   **Figure 9a**

Interpreting which is required is based on the direction of the musical line. Ascending notes are hammered, and descending notes are pulled off. This applies whether a phrase is totally hammer/pull generated (figure 10) or is launched with a pick stroke (figure 11).

Harmonics Natural harmonics – those achieved by damping a string directly over the 12th, fifth or seventh fret for example – are indicated by a diamond-shaped note in the stave accompanied by a 'Nat harms' direction and a broken line extending the length of the harmonics' duration. The same is indicated in the tab by the letters 'Nh' followed by a broken line (figure 12). Artificial harmonics – those performed by fretting a note and damping the same string 12 frets higher – are indicated in the stave with the fretted note in parentheses and the damped (harmonic) note in the shape of a diamond, an octave higher, and accompanied by the letter 'T' followed by the fret number (figure 13). In the tab, this is indicated by using a number for the fretted note followed by one for the damped note an octave higher, given in parentheses, along with the 'Ah' symbol.

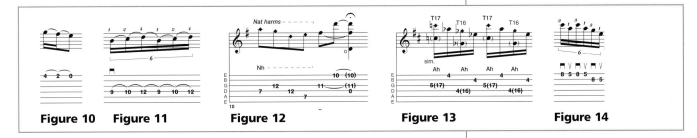

Figure 10   **Figure 11**   **Figure 12**   **Figure 13**   **Figure 14**

Picking Symbols Pick strokes are indicated with two types of symbols. They are not universally given in all exercises, but are generally included where picking direction is critical to the feel of the piece (figure 14).

∏ = downstroke   V = upstroke

Rake A rake – where the pick is dragged smoothly across the strings, hitting each string individually but in swift succession – is indicated by a wavy vertical line ending in an arrow indicating the way the pick should flow (usually from low note/string to high in these chapters). This is generally accompanied by the word 'rake' between the stave and tab line (figure 15).

Rhythm Patterns Lines representing pure rhythm patterns, without note values for pitch, occur in a couple of different forms (particularly in the 'World Music' chapter) where non-melodic rhythm patterns played by drums and/or percussion are crucial to the genre. These may be represented as one-line 'staves' with beat values given per instrument (figure 16), or as normal five-line staves with beat values given but no pitch indication or ordinary notes falling all on the same space to indicate a lack of pitch value (figure 17). The correct interpretation of each will be explained within the relevant individual chapters.

Triplets Whatever the rhythmic value of their constituent notes (which, of course, is always the same for each note in a three-note grouping), triplets are indicated by the number '3' and linking brackets above or below the appropriate notes in the stave (figure 18).

Similarly, where sextuplets occur – though a rarity – they are indicated by the number '6' and linking brackets above or below the appropriate notes in the stave (figure 19).

As for septuplets and 'fivetuplets' (quintuplets) – yes, they exist – the same applies.

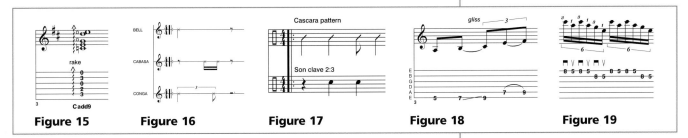

Figure 15   **Figure 16**   **Figure 17**   **Figure 18**   **Figure 19**

CHAPTER 1
Getting Started

While this entire book is dedicated to the acoustic guitar, this chapter represents an introduction to guitar playing in general – and that usually means acoustic guitar playing. It is intended to provide a thorough grounding in what many players would think of as the 'acoustic guitar' style; the rest of the book will take you a lot further. Hundreds of thousands of people the world over have gained a lifetime's enjoyment from the instrument without progressing past what this chapter offers; but it is also the perfect preparation for diving deeper into the more specialised genres that lie beyond it.

Whether it's a classical model or steel-strung 'folk' instrument, for many players the acoustic guitar is where they begin. Generations of would-be rockers have heard their parents say they should start on an acoustic before thinking about an electric, and plenty of guitarists never find a need to move on from this incredibly versatile box of tricks.

Of course much of what is learned on an acoustic guitar can be transferred to an electric and vice versa. Despite their different appearances, both types of guitar are tuned the same and have the same configurations of notes laid out on the fingerboard. If you know how to play an Am or D7 or F#m9 chord or an E major or D pentatonic minor scale on an acoustic, you can play it on an electric, and vice versa.

But working first with an acoustic can build more strength into the hands. An inexpensive acoustic guitar is more likely to be hard to play – by virtue of its heavier gauge strings and higher action (the height of the strings from the fretboard) – so it is extremely important to get an acoustic properly set up, to have its action checked, so the initial phase of learning isn't needlessly made more difficult.

You'll also find that lead guitar solos with plenty of string-bending cannot be played effectively on an acoustic, especially by the beginner, although advanced acoustic styles do sometimes include a surprising amount of such techniques. Young women in particular with smaller hands, who tend to get saddled (no guitar pun intended!) with nylon-strung 'Spanish' guitars with no regard to the type of music they want to play, should certainly take the time to shop around for a guitar of the appropriate size and neck profile (shape or diameter). Young or small-handed players are often put off playing guitar by the physical struggle involved in forming unfamiliar chords around a wide, flat neck, as experienced particularly with 'classical' type nylon-strung guitars. Steel strings might initially be harder on the fingertips, but the necks of such guitars are usually easier to wrap your hand around, and you can always begin with light

strings to ease the effort. Plenty of smaller-than-standard sizes exist out there, so get a guitar that suits you best, and don't let anyone else do the crucial shopping and testing for you.

Acoustic guitar has always been popular because it is a relatively portable instrument, and doesn't need electricity or an amp in order to function. It is ideal for accompanying yourself singing songs, and many people only desire to learn enough to take them to this point. To do this the technical requirements are straightforward: first, learn chord shapes; second, practise changing chord shapes until you can do so fast enough to keep up with a song; third, learn to strum evenly.

The chief hurdle in learning chords is getting to grips with the 'barre' chord — the chord in which several notes are held down with one finger. The barre is often first encountered with the F or B chords. Moving these a little further up the neck can assist, where string tension is not as great as it is right by the nut.

A further refinement of accompanying yourself on guitar is to be able to finger-pick the chords instead of strumming them. This is especially useful in slower, quieter material. Initially such finger patterns will be in a simple rhythm. Later, they can be syncopated and incorporate an 'alternating thumb' in the bass part. This is where the thumb moves between the bass strings while the fingers strike the higher ones, creating a tapestry of sound. Further refinements come with the ability to add little melodic phrases and riffs into the accompaniment without wholly abandoning the supporting harmony.

In this section we will look at basic rhythm and fingerpicking techniques, chords, how to use a capo, and finish with a quick look at the types of altered tunings that are so rewarding on the acoustic guitar — covering, in the process, a range of exercises appropriate to beginners, intermediates, and even some more advanced players less experienced with these styles.

RIKKY ROOKSBY

MAJOR AND MINOR CHORDS

It makes sense to start with some chords, so here are the shapes for the most-used major and minor chords. Notice that in comparison to the majors, the minors sound sad. The emotional contrast of 'bright' major with 'sad' minor is crucial to the vast bulk of Western music.

As you tackle the shapes check that each string that should be sounding *is* sounding. When the fingers are in the right place, play each string individually. If notes do not sound, the usual causes are: a finger on the metal fret, a finger too far away from the metal fret, not pressing hard enough, or a fretting finger touching and therefore muting an adjacent string.

A special word must be said about the shapes for B, Bm, F and F#m. These involve playing a barre, but you can use the version without the full barre for now, until your fingers get used to the required positions. With B and Bm the bass note on the fifth string is therefore optional.

MAJOR AND MINOR CHORDS

Master the chords on this page and you will have the most common major and minor variations at your disposal, along with some barre shapes you can move up and down the neck to create different chords. The numbers beneath each of the chords show the role each note is playing. A basic 'triad' has a root note (1) which gives it its name. The other two notes, the third (3) and the fifth (5), occupy the third and fifth steps in a scale built on the root. More complex chords add extra notes from the scale.

SEVENTHS

The next most common group of chords is the sevenths. Here are two types formed by adding a single note to the major chord. Don't worry if you can't play the B7 and F7 barre chords initially. The B7 barre version will give you a different A7 if you take off the barre and move the fingers two frets toward the nut. The little finger with F7 is optional.

The major seventh chord has a richer sound than the first type. Again, leave the Bmaj7 and Emaj7 if you find them difficult. The F#maj7 has the advantage of being a movable chord that doesn't have a barre. Make sure that all the strings that should be sounding are, otherwise you may miss the seventh!

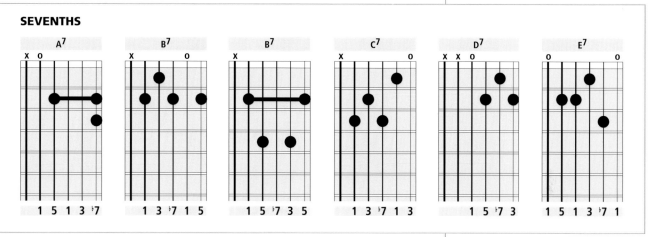

SEVENTHS

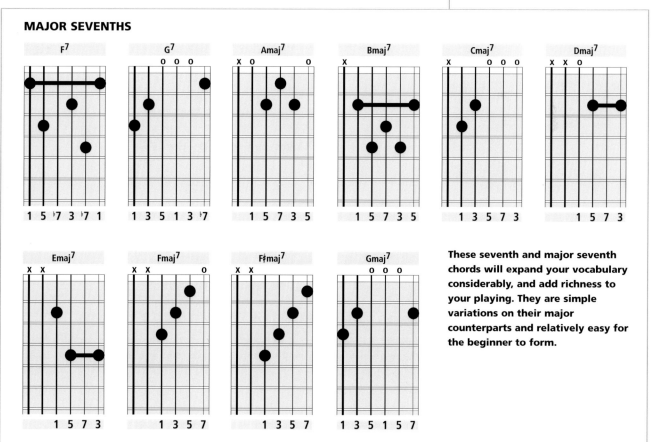

MAJOR SEVENTHS

These seventh and major seventh chords will expand your vocabulary considerably, and add richness to your playing. They are simple variations on their major counterparts and relatively easy for the beginner to form.

USING A CAPO

In order to make playing in difficult keys easier, guitarists use a device known as a 'capo'. This may look like a medieval instrument of torture but, as a guitarist, it's one of your best friends. It acts as a first finger substitute when holding a barre, or alternatively it can be thought of as a movable nut. If a key would normally mean lots of barre chords (and an aching hand) the capo will allow you to turn most of the barre chords into open string shapes.

Here's an example: you need to play a song that was recorded in A♭ major and uses A♭, B♭m, Cm, D♭, E♭ and Fm – all barre chords. If you put the capo at the first fret each chord can be played with the shape of the chord a semitone below it.

Actual pitch:	**A♭**	**B♭m**	**Cm**	**D♭**	**E♭**	**Fm**
Capo I shapes:	**G**	**Am**	**Bm**	**C**	**D**	**Em**

Much easier, and it sounds better too! And that's not the only way we could do it…

Actual pitch:	**A♭**	**B♭m**	**Cm**	**D♭**	**E♭**	**Fm**
Capo IV shapes:	**E**	**F#m**	**G#m**	**A**	**B**	**C#m**

Or, for an extreme contrast…

Actual pitch:	**A♭**	**B♭m**	**Cm**	**D♭**	**E♭**	**Fm**
Capo VIII shapes:	**C**	**Dm**	**Em**	**F**	**G**	**Am**

You will notice that as the capo goes up the neck the timbre of the guitar will change. This is something that songwriters use deliberately. They also use a capo to shift a chord sequence up or down a key to better suit their voice, which saves learning a new set of chords. Lastly, if you play guitar with a friend, using a capo high on one of the guitars can create a resonant sound with the two guitars playing the same chords high and low:

Actual pitch:	**G**	**Am**	**Bm**	**C**	**D**	**Em**	**F**

Guitar 1

Open chords	**G**	**Am**	**Bm**	**C**	**D**	**Em**	**F**

Guitar 2

Capo VII shapes	**C**	**Dm**	**Em**	**F**	**G**	**Am**	**B♭**

MINOR 7, SUSPENDED 4, SUSPENDED 2 CHORDS

By merely moving beyond the basic major chords – where appropriate – to other shapes that aren't much more difficult to play, simple songs can take on added tension and atmosphere. Here are three other types of chord that are often found in songs, and can be useful mood builders. The minor sevenths are the minor version of the A7, B7 and so on previously shown. The Bm7 will yield an alternative Am7 if you take off the barre and move the fingers two frets down toward the nut. The little finger with F#m7 is optional.

The suspended fourth chords are often used to inject drama into song accompaniment because of their tension. In the case of Asus4, Dsus4 and Esus4 all that is required is to add a note to a simple major chord shape. The Asus2 and Dsus2 are popular because the reverse happens: you just lift a finger off a string that would usually be fretted for A or D. The sus2 is not as tense and has an open, 'hollow' sound.

A MISCELLANY OF EFFECTIVE ACOUSTIC CHORDS

Here are 16 chords that sound great on an acoustic guitar. Some are created by either lifting a finger off a note with a common barre shape (Bmadd4, F#m7add11, Fmaj7add11) or moving a chord shape up (D6/9, Amaj7), or are unique 'voicings' – like the C which has a 12-string resonance because within it there are two Gs and two Es at the same pitch.

Also included are two first inversion chords – G/B and D/F# – that often feature in acoustic songs. First inversion simply means that the root note is not the lowest in the chord, the 'third' above it is played instead – the note that is two tones higher than the root in a major chord. Try these out and learn the ones you like for your own playing.

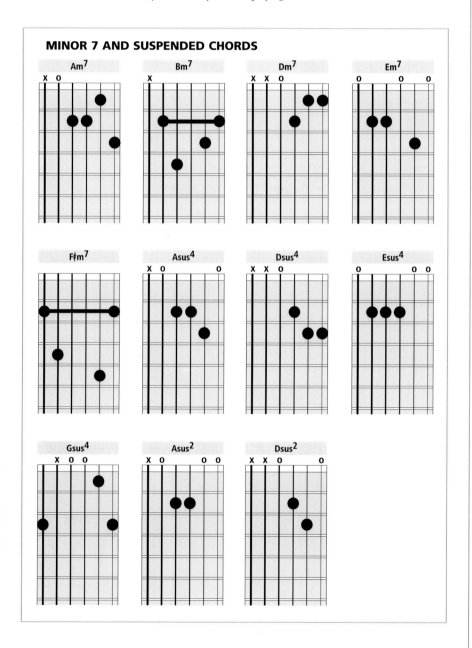

MINOR 7 AND SUSPENDED CHORDS

EFFECTIVE ACOUSTIC CHORDS

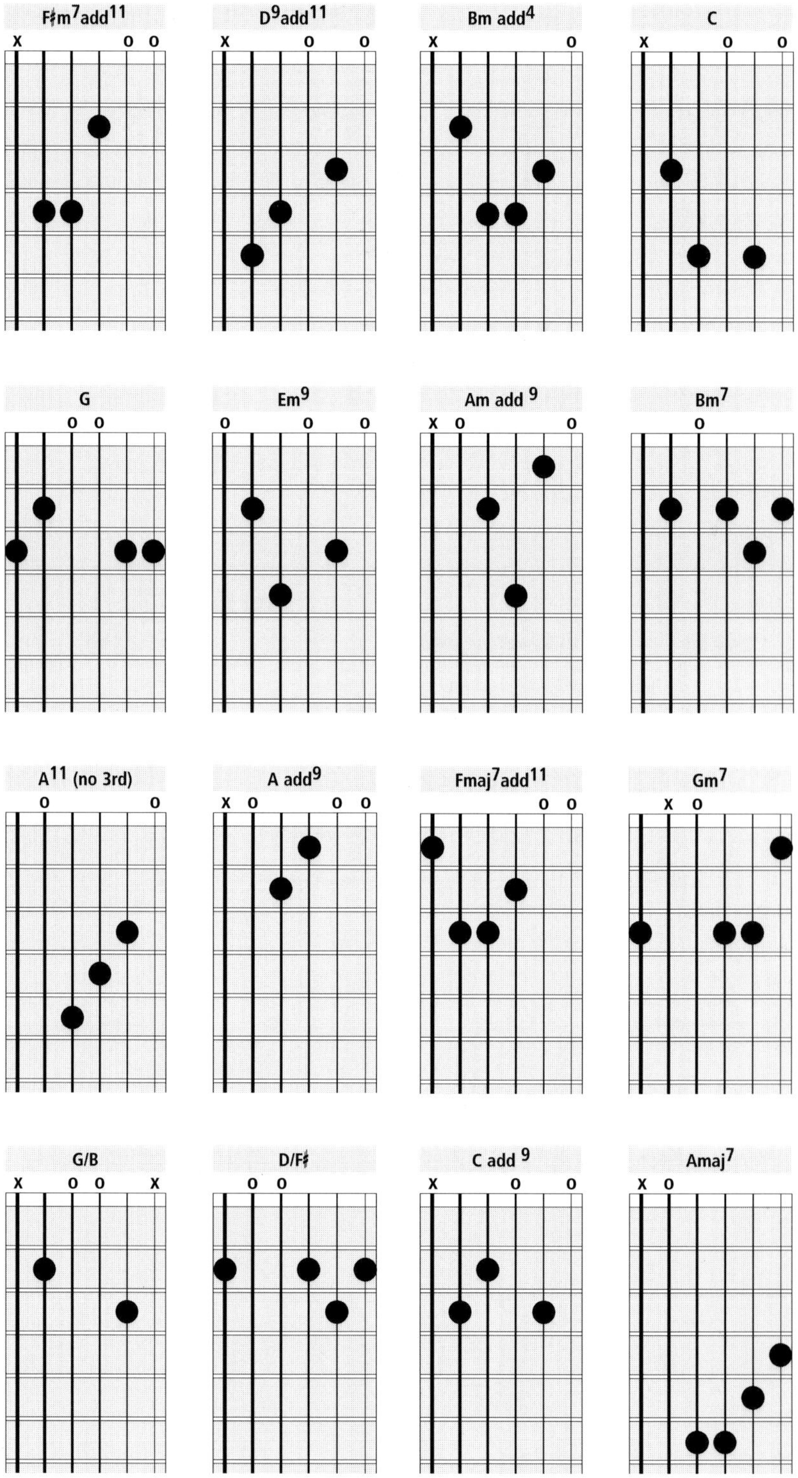

F♯m7add11

D9add11

Bm add4

C

G

Em9

Am add 9

Bm7

A11 (no 3rd)

A add9

Fmaj7add11

Gm7

G/B

D/F♯

C add 9

Amaj7

STRUMMING PATTERNS

Now you have plenty of chords to play with. So let's turn our attention to the hand that hits the strings. Although it is possible to strum with your thumb or the upperside of your fingers, the best tone for straight-on rhythm playing is produced by using a pick, or plectrum. These small pieces of plastic are held between thumb and forefinger (don't use your second finger because you might want to pluck a string with it at the same time as holding the pick). The thumb crosses the finger at approximately a right angle. Most of the pick should be gripped – there doesn't need to be much showing to hit the strings. Picks come in various shapes and thicknesses. For acoustic strumming a thin one is easiest to begin with and might give the best tone for jangly but not-too aggressive rhythm playing. Thick picks put up more resistance against the strings and take a little more effort, while also inducing a little more volume. The strumming action is mostly from the forearm as it hangs off the top of the guitar but the hand sometimes contributes a little for emphasis..

The essence of good strumming can be summarised as follows: evenness of tone, avoiding bass strings that are not meant to be hit, the ability to strum up and down with equal facility, controlling the volume, and keeping steady time. It also means knowing when and how to leave out strums.

Exercise 1 gets us started. Hold down an E major chord. Tap your foot, count to yourself, or set a metronome going at a medium tempo (around 80 to 90 bpm). This exercise is in 4/4, which means four beats to each bar. Strum downwards every other beat, then on each beat, then twice on each beat (eighth-notes or quavers), then four times on each beat (16th-notes or semi-quavers). Depending on how fast or slow you're going you may find that strumming twice and four times to a beat is too difficult just going downwards. The answer is to strum down and up, alternating.

Exercise 2 gives nine strumming patterns. The first is a strum in straight eighths. Notice how with each example some strums are taken away; the chord is allowed to ring. The rule is: the faster the tempo the longer a gap you can leave. With IV there is the introduction of a 'tie'. This is the line joining the fifth quaver to the fourth. A tie means you strike the first of the joined pair but not the second. Instead, the first lasts for the length of time of both notes. In any song you could use any one or a mixture of strumming patterns. Your choice will depend on mood, tempo and 'groove'.

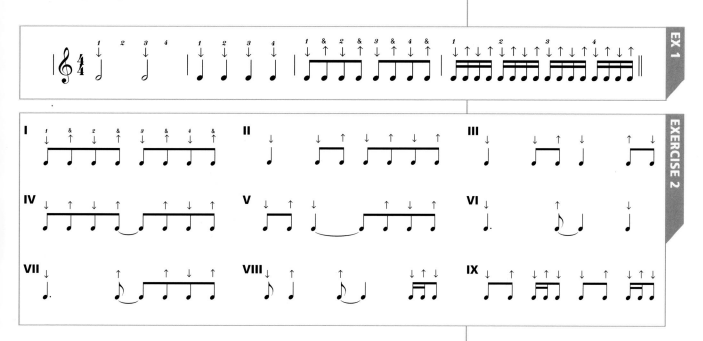

One way to make your strumming more interesting is to pick some of the bass notes of the chords individually and then hit the chord, as in **exercise 3**. This style is known as pick'n'strum. The bass note is usually the root note of the chord. Here is a well-known chord sequence that lends itself to this approach.

In **exercise 4** the bass notes are not all root notes, though the technique is the same. Introductions to songs and links between choruses and verses sometimes feature a phrase played in single notes, with chords in between, as in **exercise 5**. A song like 'Wish You Were Here' by Pink Floyd or the intro to Led Zeppelin's 'Over The Hills And Far Away' are examples of this popular approach to pick'n'strum.

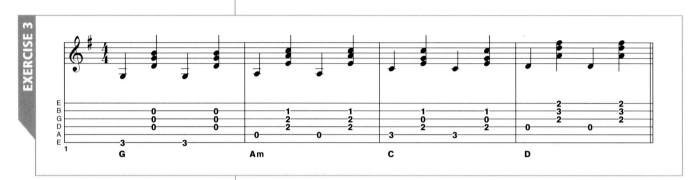

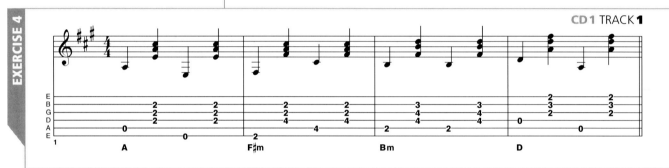

CD 1 TRACK **1**

BASIC FINGERPICKING PATTERNS

Exercise 6 shows 14 different finger-picking patterns. Notice how the thumb looks after the bass notes. In each case the notes of the chord are sounding but in a different manner to the simultaneous effect of strumming. Fingerstyle playing generates its own rhythm, too. You can easily adapt the patterns for 6/8 to 3/4. Most of the examples use a C chord, a five-string chord with its root on the fifth string. You can find variations of these patterns for chords with their root notes on the fourth or sixth strings. Obviously the more strings in a chord the more patterns you could devise to play them.

Let's continue by trying some slightly more complex fingerpicking exercises. Examples XI-XIV take a bit more work before you can do them unconsciously because of their syncopated rhythm. Remember to work out the thumb pattern first and then fit the other notes to it. Example XIV is a two-bar blues pattern in swung rhythm – each beat divides into the feel of three rather than two.

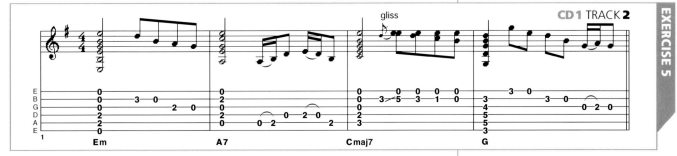

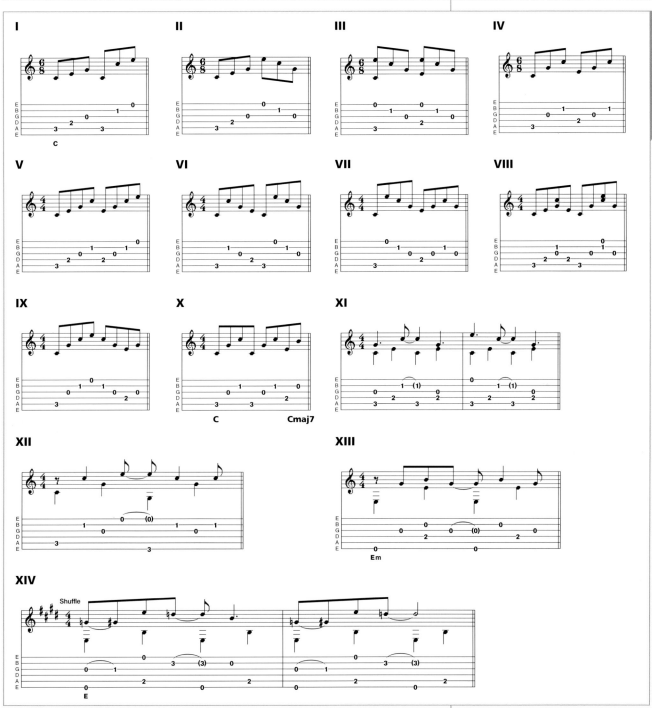

Exercise 7 is a simple ascending fingerpick applied to a popular chord progression with a descending bass-line. The 6/8 time signature means two beats in a bar, each dividing into three: 123, 456. Take it slowly at first, then build speed and play ad infinitum until you get the hang of it. It will feel repetitive, certainly, but this is the sort of exercise that really builds your fingerpicking skills.

    Exercise 8 also starts on A minor but in the later bars moves up the neck. Notice the way the open B-string is used. Initially the notes are in ascending order, but from bar three that pattern is broken up and the pitch order is less predictable.

In **exercise 9** a simple ascending finger-pick is applied to a chord sequence in which a number of inversions are used to join up root position chords. This is common in folk playing. D/F# and C/E are first inversions; the note after the forward slash sign (/) is the lowest in pitch. The Bm7/F# and Am/E are second inversion chords, in which the fifth of the chord is at the bottom. **Exercise 10** also uses some common inversions but the direction of picking is reversed. Notice also that two notes are sounded together for each group of quavers in bars 1-3. Like 3/4, 6/8 time lends itself to up-and-down patterns like this one. **Exercise 11** is another common progression with a descending bass line. **Exercise 12** (over the page) is a syncopated piece with an alternating thumb playing the bass notes (marked *p*). The progression is similar to Exercise 7. Let the notes ring for as long as possible.

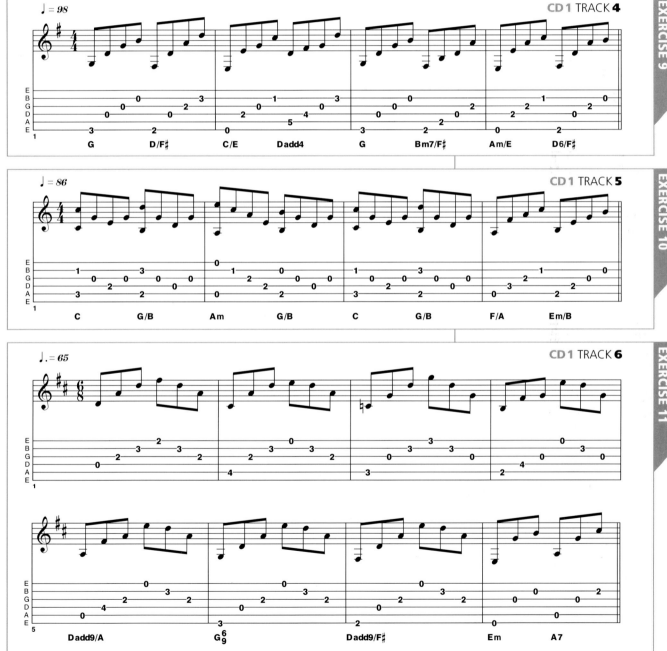

EXERCISE 12

CD 1 TRACK 7

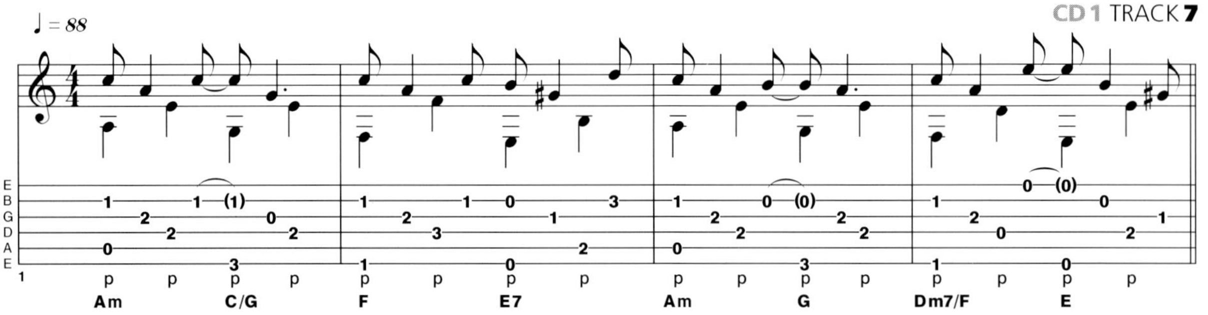

EXERCISE 13

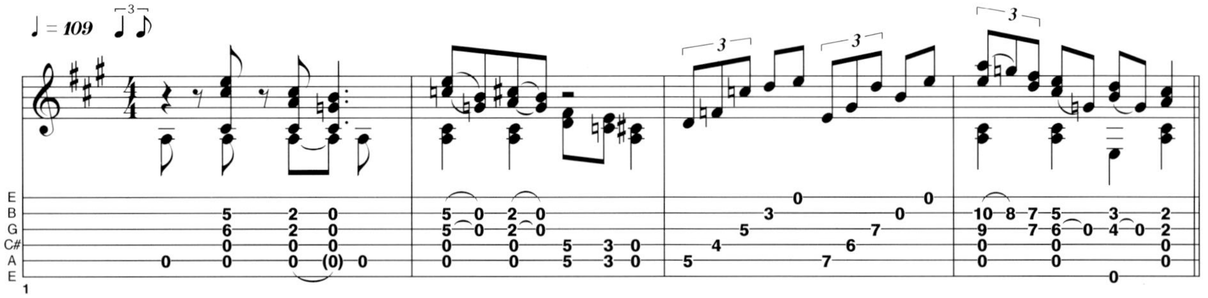

EXERCISE 14

CD 1 TRACK 8

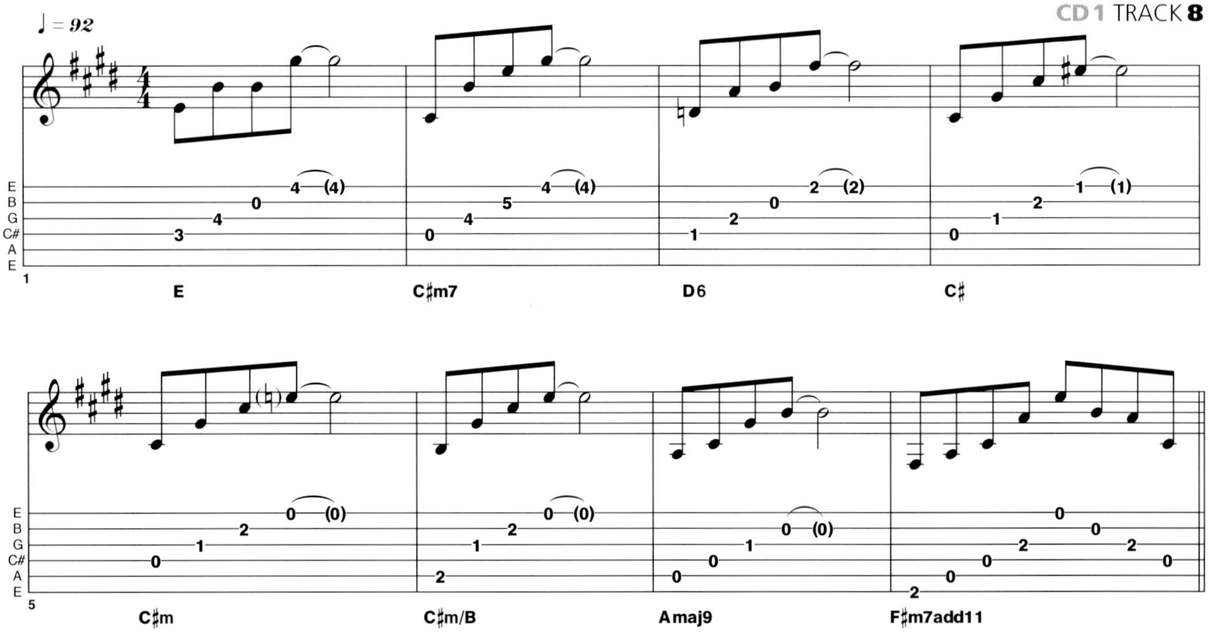

ALTERED TUNINGS

Standard tuning – EADGBE – is a wonderful compromise that allows a guitarist to work in many keys, despite its bias toward E minor. Many acoustic guitarists, however, have searched for new tones by altering this tuning. Some players stumble on altered tunings by default – no-one showed them how to tune the guitar 'properly' so they simply used their ear and tuned the strings to an open chord (Richie Havens and Joni Mitchell spring to mind). Others chased new tunings consciously to emulate the droning effects of non-Western instruments such as the sitar, or to make it easier to keep a bass going and improvise a melody.

An altered tuning can create beautiful new chords and stimulate your creativity. These new musical territories come at a price, however. First, there is the tuning in and out of them, with the attendant risk of broken strings and iffy intonation. Second, if you find some beautiful chords you had better write them down. Remembering chord shapes in ten different tunings is okay if you play the pieces regularly, but once they slip from the mind it can be a frustrating job trying to recall what they were!

SINGLE STRING ALTERATION

The simplest way to begin playing around with new tunings is simply to change one string. For this book I've invented a tuning in which the D string is detuned by a semitone to C#, giving us E A C# G B E. To do this, fret C# on the fifth string at the fourth fret and lower the open D until the two are in tune (to get back to standard reverse the process). This implies an A dominant ninth chord. I've supplied eight chord shapes and two short exercises you can play in this tuning. **Exercise 13** is a riff with a bluesy swing rhythm but some unusual chords. Try to keep the bass note steady and fit the higher parts around it. **Exercise 14** is simple upward picking. The idea is to play it slowly and let the strings ring so you can hear the unorthodox chord tones caused by the altered tuning. If these give you some new ideas, you can make up your own.

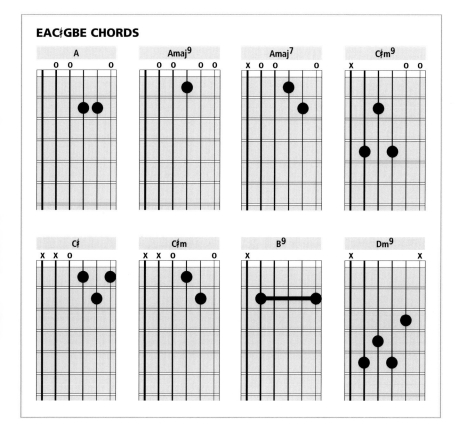

EAC#GBE CHORDS

These chords provide a quick guide to some easy shapes in the tuning of EAC#GBE, which itself makes a simple introduction to altered tunings, having only one string – the D – changed from standard tuning.

DROPPED D

The most famous single-string alteration is known, somewhat confusingly, as 'dropped D'. More accurately, the bottom E is 'dropped' – that is, tuned down a tone to D. This tuning is popular with rock players because the bottom three strings make a power-chord and the low D is good for launching heavy riffs. Folk players like it because it provides an octave open string D with the fourth string for an alternating thumb technique. The fretting hand is thus free to move wherever it wants on the neck. This tuning produces much deeper sounding six-string D and Dm chords.

In **exercise 15** the fourth and sixth open strings are played by the thumb. Above these, a series of thirds and fourths move up and down. This is one way of creating an accompaniment for a voice.

The thumb only alternates on the beat in the 12/8 piece in **exercise 16**. Above, the fingers fret a single-note melody with some decorative hammer-ons and pull-offs. Again, get your thumb working right first, then fit the melody to the steady pulse of the bass notes, not the other way around.

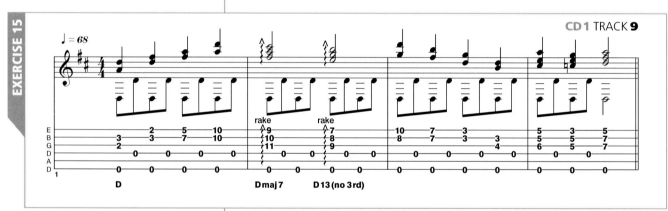

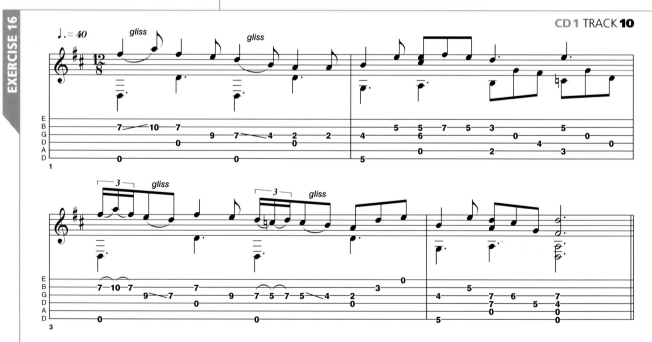

OPEN G MAJOR

After the single-string alteration we have open tuning proper, where the strings are tuned to make a simple major or minor chord. Each of the six strings is tuned to one of three chord tones. The most popular open tuning is open G (also one of the most popular tunings for five-string banjo). The notes of a G chord are G B D. Standard tuning already has those three notes on strings four, three and two, so the tuning is created by lowering strings six, five and one down until they come to the nearest of those three notes. The distance is measured in semitones.

E	A	D	G	B	E
-2	-2	–	–	–	-2
D	G	D	G	B	D

The immediate practical effect of this tuning is that a barre placed across the top five strings at any fret will create a root position major chord. The three chords needed for a 12-bar progression and many other songs will be found on the open strings, at the fifth and seventh frets, with the 12th fret giving an octave higher. Strong harmonics are also available at frets five, seven and 12 by laying a finger across the strings right over the metal fret but not pushing them against the fretboard. Strike the strings and gently pull the finger away and you will hear the ghostly, bell-like tones of harmonics.

Open G makes a very full sound if strummed. If a barre is held down various notes can be added by the other fingers. The first three chord boxes below indicate how this is done. The tuning is also used to provide drone notes, as octaves or sixths or thirds are moved up the neck. Try holding down the second fret on the first and fourth strings (an octave) and move this up and down as you strum all the strings.

Open tunings also lend themselves to slide playing. Keith Richards used open G on Rolling Stones classics such as 'Brown Sugar' and 'Start Me Up'. Use a capo with an open tuning if you wish to change its key. Open G with a capo at the third fret becomes open B♭ major.

Most accomplished players can quickly pick up some refreshing new melody lines by changing to an altered or open tuning, but finding and remembering new chord shapes can take a lot more work. These chord boxes make a handy compendium of fingerings to get you started in open G. Some even make useful 'movable chords' to take you to new positions.

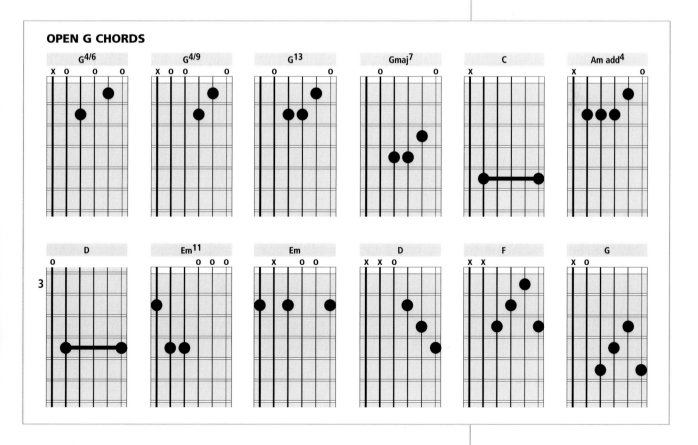

OPEN G CHORDS

DADGAD

Altered tunings need not make a simple major or minor open chord. 'DADGAD' is one of the most popular examples of a more complex tuning. It has misleadingly been called a 'modal' tuning. In fact, it's a Dsus4 chord. DADGAD was introduced into the world of folk guitar in the early 1960s by Davey Graham, a key figure in the English folk scene. It has been used by many players since, including Pierre Bensusan, for whom it is now 'standard tuning', and in a rock context by Jimmy Page, who used it for the mighty Led Zep epic 'Kashmir'.

Here are some DADGAD chord boxes for you to strum or finger-pick.

To conclude, **exercise 17** is a composition entitled 'Postcard To Denys', a fun piece with lots of bends and decorative hammer-on/pull-off figures typical of the style known as 'folk baroque'. It should be played with a slightly sloppy touch. In keeping with its humorous spirit the intro alludes to 'Purple Haze'.

DADGAD CHORDS

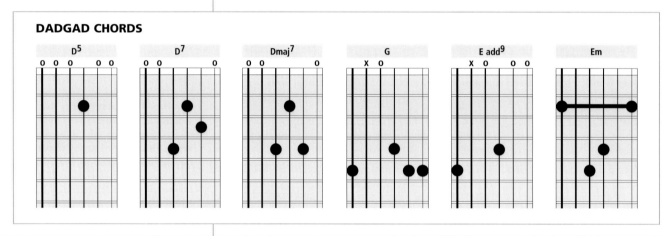

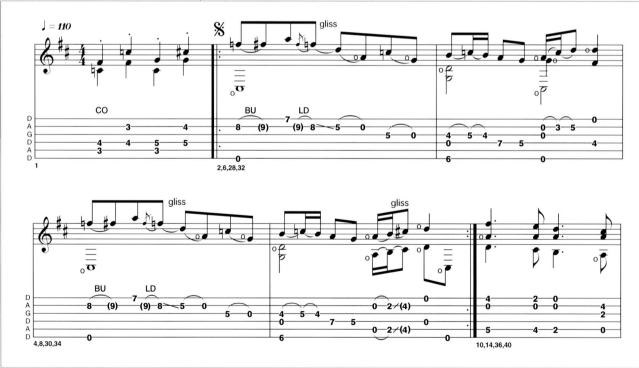

58

CHAPTER 2

Rock & Pop

There is no rigid boundary between pop and rock music, so this chapter will deal with playing a range of musical forms across the two styles, from the late 1950s to the present; in short, the bulk of the most popular music played and enjoyed today. There's nothing to stop you playing most pop and rock styles on the acoustic guitar, although extreme bends can be difficult, and of course distorted styles won't sound the same. Plenty of people enjoy playing popular tunes in this style, or writing their own, whether they eventually eventually take it electric with a full band set-up, or keep it unplugged for their own enjoyment.

By 'pop' we generally mean a lighter, less aggressive type of song, more suited to being chart material, possibly with more conservative lyrics, and with less reliance on the blues element that was brought into rock by 1950s rock'n'roll. There are also production differences, of course. Rock guitar tends to make more use of distortion, but even in full-blown rock recordings today the acoustic guitar often plays a big part, and the 'acoustic rock ballad' has almost become a genre in itself. Despite the development of many sub-genres within rock and pop the guitar basics remain quite stable. Eddie Cochran and Kurt Cobain might have had 30 years of rock between them, but from a guitar playing perspective they are still recognisably connected.

It was in the mainstream rock'n'roll of the 1950s rockers like Elvis Presley, Chuck Berry, Buddy Holly, and Eddie Cochran that the guitar really came to fame as a popular instrument (reinforced by the folk boom of the late 1950s and early 1960s). Accompanying this cultural revolution, a new group format was created around the new instrument: two electric guitars, electric bass and drums. This quartet was easy to form among your friends, and the combination of amps and hard-hit drums gave it a strong and dynamic presence. The two guitars could punch out a thick, resonant harmony, underpinned by the bass (up to 16 strings sounding together). In this format, one guitar could play a solo or melody and be supported by the other's chords – thus the roles of rhythm and lead guitar were born. Playing at home for your own enjoyment, you can easily take both roles on a single acoustic guitar, or get together with other musicians for an unplugged approximation of the classic set-up.

Players like Duane Eddy, The Ventures, Hank Marvin and Vic Flick (who played the James Bond theme) recorded many guitar-led, echo-haunted instrumentals. Instrumental guitar groups were everywhere in the early 1960s, until the triple-voice double-guitar songs of The Beatles and countless followers pushed them aside.

Mid-1960s bands like the Stones, The Kinks, The Who, The Animals and The Yardbirds made the guitar riff more of a feature. By the late 1960s blues-rock and heavy rock were pushing

into the mainstream, their groups invariably built around the first generation of guitar heroes who paraded their virtuosity in long, often improvised solos: Hendrix, Clapton, Page, Beck, Kossoff, Iommi, Blackmore, West, Garcia, Santana, and many others. Since then glam rock, late-1970s punk, early-1980s new wave, 1980s rock, indie, grunge, alternative rock, Brit-pop and nu-metal have all recycled riffs and ideas. While the electric guitar's possibilities have been expanded with the advancement of digital amplification and MIDI-controlled effects units, the electro-acoustic has also been improved to permit an acoustic guitar sound in an amplified quartet. Plenty of contemporary players – Dave Matthews comes to mind, for one – have proved you can make a big sound on stage without ever plugging in a 'conventional' electric guitar.

The relatively limited harmony used in many rock and pop songs means you can play most styles with a small number of chord shapes. When learning chords, first learn the open string shapes. These are easiest to finger and create a resonant, satisfying tone. The most common chords used in songs are A, C, D, E, F, G; Am, Bm, Dm, Em, F#m; A7, B7, C7, D7, E7, G7; Amaj7, Cmaj7, Dmaj7, Fmaj7, Gmaj7; Am7, Dm7, Em7; Asus4, Dsus4, Esus4, Gsus4; Asus2, Dsus2; and Cadd9. All these, and more, can be found in the previous section, 'Getting Started'. One essential task will be to master the barre chord. A barre chord involves holding more than one string down with a single finger, usually the first. Your aim should be to have two shapes for each type of chord, one with the root note on the sixth string, and the other with the root on the fifth. This will give two options for any required barre chord in any key, including all the sharps and flats. The four most important are derived from open string A, E, Am and Em shapes. At the first fret, turned into barre chords, these become Bb, F, Bbm and Fm. In the exercises that follow we'll look at many of the key techniques and ideas used in rock and pop since the early 1960s. The pages that follow include subsections on Rhythm Playing, Riffs, Triads, Intervals, Fifths, Scales and Lead.

RIKKY ROOKSBY

THE EXERCISES

A tempo indication in 'beats per minute' (bpm) is given for each exercise. With a metronome or drum machine you can hear how fast it should be played. Chord indications are given below the stave. These do not necessarily apply to the notes of the exercise. They may be implied chords or chords for a backing. To hear the full tone-colour of these exercises get a friend to play the chords for you, or record them on tape and then play along.

RHYTHM

Let's begin with an easy-to-play rock figure that has been around since the 1950s and almost defines the word 'boogie'. It's important to master this playing feel for all sorts of music you might want to tackle. For **exercise 1**, play to a steady rhythm, at first with downstrokes of the pick. Later try alternate down/up picking for a somewhat different rhythmic feel. (The

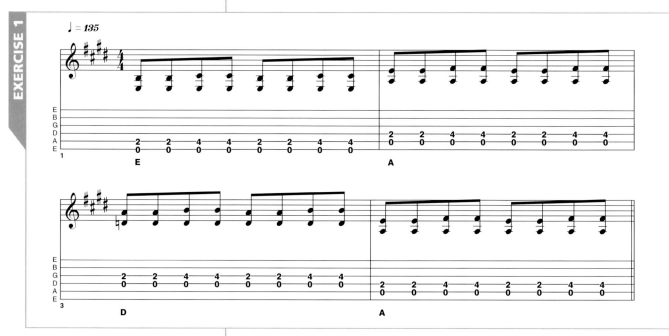

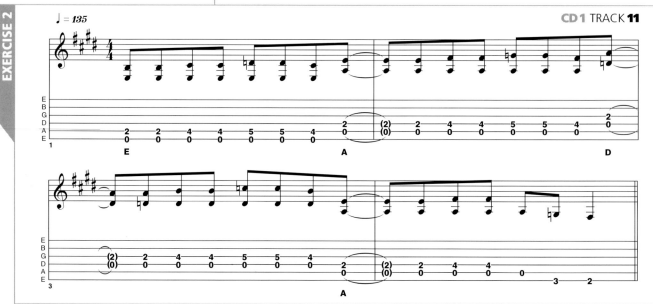

'shuffle' variation of this figure can be found in the 'Blues' section.) This popular rhythm has powered great rock playing from Chuck Berry to Oasis.

Exercise 2 is a variation where the note on the fretted string goes a further semitone up. Notice also the change from E to A comes on the last off-beat of bar one. This syncopation – with its distinctive 'pull' across the bar-line, is typical of rock. Remember to try to get each pair of notes the same volume.

Exercise 3 shows a subtle yet distinctive third variation on this theme, where two notes are introduced that temporarily eclipse the root note in each bar. Syncopation is once again present on the last off-beat.

It is also possible to use this rhythm figure in a new way by turning it into a set of single notes instead of striking two notes at a time, as in **exercise 4**. Watch out for the transition in bar four from hitting the sixth string to hitting the fourth string.

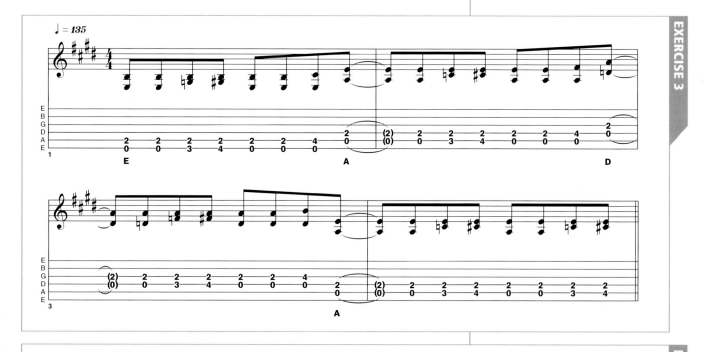

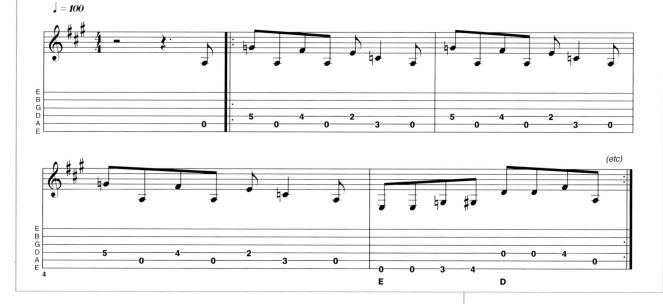

Exercises 1-4 work well in the key of A major. But what if we want to play this rhythm figure in other keys? The answer is to convert it into a fretted figure with no open strings. Don't worry if you find this a bit of a stretch at first. Drop your thumb well behind the neck. That will help your fretting hand open out. **Exercise 5** shows the boogie figure following a common chord progression (chords I, IV and V in B major).

Exercise 6 displays the same idea in E major starting on the fifth string. Starting on either the fifth or the sixth strings enables you to play it in any major key, and to pitch it higher or lower. Songs like Status Quo's 'Paper Plane,' Queen's 'Now I'm Here' and Super Furry Animals' 'Rings Around The World' feature this.

To help you memorise the pattern that governs the I-IV-V changes, **Exercise 7** isolates the root notes. Bars 1-2 give the pattern for starting on the sixth string; bars 3-4 for starting on the fifth. **Exercise 8** shows how original effects can be had with this rhythm figure by moving between less related root notes. Chord VI in E major should be C# minor, not C#, and there is no A# in the key of E, which is what the boogie figure demands. You can hear this change in T.Rex's 'Mambo Sun' from the album *Electric Warrior* (1971). A further innovation is to flatten the expected note, as in bar four.

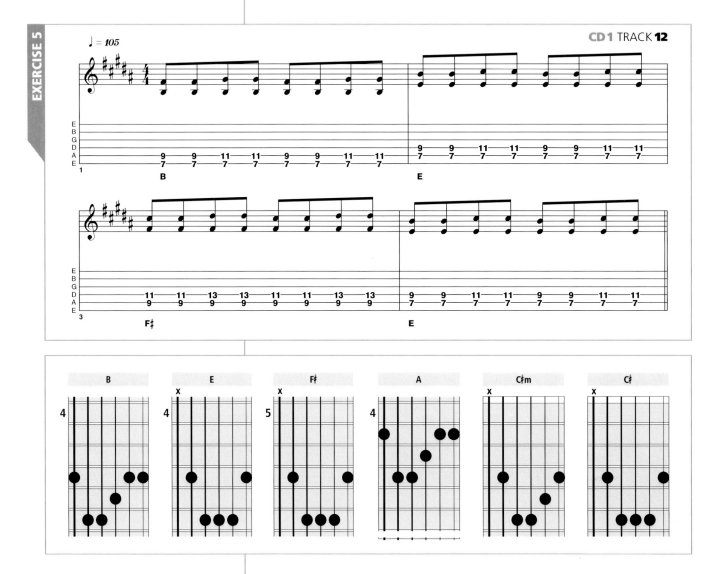

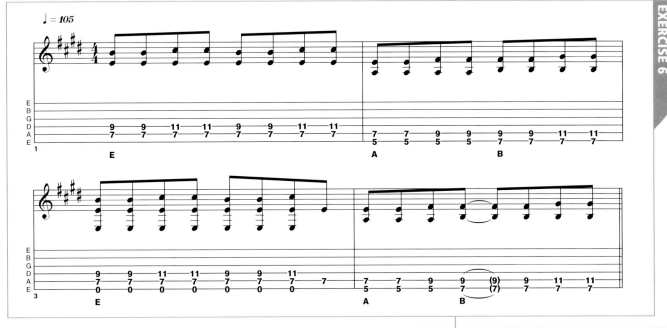

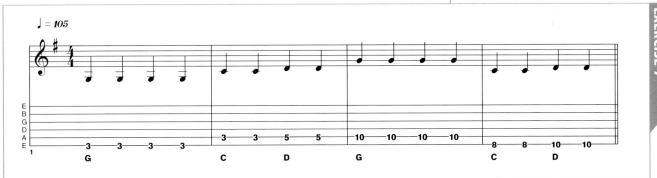

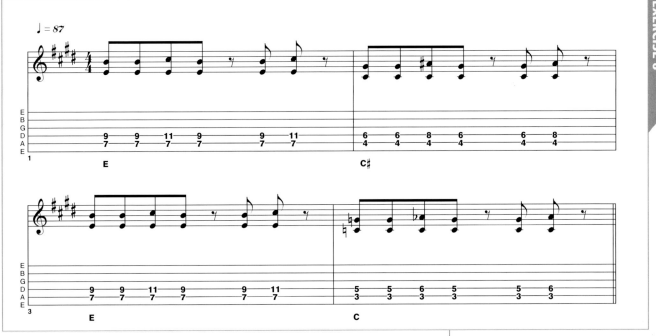

A related version of the rhythm figure we have been playing occurs on the higher strings and is based on a major triad held by the first finger. Play **exercise 9** to try it in C major.

Exercise 10 is a variation related to Exercise 2 where the finger goes up one additional fret. The note you added to each chord in Exercise 9 is known as the sixth of the chord. If we add the fourth as well as the sixth we get the rock rhythm figure displayed in **exercise 11**. Bars 1-2 lack a root note. This is suggested in bars 3-4. It is possible but awkward: the little finger must hold down the root and damp the fifth string. In **exercise 12** a related figure adds the fourth and the ninth to the basic triad. Notice the A chord in bar two has a powerful sound because the root note is merely the open fifth string. This figure on A is very popular for this reason. Exercises 9-12 will remind you of the Rolling Stones, the Faces, and the Black Crowes – good-time rock'n'roll. They are standard tuning versions of figures that occur in open tunings (the 'Getting Started' section deals further with open G).

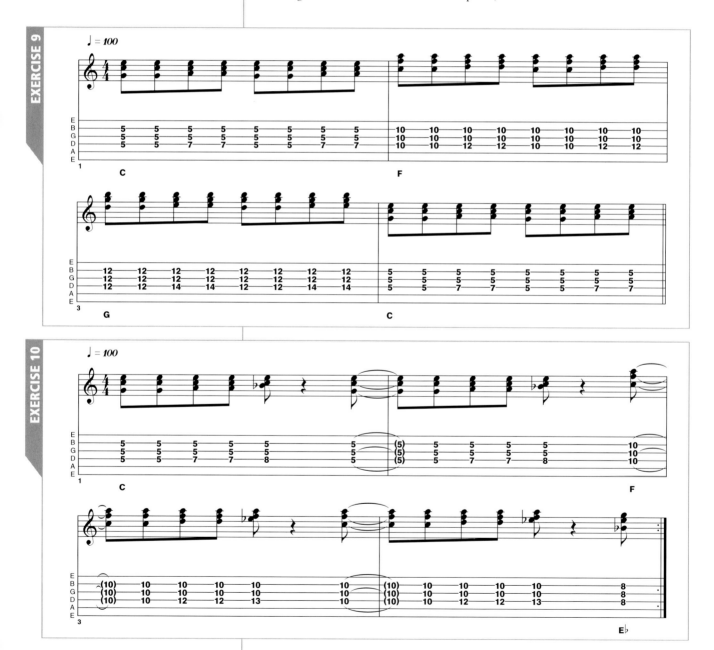

Apart from the A chord in the last example, the other open-string chord that yields excellent results with these 4/6, 4/9 shapes is G. In **exercise 13** bar one adds just the sixth, bar two the sixth and fourth, bar three the ninth and fourth, and bar 4 shows a common pull-off fill making good use of the open strings. Listen to 'John, I'm Only Dancing' by David Bowie, or 'If It Makes You Happy' by Sheryl Crow.

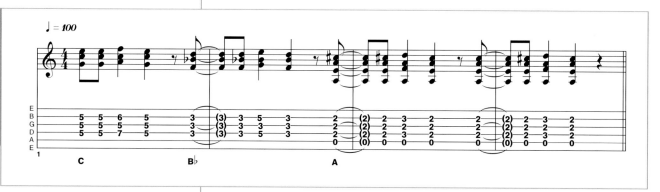

Exercise 14 shows how new effects can be had by giving these shapes a less predictable twist. Bar two has an E where we would expect an E♭, and bar three has an F where we would expect F#. This is now less Keith Richards and more Jimmy Page.

RHYTHM FIFTHS

Many of the above exercises are dominated by the interval of a perfect fifth (seven semitones), from E-B, A-E and D-A. The perfect fifth is crucial to rock guitar. It has a bare, tough, assertive sound and tolerates any amount of distortion. You may already know it under the name commonly used by rock guitarists, the 'power chord', and it is essential to master for comprehensive rock playing. While these are employed by many players as a means of keeping heavy, distorted sounds from overwhelming the mix – as can happen with a distorted full-barre chord, for example – they are also surprisingly effective on acoustic.

Strum this sequence in **exercise 15** with open-string chords. Then play it as fifths, as written out. Notice the difference. Even on an acoustic guitar the fifths toughen up the progression if a second guitar plays full chords. Played at various speeds, with or without damping (to give more 'thud'), rhythm fifths are a surprisingly diverse tool which occurs in rock, metal, punk, new wave and grunge – heard in the music of everyone from Soundgarden to Devo. If you play any form of rock, you'll find a use for them sooner or later.

In **exercise 16** damp all the strings on beats two and four. If you use your little finger to fret the higher of the two notes in each pair it will lie flat enough to stop most of the strings sounding when needed. To damp the lower note just let the string come off the fingerboard but keep your first finger on it. Notice the F5 occurs in bar four an octave lower than in bar two.

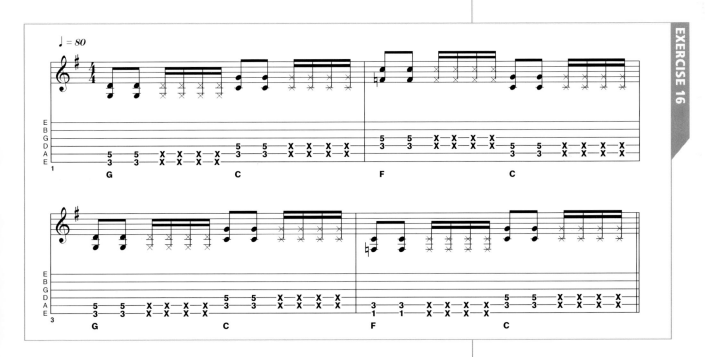

Fifths can be found in the same shape on all string pairs except three and two. **Exercise 17** shows how U2's guitarist The Edge might use a high fifth with an open G-string, which is characteristic of his guitar playing and a significant factor of his band's sound in general.

Exercise 18 gives us a fifth with an open G-string inside it. As you move the fifth the open G forms different relationships with the other notes, with a moody effect.

Fifths on four and three can be moved up and down in the key of E or E minor to combine with the top two open strings. Notice the resonance in bar one of **exercise 19** where there are two Bs at the same pitch. As you move the fifths try to let the open strings ring for as long as possible.

Fifths also combine well with sixths. A sixth is produced when you move either the first finger down a fret or the little finger up a fret, as in **exercise 20**. This is an idea frequently explored by Paul Kossoff, the late guitarist of Free.

If you invert a fifth you get a fourth: A-E (a fifth) becomes E-A (a fourth). Fourths combine well with fifths. In **exercise 21** fourths appear in bar four, but watch out for the way open bass strings add extra interest; this could be Eddie Cochran, Mick Ronson or Green Day.

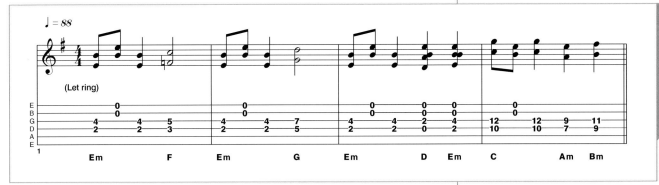

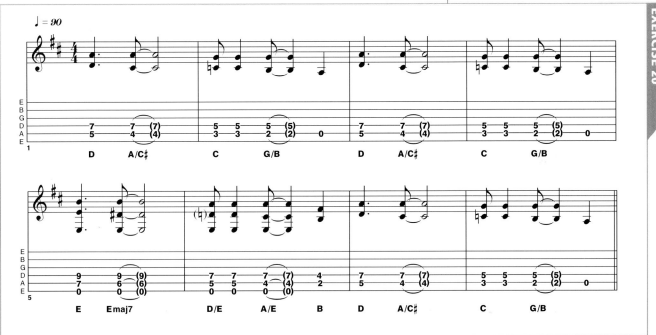

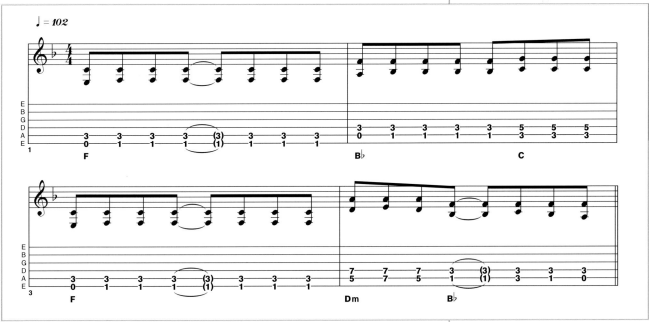

♩ = 108

G add9

C♯ add9

A add9

E♭ add9

If you take a fifth and 'copy' its shape onto the next string an add9 figure is the result. The chords in **exercise 22** are excellent stretching practice and spice up a sequence of fifths. They are associated with Andy Summers, who used them on Police hits like 'Message In A Bottle'.

TRIADS

Though much guitar-playing uses full chords, guitarists should not forget the humble triad. It only takes three notes to make a major or minor chord. This builds directly on the fifths, adding just one extra note – but it's a crucial addition, changing the mood of the chord dramatically between major and minor. Triads are easy to play and lend themselves to rhythm parts, fills, riffs and even lead solos. (In the 'Jazz' chapter, you will see how triads can allow you to play convincing jazz-style rhythm parts without needing to learn complicated chord forms.)

The fretted notes of an ordinary D chord make a D triad. In **exercise 23** that shape is moved up the neck in a chordal riff. The open D-string remains, an example of a 'pedal' note (a note which remains unchanged while chords or melody lines change around it). The major triads form different relationships with that D. Watch out for the open top string at the end of bars one and two. This simple but effective approach is used by Pete Townshend in many Who songs.

The chord block diagrams below offer an added visual approach to some of the concepts explained on this page. Though the chords in these exercises are written out in the notation of each individual example, it might help some readers to try them in this familiar form before going on to explore the exercises fully.

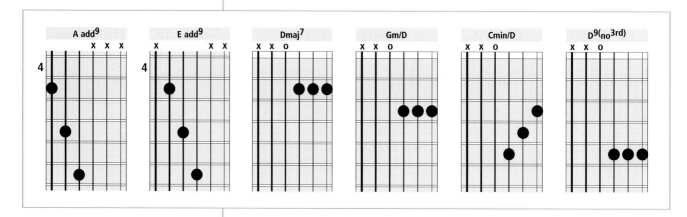

There are three major triad shapes on the top three strings. **Exercise 24** shows them over a D pedal. Compare this progression with strumming D, C and G in full chords. You can hear similar effects in Focus's 'Sylvia' (intro) and Wishbone Ash's 'Blowin' Free'. There are also three minor triad shapes on the top three strings.

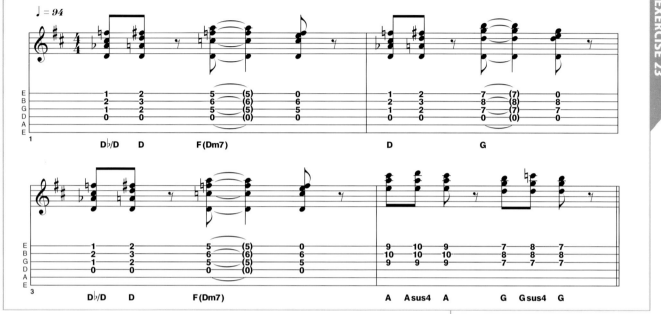

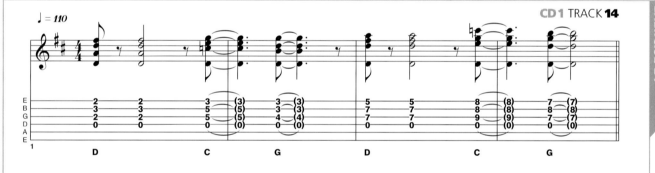

73

In **exercise 25**, notice how the D string modifies their sound at certain points, turning the F# minor triad of bar one into a Dmaj7 chord in bar two.

Exercise 26 uses major and minor triad shapes as they occur on strings two, three and four. This time the pedal note is A. Mark Knopfler of Dire Straits is a guitarist whose idiosyncratic picking technique led him to use triads for songs like 'Sultans Of Swing' and 'Lady Writer', as in **exercise 27**. It was easy for him to choose triads because he was plucking the strings with his thumb, index finger and middle finger only. This time there is no pedal note.

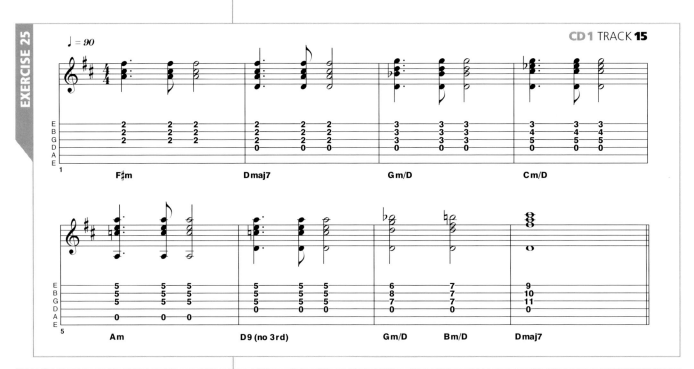

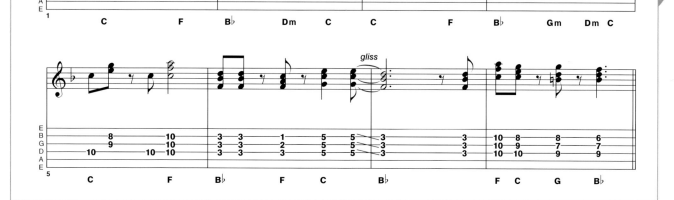

FOUR-NOTE CHORDS

Sometimes it's not necessary to include the lower strings. With a strong bass line it can be sufficient for the guitar to play chords on the top four strings only. The Spin Doctors' 'Two Princes' is a fine example. A well-known pop and soul recording trick is to put a 'stab' guitar chord on beats two and four, as in **exercise 28**. A bright, clean tone is used and the chord is immediately followed by a rest. This chord will often sit with the snare drum. Listen to many 1960s soul records, especially from Motown, where the high stab guitar was often played by Joe Messina on a Telecaster.

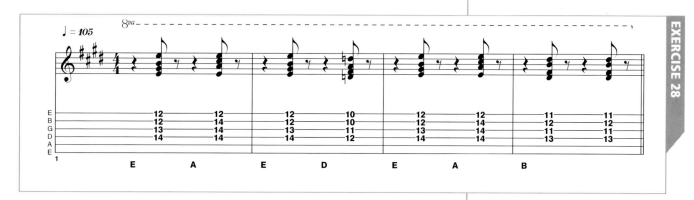

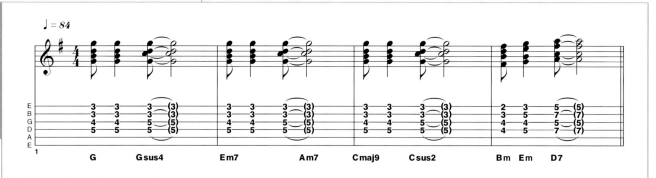

One of the tricks of professional song-arranging is to know when you don't need to change a chord but can let the bass guitar do the work. The G-Gsus4 change stays the same throughout bars 1-3 in **exercise 29**, yet the chords written below change. To hear the effect either get someone to play the root notes of G, E minor, A minor and C, or play those chords on guitar or keyboard while you play the written part. The changing root notes change the harmonic value of the written G-Gsus4 change even though it stays the same, so it sounds different in each bar.

RIFFS

A riff is a memorable phrase of between one and four bars. In rock it often focuses much of the energy of the song, and is generally repeated as a central 'hook' of the guitar part. Riffs occur in almost all guitar music from 1950s rock'n'roll to contemporary nu-metal, and in other genres like reggae, soul, blues and folk; they're the building blocks of countless pop and rock guitar parts. Riffs are quick to write and learn, and great fun to play – and chances are you know a few good ones already.

Many riffs are derived from the same scales used for rock and blues lead. Bars one and two of **exercise 30** ascend E pentatonic minor. 'Pentatonic' means five notes – in this case, E G A B D. Bars three and four provide the riff itself, using the lower notes of this scale.

By adding one note to the previous pentatonic scale – B♭ – we get the E blues scale, as used in **exercise 31**. This extra note is called a flattened fifth and it is important for its dissonance: it sounds mean. This note allows a riff with creeping semitone movement.

E/E minor are popular keys for the guitar because the strings are naturally biased toward E. However, a pentatonic scale can be played from any note. Since the second lowest open string is A, A pentatonic minor (A C D E G) is also popular. **Exercise 32** is a riff on that scale. Watch out for the powerful A5 chord in bars two and four, and the flattened fifth (E♭) that appears in bars three and four.

Fifths are popular for riffs. In **exercise 33** the fifths are strengthened by the open A and E strings. You can hear this in rock bands like Thin Lizzy and Iron Maiden.

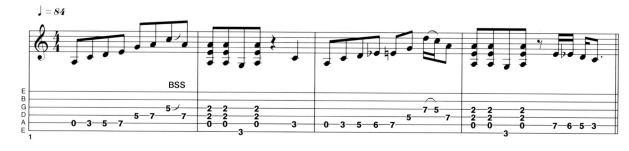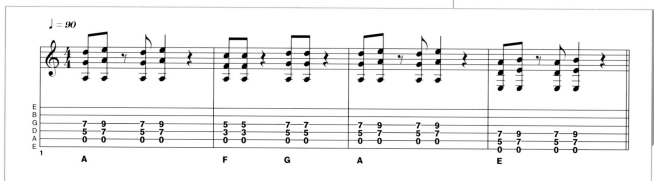

Exercise 34 is a riff that uses fifths, fourths (the pairs of notes here with the same fret number) and octaves (bars two and four). The riff sequence in **exercise 35** uses fourths. Fourths have their own flavour. They are less stable than fifths because the root note is no longer the lower of the two. Ritchie Blackmore used fourths for many Deep Purple and Rainbow riffs.

Transferred to the top two strings, as in **exercise 36**, fourths become less heavy rock and more new wave. Their slightly 'oriental' color was exploited by Television on *Marquee Moon*, and in Wings' 'Band On The Run'. Meanwhile, bands like Led Zeppelin have forged memorable rock songs from riffs built on octaves, not unlike those in **exercise 37**. This type of riff is especially effective when the guitar and bass are together on the riff. Octave riffs can also make a good accompaniment during a verse structure, as in **exercise 38**. Bars 1-4 feature a basic figure of an octave that falls to the flattened seventh and then the fifth. In bars 5-8 a variation introduces the flattened fifth note previously featured. Here, it's the C# in bars five and six.

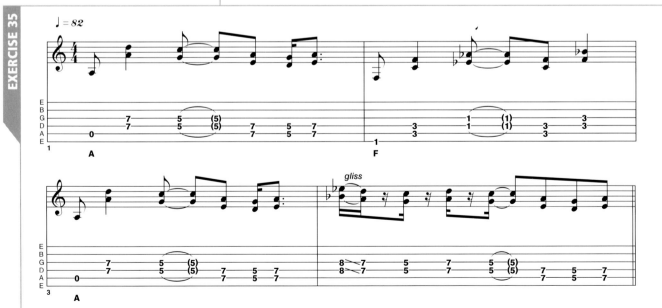

Riffs can use single notes over a pedal note, as in **exercise 39**. The pedal note is supplied by an open string. Here over D is a scale known as the 'Mixolydian mode'. You can read more about this mode later in the chapter. It differs from the D major scale (D E F# G A B C#) merely in having the seventh note flattened to C. This effect is featured on The Cult's 'She Sells Sanctuary' and R.E.M.'s 'Green Grow The Rushes'.

Exercise 40 is a similar pedal riff, this time using A and having two notes at a time above it. Rock music favours the sus4 chord because of its tension (great for building drama) and its neutrality. Like fifths and fourths, the suspended fourth chord, explored in **exercise 41**, is neither major nor minor. This riff takes a triadic form and moves it down through small changes. Sus4 chords feature strongly in the Who's 'Pinball Wizard', T.Rex's 'Cadillac', Argent's 'Hold Your Head Up', and John Lennon's 'Happy Xmas (War Is Over)'. The bends in **exercise 42** – two strings bent together – were established in rock guitar by Chuck Berry and have been used by many other players ever since. They are very effective at faster tempos, as in Motorhead's 'Ace Of Spades'.

No look at riffs would be complete without the 1-3-5-6 figure, so called after the notes of the scale and explored here in **exercise 43**, which is closely related to the rock'n'roll rhythm parts you played in exercises 1-4. **Exercise 44** is a slightly decorated version. You can hear something similar on Roy Orbison's 'Pretty Woman', though in that song the riff stays on E.

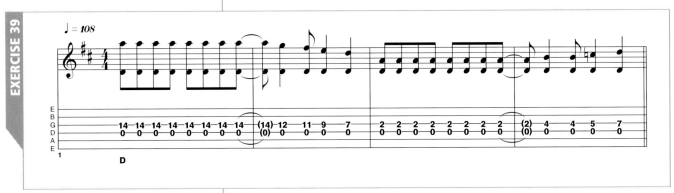

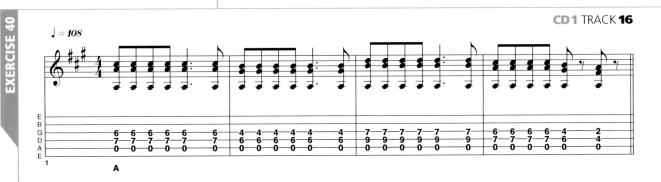

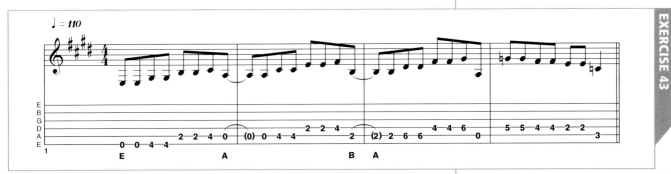

The term 'chromatic' refers to the use of extra notes that do not belong to the key, as employed in **exercise 45**. Chromatic riffs have an element of surprise about them. They can sound 'jazzy' – as in Pink Floyd's 'Money' or toward the end of Hendrix's 'Hey Joe' – or sinister, as in Led Zep's 'Dazed And Confused'. Look for a fingering that will make use of all your fretting fingers.

USING INTERVALS

Already we've played exercises that use significant intervals. In a major scale the intervals are major second (C-D), major third (C-E), perfect fourth (C-F), perfect fifth (C-G), major sixth (C-A), major seventh (C-B) and perfect octave (C-C). We have seen how fourths and fifths are used in rhythms and riffs. Seconds and sevenths are not harmonious enough for consecutive playing, but octaves can thicken a melody or melodic phrase, as Hendrix did in 'Third Stone From The Sun'. For **exercise 46** use a pick and your middle finger, or damp any strings in between and just use a pick. Octaves lend themselves to sliding up or down. **Exercise 47** gives you a chance to practice a 16th-note strum of 'damped' octaves. Mute all four of the other strings with your fretting hand, then strum up and down in groups of four with the first of each group accented. When you get comfortable with this you can try cutting out some of the fretted 16ths. By muting more of them in the bar you can generate funk rhythms. There is a hint of this in the last bar. There's more muting practice for octave riffs in **exercise 48** – but listen for the altered intervals in the last bar.

Octaves are crucial to the sound of a 12-string guitar. But what if you don't own a 12-string? Well, **exercise 49** shows a way of generating a 12-string effect on a six-string. It requires some nimble finger-work in both hands but it's a valuable technique, and a great skill builder in itself. Use a pick and a finger and let strings ring as long as you can.

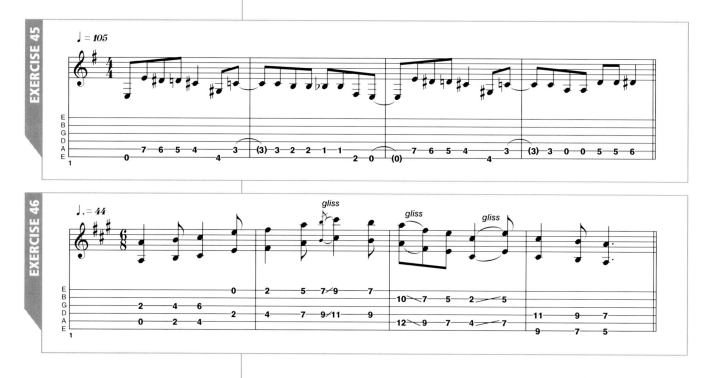

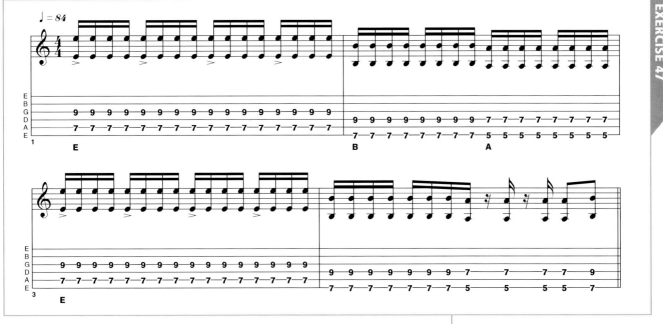

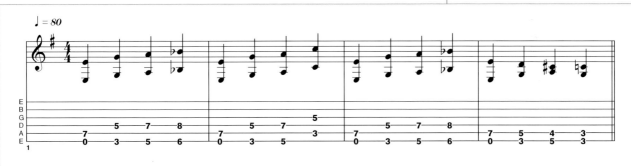

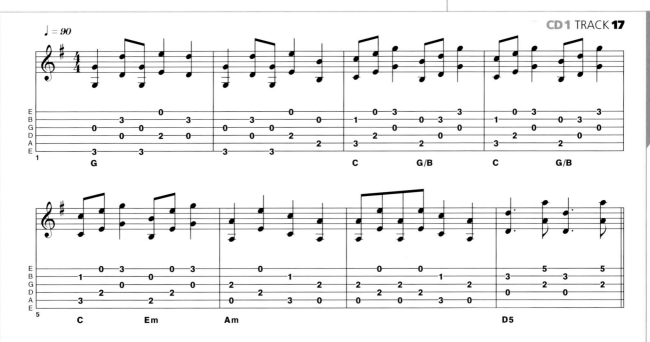

THIRDS AND SIXTHS

The only useful intervals we haven't touched on yet are thirds and sixths. Both have major and minor forms. A major third is four semitones (C-E); a minor third is three (C-E♭). A major sixth is nine (C-A); a minor sixth is eight (C-A♭).

Exercise 50 shows a sequence of thirds in D major on the top two strings. All the notes on the top string should be fingered with the first finger; those underneath are either the second or the third. The first finger acts as a guide when you shift position. The key note for the sequence is on the second string at the starting position. If you want to transpose this to another major key, locate the new key note on the second string and play the same sequence from there.

Exercise 51 is the equivalent sequence in A major on the second and third strings. The guide finger is the second, which plays all the notes on the lower string; the second string notes are either first or second finger. If this were played from the seventh fret you would have the same notes as in exercise 50.

Thirds have a sweetening effect, and can be used for guitar fills and lead solos. Van Morrison's 'Brown-Eyed Girl' and The Smiths' 'This Charming Man' use them. They can be played either simultaneously or one after the other, as **exercise 52** shows.

Remember: the harmonic value of notes depends on the underlying harmony. Change the harmony and you effectively change the notes even if they stay still. **Exercise 53** has a two-bar phrase in thirds. Each time the chord changes it will sound different. Try continuing this riff through another four bars – two bars each against the underlying chords F and G – to hear this effect even further.

Exercise 54 is a sequence of sixths in G major on the first and third strings. All the notes on the third string should be fingered with the second finger; those above are either the first or the third. The key note for the sequence is on the first string at the starting position. To transpose this to another major key simply find the new key note on the first string and play the same sequence from there.

Exercise 55 is the equivalent sequence in D major on the second and fourth strings. The guide finger is the second which plays all the notes on the lower string; the second string notes are either first or third finger. If this were played from the eighth fret you would have the same notes as in exercise 54. Sixths are also used for fills and lead solos, though they don't sound as sweet as thirds. Soul guitarist Steve Cropper is renowned for his use of sixths on many 1960s recordings like 'Soul Man' and 'Dock Of The Bay'.

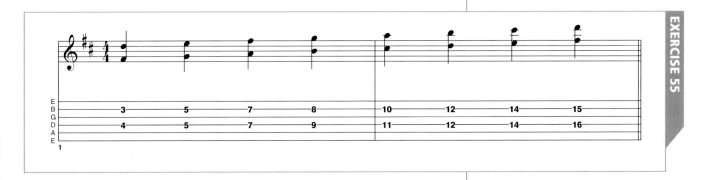

In **exercise 56** the addition of a couple of chromatic sixths emulates Cropper's slinky feel. This is yet another technique that can be simple to master, but has an extremely effective, melodic feel with a little extra bluesy groove to it too – and it usually yields positive results when employed tastefully.

Sometimes in a riff sixths make a refreshing change from fifths or fourths. In **exercise 57** the D G F D change could have been done with either – but here it is in sixths, combined with a D pentatonic minor single-note phrase.

Exercise 58 gives us a look at some thirds combined with an open G-string.

Clever choice of key makes it possible to put the open B string in the middle of a run of sixths in **exercise 59**. Taking B as the key note, it is only necessary to find a run of sixths in B major. Andy Summers used the technique in E minor in The Police's 'Bring On The Night', where sixths in E minor straddle the open G string (the middle note of an E minor chord).

Learn each of these approaches to sixths, then see if you can make up a few in these keys and others. Use them to spice up your riffs and tunes where appropriate.

THE 'JANGLE' STYLE

The last two exercises are reminiscent of a popular style which has become known as 'jangle'. It is associated with the 12-string sound of The Byrds' Roger McGuinn, Peter Buck's playing with R.E.M. in the 1980s, Johnny Marr's work with The Smiths, and many 'indie' bands of the 1990s. The La's 'There She Goes' is a superb example.

Jangle is a clean, shimmery, ringing guitar texture, aided by sustaining effects like compression, chorus, echo and reverb, and needing a certain approach to chord shapes and picking.

Jangle guitar requires open strings to ring out between changes, while chords are turned into arpeggios, the strings picked one at a time, as typified by **exercise 60**. The shapes can be simple but the end result pleasing to the ear and extremely effective in the right context.

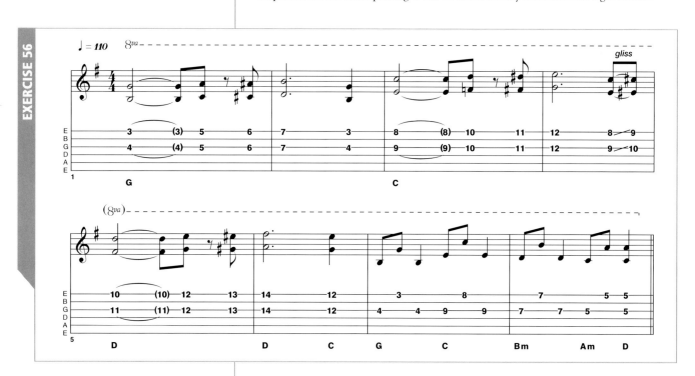

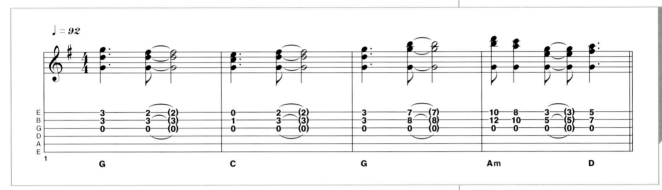

CD 1 TRACK **18**

In the early playing of Peter Buck there is often a quick picking of the chord to give drive and motion to otherwise fairly simple progressions, and that's the way to approach **exercise 61**. Make good use of up and down pick strokes as you weave among the strings. Notice in bar three the 'harp' effect of having three notes each a tone apart all sounding at once. Hear Buck's jangle in songs such as 'Radio Free Europe' from the album *Murmur* and 'Good Advices' from *Fables Of The Reconstruction*.

    Exercise 62 demonstrates another of those 'weaving' picking patterns, with a harp effect in bar four. Notice the introduction of the open E into the D chord in bars one and two, and the hollow ring of the Asus2 in bar seven. Take care that all the notes in bar six ring as long as they can for the full effect.

    In **exercise 63** chord shapes are devised away from first position so that open strings can combine with higher fretted notes. This offers a pleasing contrast to the lower-position jangle phrases so often heard.

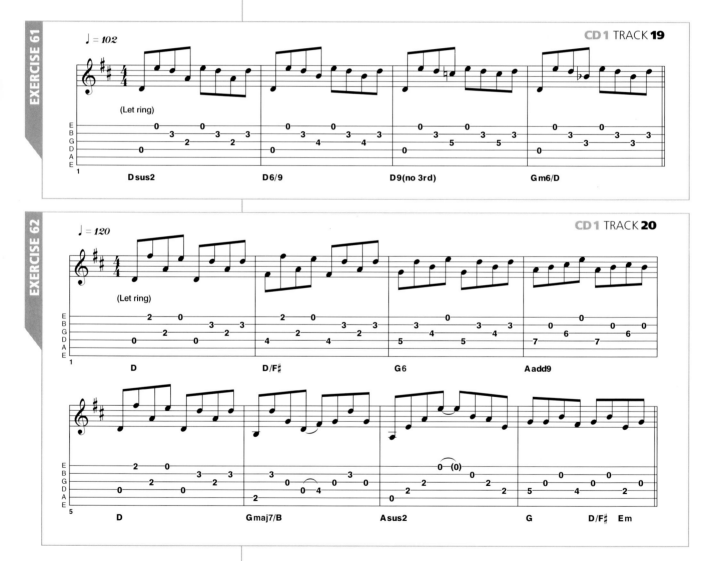

ARPEGGIOS

The jangle style plays the notes of a chord one after the other to generate an 'arpeggio'. Arpeggios are found elsewhere in rock and pop guitar. They are crucial in songs such as Cream's 'Badge', The Beatles' 'Here Comes The Sun' and 'I Want You', Bebop Deluxe's 'Maid In Heaven' and The Jam's 'When You're Young'.

The figures in **exercise 64** exploit the slightly murky tone of low thirds on the guitar. Bryan Adams's 'Run To You' and Nirvana's 'Come As You Are' do likewise. In **exercise 65** most of the arpeggios are based on a triad, but watch for the C#m7 in bar seven.

EXERCISE 63

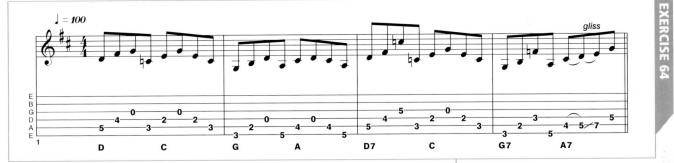

EXERCISE 64

EXERCISE 65

In **exercise 66** a common sequence moving from C down to G is transformed by the use of arpeggios. This might make a suitable conclusion to a chorus or a whole song.

Arpeggios can also be included in a guitar solo. Many of the lead solos on Dire Straits' *Brothers In Arms* begin with a rising arpeggio. The triad in bar four of **exercise 67** is played with a 'rake': the notes are not struck altogether but fractionally one after the other, either by pushing the pick through the strings, or 'rolling' the notes with the pick and two fingers.

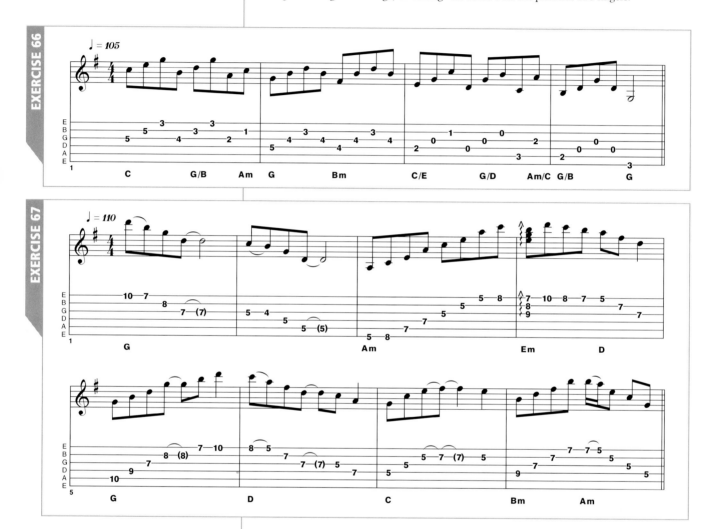

LEAD GUITAR

Playing lead guitar competently is a matter of learning a small number of scales and scale patterns; mastering the art of bending and left-hand techniques like vibrato, hammering-on, pulling-off and slides; and gradually finding out which notes work over any given chord sequence.

BENDS

Exercise 68 features four of the commonest bends, one per bar, arranged in order of their rise in pitch. (Players do occasionally bend further than three semitones – but string breakage is always a risk!) In each bar you first play the target note by fretting it; then you bend the previous note up. This 'primes' your ear each time so you can listen for when you're in tune. The exception is the final quarter-tone bend which is actually a fraction lower than the C# you play on the first beat. In Ex.68 the bends are all done with the third finger, with the first and second on the same string behind it. This means you can push with all three. Try also having your thumb on the top edge of the neck to get more grip. Bends are undoubtedly more difficult to execute on acoustic guitar than on electric, but many skilled players still make good use of them, and they are an effective technique in many styles.

   Exercise 69 displays a single bend with two notes above it that will generate either a major or a minor chord depending on how far you push the bend. Hold the top two notes down with a little finger barre, and bend with the third finger with first and second supporting behind it. You can also play this progression hitting all the notes at once for a slightly different feel. The note on the top string is your root note. Select the root note for the chord you want on the top string, then bend a semitone or a tone to produce the minor or major chord on that note.

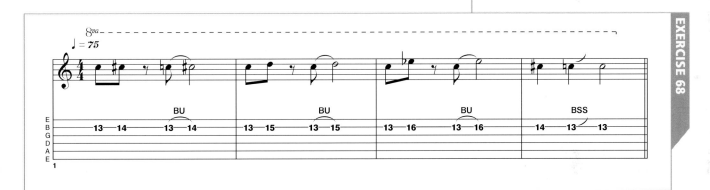

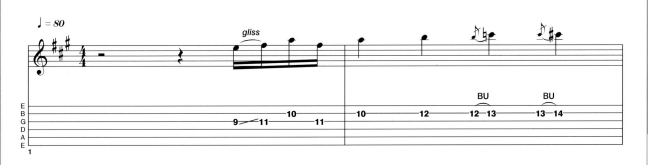

It is possible to push a bend up a semitone at a time in order to get a sequence of notes, as in **exercise 70**. The B in bar 2 is pushed up first to C, then C#, then D, after which the E is supplied by the 12th fret on the top string. In bar three the idea is used in reverse. The bent E is dropped first a semitone from F# to F and then down to E. You'll see that a similar technique occurs again in bar five.

Exercise 71 is a two-octave A pentatonic minor scale pattern starting on the fifth string. This exercise uses triplets – a group of three quavers played on the beat – and will take some stretching to reach the top if you haven't got a cutaway guitar. (With a 12th-fret neck join, forget it!)

THE 'CASCADE'

In order to make a scale pattern last longer when playing quickly, guitarists sometimes use a technique which we can dub the 'cascade'. The idea is to play down a few notes and then go back up one or two less. **Exercise 72** is a triplet cascade down the A pentatonic minor scale. You'll notice right away how the cascade helps to give the impression that you're not just running down a scale, but playing a more considered lead line. **Exercise 73** is an eighth-note cascade down the same scale. In bar two the flattened fifth (E♭) is added to make the A blues scale. Bar three is the same cascade idea starting one string lower than bar one. In bar four the same flattened fifth occurs but this time it is bent rather than fretted. Notice the difference in tone.

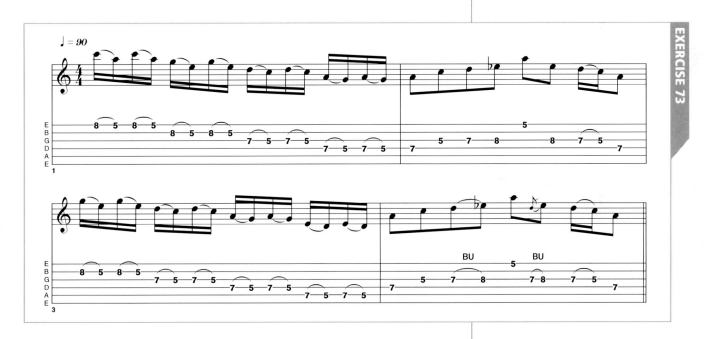

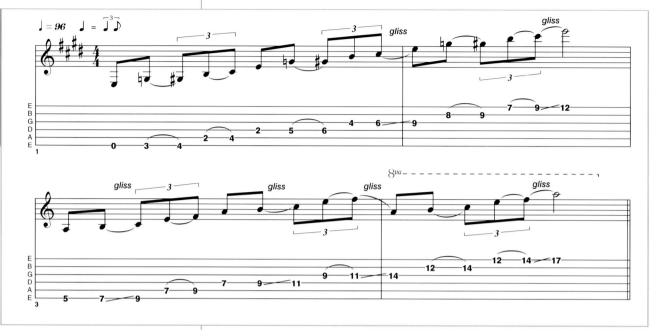

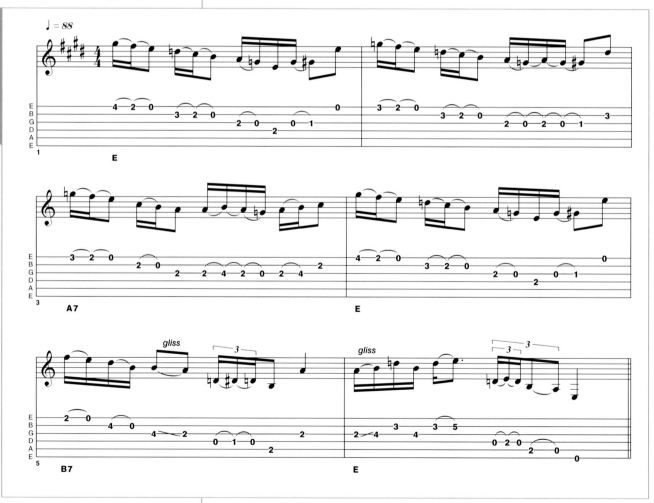

Exercise 74 is a three-octave E blues scale based on the E pentatonic major (E F# G# B C#) but with the addition of a flattened third, in this case G. This scale has an upbeat feel and is found in lead guitar solos that derive from 1950s rock'n'roll.

Apart from string-bending, another decoration used by lead players is the hammer-on/pull-off, seen here in **exercise 75**, where notes are created by the fretting hand. This is based on a six-bar blues pattern. The scale is E Mixolydian (E F# G# A B C D) but with the flattened third G also appearing.

REPEAT LICKS

Like the cascade, the repeat lick is a way of getting more from a small group of notes. The idea is to make a short phrase and repeat it for several bars. The one in **exercise 76** uses several that are based on a triad. Mark Knopfler used this idea very effectively at the close of 'Sultans Of Swing'. In the right place, as in his energetic solo, these can sound more dynamic and driving than merely repetitive.

Exercise 77 is a five-note repeat lick that is based on A dorian (A B C D E F# G). Notice the shift up a minor third – a favourite trick of Jimmy Page.

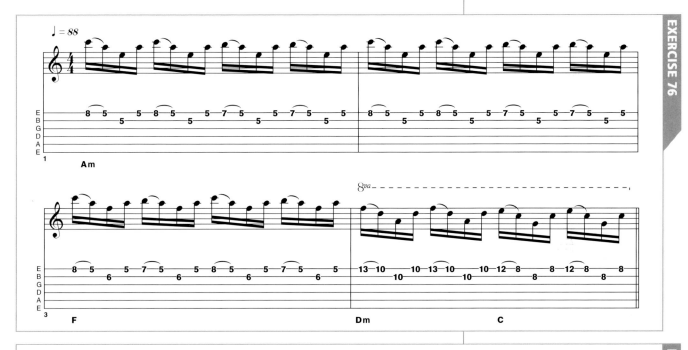

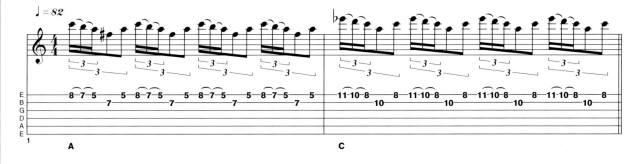

Once you've mastered exercise 77, try squeezing one more note onto the beat to get six – voila, **exercise 78**!

THE MODES

The pentatonic patterns are the most used by rock guitarists. A brief look at the group of scales known as the modes, however, will suggest some extra 'colour'. Whether you can use these in a solo will partly depend on the chords you're playing over.

The Aeolian mode, **exercise 79**, is also known as the natural minor scale. In A it would be A B C D E F G. Listen for the sadness of the second and sixth of this scale (B and F).

Contrast exercise 79 with the non-modal harmonic minor scale in **exercise 80**, where the seventh note is raised a semitone. Rock guitarists sometimes exploit the last four notes of this scale – E F G# A – to get an 'Eastern' sound. The Dorian mode, **exercise 81**, can be thought of as the natural minor with a sharpened sixth: A B C D E F# G. It is favoured by Carlos Santana in much of his lead playing. **Exercise 82** shows the Phrygian mode, which can be thought of as a natural minor with a flattened second: A B♭ C D E F G. Many players consider it to have a Spanish sound. The Aeolian, Dorian and Phrygian are all minor modes.

96

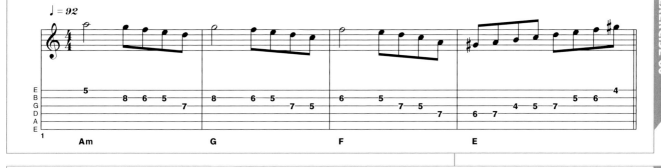

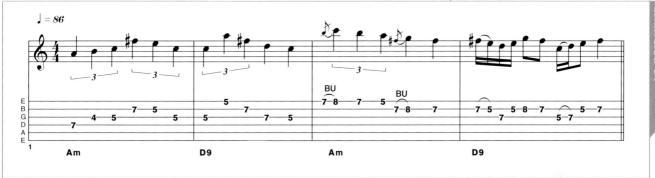

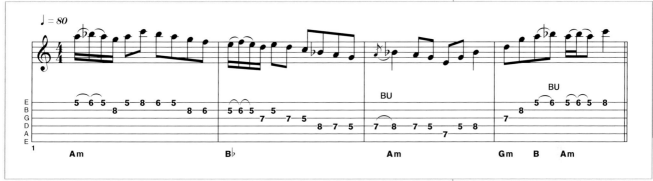

There are three major modes. The Ionian is our major scale (in G: G A B C D E F# G). The Mixolydian is a major scale with a flattened seventh: G A B C D E F G. This is very common in pop and rock. **Exercise 83** shows it in various positions to fit the chord progression.

The Lydian mode, **exercise 84**, is the major scale with a raised fourth: G A B C# D E F# G. The raised fourth gives this mode an edgy, unsettling quality.

To finish, try **exercise 85**, chock-full of well-used bends. It is based around the tenth fret and lends itself to playing in D and A. Listen for the bluesy sound of the half bends. When you are working out a solo always check the chords you're playing over. If the progression is in a single key, with no odd chords, a single scale will usually work all the way through. Any unusual chords may need an additional scale or perhaps just the adjustment of one note.

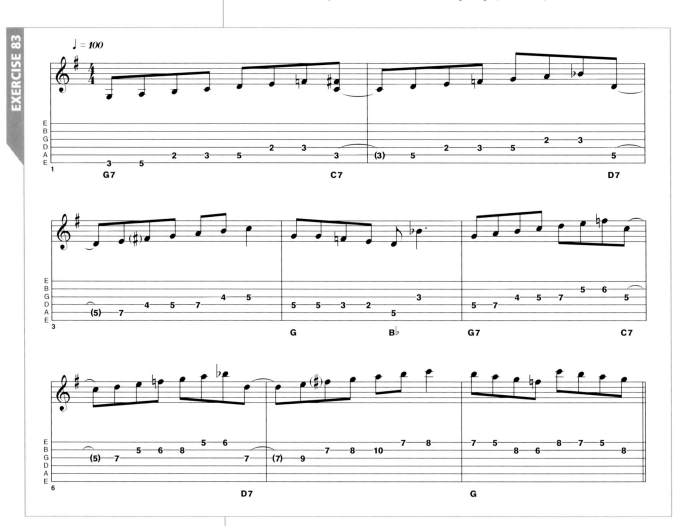

CHAPTER 3

Blues

Blues music in its various forms has influenced many strands of popular music and guitar playing since the 1950s. The blues originated as an acoustic folk music through which African Americans expressed their misfortunes as a disenfranchised people, as well as the perennial human themes of frustration, love, sex and loss. Perhaps the greatest voice in this style was Robert Johnson in the 1930s, though other early blues giants include Elmore James, T-Bone Walker, Son House and Charley Patton.

The migration of many African-Americans from the rural south to cities further to the north eventually led to the development of an electric, urban-based blues, most famously in Chicago. During the 1950s and early 1960s, performers such as Muddy Waters, Willie Dixon, Albert King, Buddy Guy, B.B. King, Albert Collins, Otis Rush, Hubert Sumlin and John Lee Hooker made their mark with blues played on an electric guitar. But the acoustic form of the music remains tremendously popular today too – both in the rediscovery of the great original acoustic artists and in the resurgence of electric 'Chicago' or 'Texas' blues played 'unplugged'.

The sound and songs of many blues originators were emulated in the early to mid 1960s by a younger generation of singers and guitarists attracted to the earthy directness of blues, finding in it a raw energy and authenticity of experience that much pop and rock music lacked. This was especially true in the UK, where a blues boom occurred. Artists such as The Rolling Stones, Eric Clapton, John Mayall, The Animals, The Yardbirds, Peter Green's Fleetwood Mac, Cream, and Free all either covered blues songs or wrote music in the same vein. In the USA a similar phenomenon brought forward talents such as Mike Bloomfield and Johnny Winter. It was highly significant that the most high-profile rock guitarist of the 1960s, Jimi Hendrix, played some blues and wrote several classic blues-rock tracks, such as 'Red House', 'Voodoo Chile' and 'Hear My Train A-Comin''.

Despite charges of plagiarism and the accusation that their music was only a pale imitation of the real thing, the white musicians' interest in blues boosted the record sales and concert-drawing power of the older generation of bluesmen, enabling the latter to enjoy career success and longevity beyond their former expectations. Whatever critics think about the way Led Zeppelin played the blues on their 1969 debut album, there can be no doubt that that album (and others like it) introduced the blues to a vast number of listeners. The effects of this new interest panned out through the 1970s and 1980s, with the result that the blues has taken its place in the broader range of commercial music styles, its legacy carried on by newer talents such

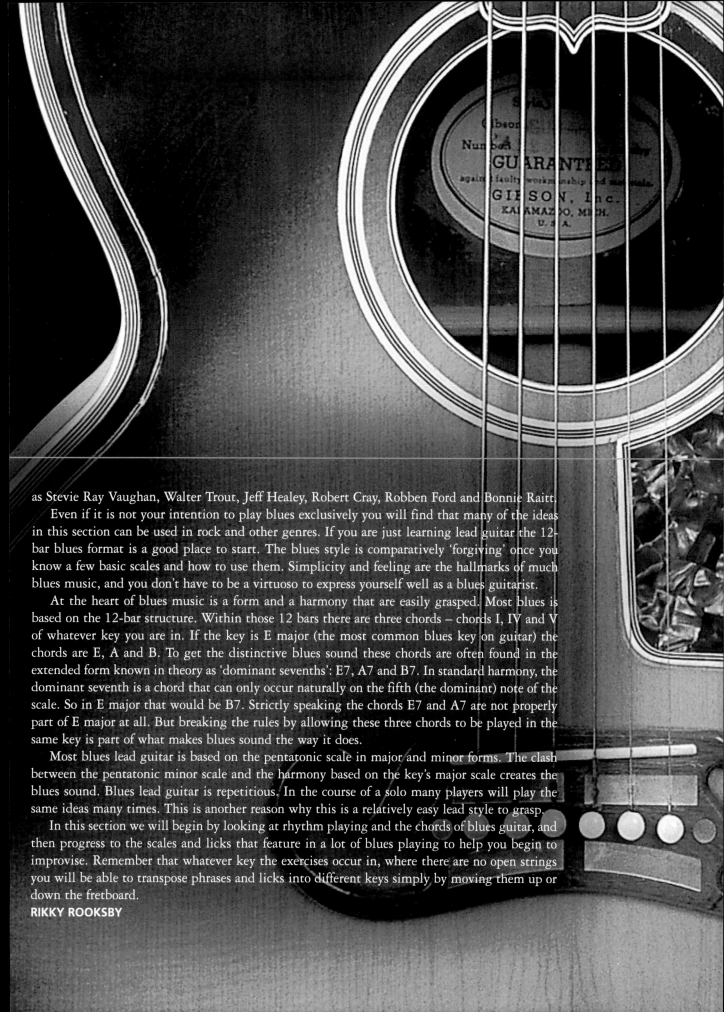

as Stevie Ray Vaughan, Walter Trout, Jeff Healey, Robert Cray, Robben Ford and Bonnie Raitt.

Even if it is not your intention to play blues exclusively you will find that many of the ideas in this section can be used in rock and other genres. If you are just learning lead guitar the 12-bar blues format is a good place to start. The blues style is comparatively 'forgiving' once you know a few basic scales and how to use them. Simplicity and feeling are the hallmarks of much blues music, and you don't have to be a virtuoso to express yourself well as a blues guitarist.

At the heart of blues music is a form and a harmony that are easily grasped. Most blues is based on the 12-bar structure. Within those 12 bars there are three chords – chords I, IV and V of whatever key you are in. If the key is E major (the most common blues key on guitar) the chords are E, A and B. To get the distinctive blues sound these chords are often found in the extended form known in theory as 'dominant sevenths': E7, A7 and B7. In standard harmony, the dominant seventh is a chord that can only occur naturally on the fifth (the dominant) note of the scale. So in E major that would be B7. Strictly speaking the chords E7 and A7 are not properly part of E major at all. But breaking the rules by allowing these three chords to be played in the same key is part of what makes blues sound the way it does.

Most blues lead guitar is based on the pentatonic scale in major and minor forms. The clash between the pentatonic minor scale and the harmony based on the key's major scale creates the blues sound. Blues lead guitar is repetitious. In the course of a solo many players will play the same ideas many times. This is another reason why this is a relatively easy lead style to grasp.

In this section we will begin by looking at rhythm playing and the chords of blues guitar, and then progress to the scales and licks that feature in a lot of blues playing to help you begin to improvise. Remember that whatever key the exercises occur in, where there are no open strings you will be able to transpose phrases and licks into different keys simply by moving them up or down the fretboard.

RIKKY ROOKSBY

RHYTHM

We'll begin with a single-note blues idea. **Exercise 1** has the distinctive 'swinging' rhythm so often heard in blues. In 4/4 time each beat can be divided into two eighth-notes (quavers), or four 16th-notes (semiquavers), and so on. The 4/4 bar of eighth-notes – counted as 'one-and two-and three-and four-and' – is common in rock. In blues it is more usual to divide the beat into three eighth-notes . Two eighth-notes are thus played as if the first was a quarter-note and the second an eighth-note, giving the rhythm 'one-and-uh two-and-uh three-and-uh four-and-uh'; the middle note of each three-note set is silent – it's there for rhythmic feel. There is a time signature – 12/8 – which expresses this. But for ease of notation reading we will use 4/4 for most of these examples and add the direction to treat the rhythm as a shuffle', displayed as:

This example is in A major, whose scale is A B C# D E F# G#. In bar one you will see a C. This flattened third note is a 'blue' note. It clashes with the underlying harmony based on the major scale. In bar five there is an F which is the flattened third of the D major chord and in bar nine there is G, which is the flattened third of an E major chord. Listen for the 'tough' quality of these notes. This type of single-note progression will sound good if it is doubled by bass guitar. Just add a drumbeat and away you go: instant blues power trio!

Exercise 2 is another single-note 12-bar, this time in E. Watch out for the syncopation across bars 1-2 and 3-4, 5-6, 7-8, and 10-11. Like exercise 1 this sounds good when doubled with a bass guitar. If you want to solo over either, let the bass continue playing the notated progression.

Chord symbols are given in the exercise merely as guides to what you would be playing over. To get an early taste of chordal blues rhythm you can try playing through the exercise not with the straight chord forms below, but using the dominant sevenths as discussed in the introduction – basic examples of which are on next page.

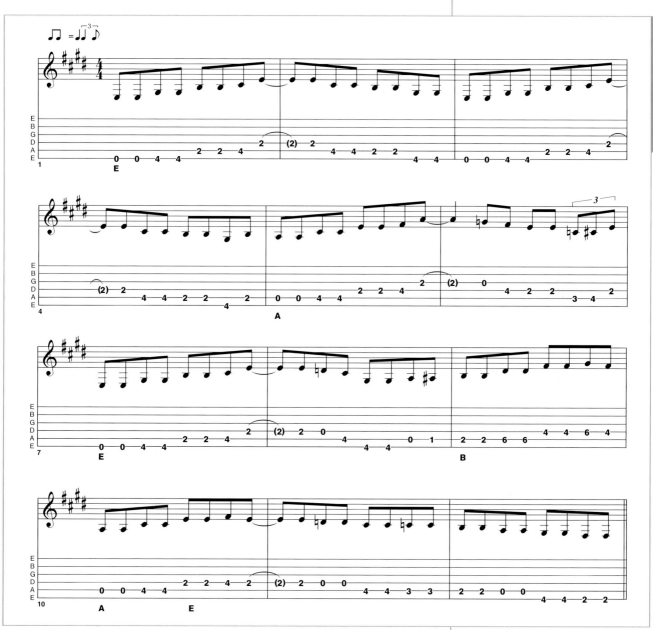

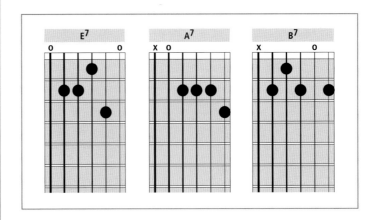

CD 1 TRACK **22**

THE SHUFFLE

Here's the easy rhythm figure that you will find at the start of the 'Rock & Pop' section too. The difference in **exercise 3** is the shuffle rhythm. Watch out for the variation in bar five, another in bar six, and a third in bar 12. Notice that in bar ten the music does not return to D as it did in exercise 1. Staying on E for two bars is a valid alternative at this point in a 12-bar.

We need to be able to play this shuffle figure in any key, so **exercise 4** converts this six-bar blues into a fretted figure with no open strings. If you find this a bit of a stretch drop your thumb well behind the neck. This will help your fretting hand open out. Exercise 4 shows the 'boogie' figure starting with the root note on the fifth string.

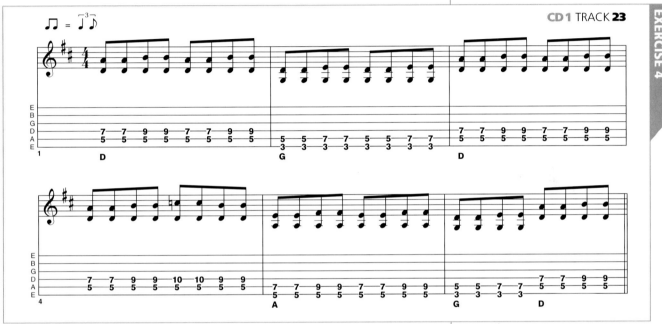

Exercise 5 shows the same idea in G major, over eight bars, starting on the sixth string. Starting on either the fifth or the sixth string enables you to play it in any major key, and to pitch it higher or lower. Notice the G figure in the final bars is an octave above the G figure at the start. Once you've got these down you'll be equipped to transpose this essential blues rhythm into any key required.

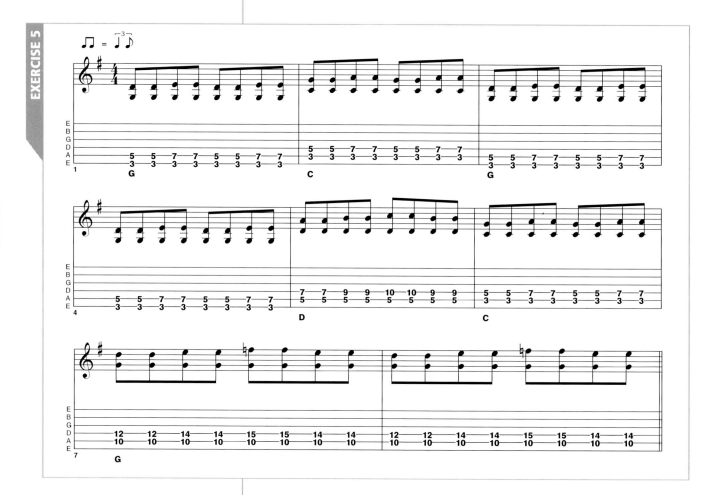

THE IV-bIII-I CHANGE

In blues, movement between the first note of the scale and the flattened third is very common. It occurs in vocal lines, in single-note riffs, in lead solos and in chords. Muddy Waters, for example, features it heavily in songs like 'Mannish Boy', and Hendrix songs like 'Voodoo Chile' and 'Hear My Train A-Comin'' likewise.

Exercise 6 takes us through a set of variations on the E-A-G change, where G is the flattened third blues note or chord. In bar one it occurs as single notes, in bar two as thirds, in bar three thirds with a different termination (in bar four), in bar four as fifths, in bar five as triads, and in bar six as four-note chords. Each one has a different effect. You can combine these in any way you like during a blues number using the I-IV-♭III change.

We have already discussed a couple of times how the dominant seventh chord is central to blues. Before moving on, let's reinforce that further with another short exercise on its variations. In **exercise 7** D7 is D F# A C. In bar one, F# and C are played together. By moving them down one fret we get part of G7 and by moving them up one fret part of A7.

CD1 TRACK **24**

EXERCISE 6

EXERCISE 7

TURNAROUNDS

In many blues tunes a musical phrase signals that the 12-bar is reaching its end and is about to start again. It's a short phrase, often going down by steps, sometimes going up. This is the 'turnaround'. Turnarounds are mainly used in rhythm parts but if you are quick-witted enough you can put them into a lead solo at the end of each 12-bar. Here are eight typical turnarounds, seven in E and one in A.

Imagine that you have already played ten bars of a 12-bar sequence. Each of these examples represents bars 11-12. When playing turnaround figures, use alternate picking: strike the lower note of a triplet with a downstroke and the upper note with an upstroke. In **exercise 8** the note moves down the third string alone. **Exercise 9** displays a third moving down the second and third strings.

Exercise 10 is an equally effective turnaround, and is much like exercise 8 but with an ascending movement. **Exercise 11** is also like exercise 8 except notes are coming down in sixths on the first and third strings. At this point, you should begin to see the subtle variation with which this seemingly simple figure can be played.

Exercise 12 continues our exploration of turnarounds with a pattern higher up the neck, which takes advantage of the open top E string.

Here are two patterns in descending sixths, one high, one low, grouped together in **exercise 13**. Use one or the other and then move to the expected B chord in the last bar. The example in **exercise 14**, moving upwards, is in the key of A major.

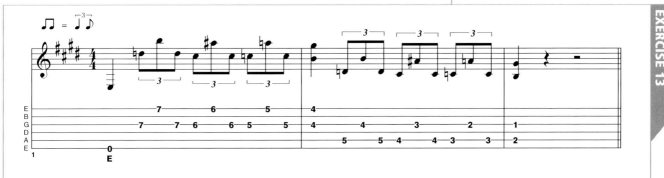

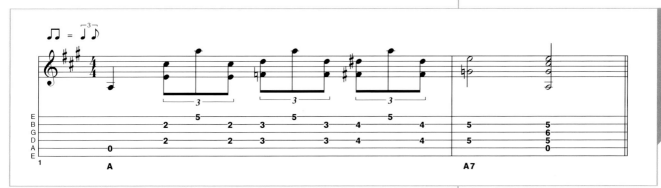

Turnarounds can also be made of a fast single-note run. **Exercise 15** is a typical example, with pull-offs, going down the E pentatonic minor scale in first position. It is similar to those heard throughout Stevie Ray Vaughan's 'Rude Mood', and is getting you into some fancier playing of this generally simple form. Check out more of Vaughan's playing for further examples of hot-rodded turnarounds.

BLUES LEAD GUITAR SCALES

Playing blues lead guitar competently is a matter of learning a small number of scales and scale patterns; mastering the art of bending and fretting-hand techniques like vibrato, hammering-on, pulling-off and slides; and gradually finding out which notes sound stronger over any given 12-bar sequence.

THE PENTATONIC MINOR

This is the most important scale for blues (and rock). The pentatonic minor on E is E G A B D. Compare this with E major: E F# G# A B C# D#. Three notes – E A and B – are the same. Two – F# and C# – have been omitted, and two – G and D – are a semi-tone lower. When the pentatonic minor is played over a 12-bar in E major the ear picks up the G and D 'blue' notes but accepts this clash as the blues sound. Here are two open string patterns for this scale. The second has a small extension to it. Instead of playing the open B string, the same note is found at the fourth fret. This establishes the hand in third position. The pattern that follows for the last six notes of the bar is very important to blues.

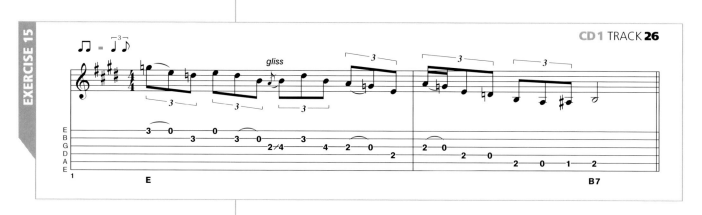

EXERCISE 15

CD 1 TRACK **26**

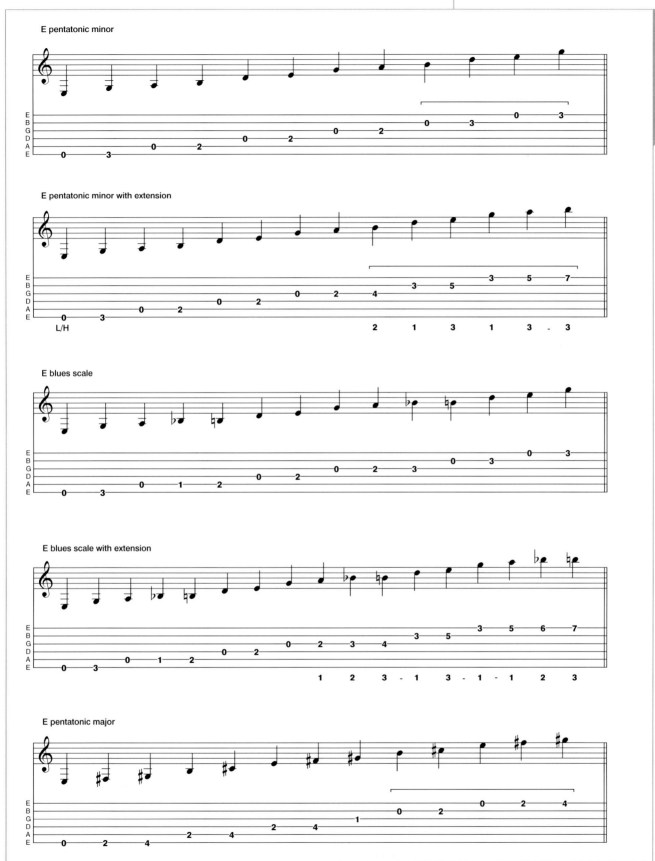

THE E BLUES SCALE

The next two scale patterns repeat the previous two but add an extra note: B♭. Although this is not on the pentatonic minor, it is another blues note – the flattened fifth. This results in what is known as the blues scale. In a solo this flattened fifth can be approached either by fretting it or by bending a note up to it; the effect is slightly different with each approach.

Exercise 16 puts some of what we just learned into action, using the scale notes in first position. Notice that the open strings of the guitar – E A D G B E – have all the notes for E pentatonic minor. This is one reason why E is the most popular key for blues music on guitar. Each bar starts with a bass note. Let this ring throughout the bar, as it will give a 'context' for the lead notes. Notice that bar seven has the added flat note B♭, which you will begin to find familiar as another typical blues element.

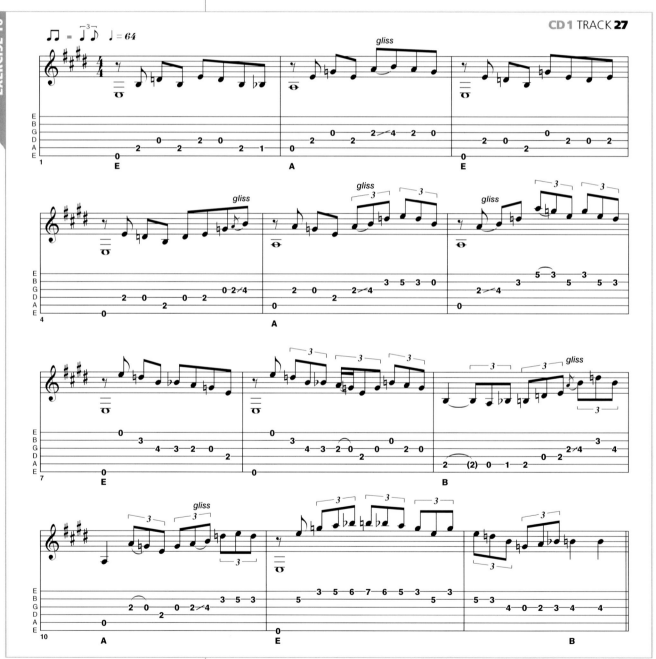

THE PENTATONIC MAJOR

There is also a pentatonic scale drawn directly from the major scale. E pentatonic major is E F#
G# B C#. Compare this with E major: E F# G# A B C# D#. Two notes – A and D# – have been
omitted, but otherwise the scales use the same notes. When the pentatonic major is played over
a 12-bar in E major there are no clashing 'blue' notes; the notes fit harmoniously with the
chords. An important part of playing good blues lead is contrasting the pentatonic's minor and
major forms to add greater interest to your solos. Here are two open string patterns for this scale.
The second has a slight extension to it. Instead of playing the open B string, the same note is
found at the fourth fret. This establishes the hand in third position.

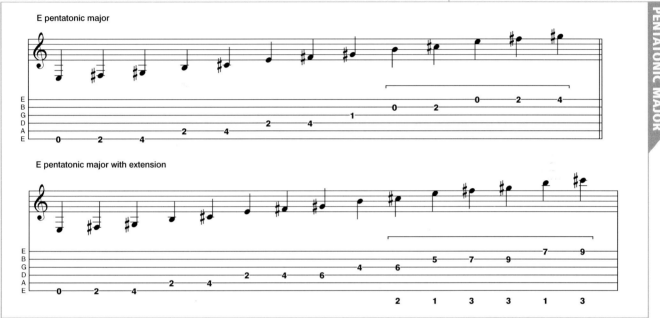

THE E MAJOR BLUES SCALE

The third of these scale patterns adds an extra note: G. This is the flattened third note we
have already encountered. This results in what is known as the E major blues scale.

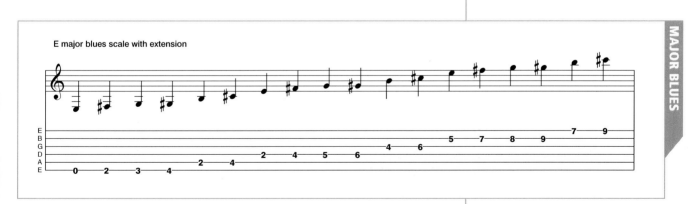

To further practise these scales, **exercise 17** is a 12-bar solo in E that uses the pentatonic major and major blues scales. The flattened third is easy to see in the music because of the 'natural' accidental added to G. Sometimes this G is fretted; sometimes, as in bar ten, it is reached with a bend. This break employs a 'call-and-answer' technique, whereby the first five notes of bars 1-3, 5 and 6 make a phrase that is 'answered' by whatever follows.

RULES OF THUMB FOR USING THE PENTATONICS

1. In a minor-key 12-bar you can play the pentatonic minor but not the major. Note that the pentatonic minor will not sound as bluesy as it does in a major key because the notes are no longer flattened versions of notes on the key scale. Compare E natural minor – E F# G A B C D – with E pentatonic minor: E G A B D. All the latter's notes are in the former.

2. In a major-key 12-bar you can play the pentatonic minor *and* the major. However, if the piece you are soloing over uses any of the three minor chords of the major key (in E these are F# minor G# minor C# minor) the pentatonic minor will clash with them in an undesirable manner. The

easiest solution is to use the pentatonic major wherever those minor chords occur.

3. Any pentatonic minor scale pattern moved down three frets will automatically 'convert' to a pentatonic major on the same root note. Remember this to switch scales in a solo.

THE 'EXTENSION' BOX

Let's just concentrate for a moment on the pattern found at the top of the previous set of scales. It is good discipline to restrict yourself to playing a 12-bar solo using only these five notes and nothing else, as in **exercise 18**. It will make you think more carefully about the way each note sounds against the harmony. By this method you get an appreciation of 'chord tones.' (A similar approach to basic soloing will be taken in the 'Jazz' chapter.) These are the notes on the scale that belong to each of the three chords in the 12-bar. Whenever you strike one of these over a chord to which it belongs, that note seems a strong fit. Notice in particular here in bars 1-4 the stress placed on E, the timing of the run that leads up to an A in bar five just as the chord changes to A, and in bar nine the emphasised B.

Exercise 19 presents the same extension box but with a few notes added – either by fretting or by bending – that lie within the box. We are still working with a small area of the fretboard to get the maximum musical possibilities out of it. This solo is full of blue notes.

Another important rule to remember is that every pentatonic minor scale shares its notes with the pentatonic major of the note a minor third above it (three semitones). Thus E G A B D is the same notes as G pentatonic major: G A B D E. This means that over the chords of G, C and D we can put the extension box to a different harmonic use, as **exercise 20** shows. Notice the solo moves the patterns up for the C and D chords. (Also note here the melodic elements that the pentatonic major blues shares with country guitar styles: the main contrast is the radically different rhythmic feel.)

116

Exercise 21 shows you how the pentatonic minor and major scales in G can be put in a sequence of answering phrases. **Exercise 22** is another 'chord tone' example, this time in G. The starting position is the extension box that lies at the top of a pentatonic minor scale that would start at the third fret: the scale pattern for that is given above the exercise. A variant has been added to this scale: instead of moving to D at the seventh fret, the D is played at the third on the B string. This is the most common pentatonic pattern. With no open strings it is movable and gives the pentatonic minor of any key from G upwards. Move this up 12 frets to create a pentatonic minor one octave higher; or start it on the second note for a pentatonic major from that note. Here the second note is B♭, so starting there gives B♭ pentatonic major.

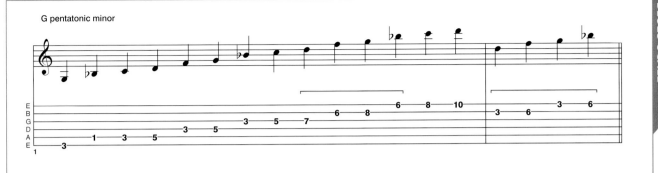

EXERCISE 23

WHEN CHORDS CHANGE: BARS TWO, FIVE AND NINE

Your lead playing will sound more confident if you are able to reflect in your choice of notes the moments in the 12-bar when there is a chord change. The first of these will be the change from chord I to chord IV in bar five, or bar two if it is a 'quick-change' blues. The five examples in **exercise 23** show how to navigate the I-IV change (here the change is from A to D).

A similar moment occurs in most 12-bars at bar nine where chord V appears. In the key of A this is an E chord. Many players find that continuing to solo over the pentatonic minor at this point does not sound as effective as elsewhere in the 12-bar. **Exercise 24** shows eight ways of making the transition. Play bar one in each case, followed by any one of the E bars.

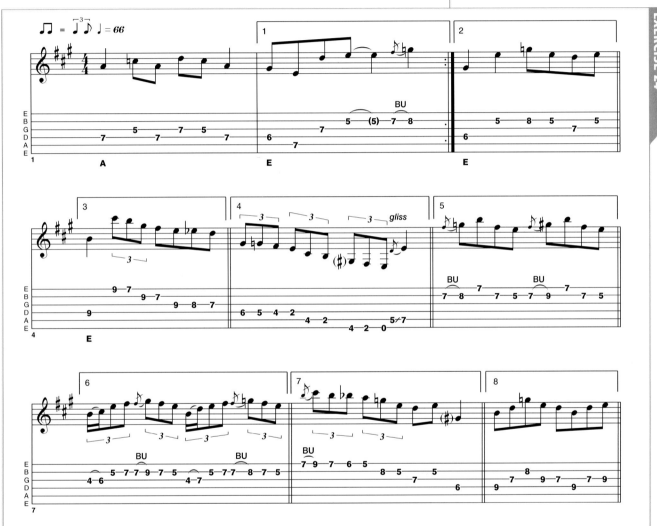

INTERVALS AND QUARTER BENDS

String bending is a significant part of blues lead playing. The usual bends are up a semitone or a whole tone; some players go higher, though rarely on the acoustic guitar. It is important to be able to bend either a semitone or tone accurately, because in practice this can mean the difference between playing a C against an A chord (the flattened third) or a C# (the normal third in A). Remember the golden rule of bending: always support the finger that is bending by putting the other fingers down, where possible, on the same string and pushing with two or three. Bends are almost never done with the fourth finger.

Blues guitar also employs a bend actually smaller than a semitone, the quarter-tone bend, and most acoustic players can make liberal use of these with little difficulty. It amounts to little more than a 'smudging' of pitch but it can be effective. Try it on the thirds that crop up throughout **exercise 25**. Another example of some typical blues double-stops is shown in **exercise 26**. They are mostly thirds, but there are sixths in bar four.

MINOR KEY BLUES

Blues music is also found in the minor key. The first of two minor blues examples, **exercise 27** is in an elongated form and 6/8 time, where there are two beats in each bar and each beat divides into three. Notice that the half bend in bar one becomes a full bend in bar five. Although some of the phrases are pentatonic minor (A C D E G), there are also bars like eight where the A natural minor scale (A B C D E F G) is used.

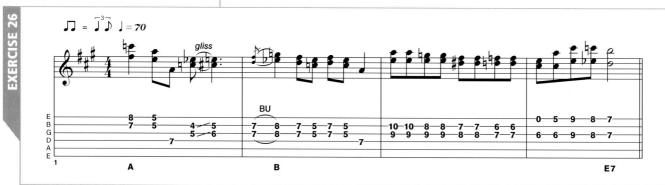

Exercise 28 is an example of a minor-key blues progression that has more advanced harmony. For the first four bars you play chord tones that give the full flavour of the chords. Bars 5-8 repeat the progression but shift to a lead solo. As with the previous exercise, both the pentatonic and the natural minor scales are used. The chords backing this example are somewhat more complex than we have seen so far, so some suggestions are given beneath the music.

MORE BLUES RHYTHM

A traditional rhythm, **exercise 29** is in the style of an acoustic blues and is best played with fingers or fingers and a pick. **Exercise 30** (see over) is a funky blues style with rhythm chord and single note fills. Many of the chord shapes require you to damp the fifth string with your fretting hand thumb. It's a different sort of rhythmic feel than we have yet encountered: now that you've developed a good blues vocabulary, record a few bars to practise soloing over it.

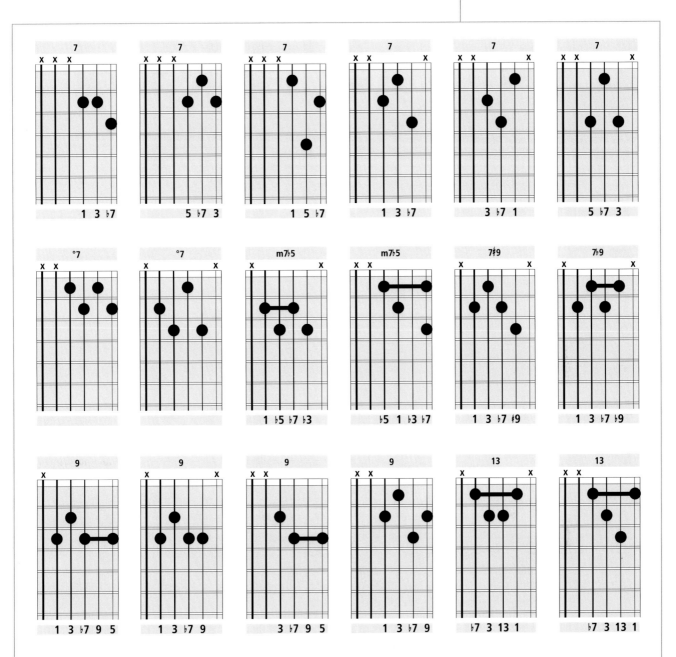

CHORD BOXES

Here are a number of movable chord types that are useful in blues playing. Learn them in different positions relative to the root note (the I) given and, when you play a 12-bar, try occasionally substituting these for the straight majors you would otherwise play.

When playing with a band or a bass guitar it is not always necessary to play full chords. The **dominant seventh (7)** triads are useful for this purpose and for putting into solos for a rhythmic effect. Notice that some of them are missing a root note, which will often be played by the bassist anyway.

The **diminished seventh (°7)** chord is an oddity – because any of its notes can be treated as the root! The **minor7♭5**, also known as the half-diminished chord, is a colourful variation on the usual minor seventh. The flattened fifth is the same note you would be playing on the blues scale for that key.

The **7#9** (now popularly known as the 'Hendrix chord') gives real edge; the **7♭9** is more gloomy and resigned.

Ninths and **thirteenths** become increasingly difficult to finger on the guitar so they are often found in incomplete forms. They will substitute for the dominant seventh.

CHAPTER 4

Bottleneck

The sound of bottleneck acoustic blues is one of the most distinctive voices in all of guitar playing. It encompasses a wide range of emotions, all of them evocative, all of them straight from the heart. Over the past couple of decades the great originators of the style, from the Mississippi Delta right on up to Chicago and beyond, have come to be appreciated more than ever before. Their playing techniques can sometimes be tricky to master, but plenty of them are easy enough to get started with, and it is probably simpler than you think to learn a few authentic licks that will get you sounding like the real thing in no time.

As ever, anyone new to the style is best advised to listen to the many greats who have gone before. In the blues tradition the obvious place to start is with Robert Johnson. Johnson's distinctive style combined rhythm, single note runs and a mournful voice that the slide accentuated.

Blind Willie Johnson and Son House blended their slide playing with growling vocals – a very primitive sound which seemed to come straight from the ground and seep into the soul. Charlie Patton, who was actually an early influence on Robert Johnson and whom some would call the 'King of the Delta Blues', played a driving rhythm, and married ragtime and other musical forms of the day into a unique voice in the blues. Like Son House and Willie Johnson, Patton had a rough voice that spoke of the hard times he lived. He was also considered quite an entertainer, known for playing the guitar behind his back... I always wondered where Jimi Hendrix got that idea. Most of what we hear today from these players exists as solo recordings, although others worked with a range of musicians and ensembles. Tampa Red, for one, did much of his slide playing with an orchestra and worked with many different singers.

Today, slide guitar is well represented by players such as Leo Kottke and Bob Brozman. Kottke used the technique of the early blues players and shoved it into overdrive with speedy runs and virtuosity unparalleled in the field. Brozman has continued to develop the form, using blues and early Hawaiian players for inspiration, adding complicated African rhythms and borrowing melodic influences from the Middle and Far East.

The choice of materials for slides runs from glass to brass, steel to ceramic – pretty much anything you can run across the strings that makes a sustained glissando can be used. Often the best choice is to use material that has a little weight (metal or ceramic) and match that with heavier gauge strings (.013 to .056, or even just a little heavier). You need to be careful with putting too heavy a gauge of strings on your guitar, since increased gauge means increased tension on the neck and bridge. The heavier tension is frequently compensated for by the fact that you are often tuning the strings down (to open G or open D, both explored below), but again, be careful. Consult a knowledgeable luthier if you plan on using strings gauged heavier than .013 to .056.

Any guitar set up properly will work for slide playing, but many players choose to set up a guitar specifically for slide and nothing else. This might first sound a bit costly, but fortunately a lot of cheap guitars actually sound really good for slide. If you set up a guitar just for slide you will want to raise the action (ideally by raising both the bridge saddle and the nut) and put heavier strings on it. In open tunings, lighter strings will not have the tension you need to produce a solid tone and good volume, and the sound will be harder to control.

Many of the early blues guitarists used a National resonator guitar to get what we think of today as a distinctive Delta Blues sound. Nationals were – and still are – traditionally made from brass or steel, and there are also wood-bodied variations on the format, although the latter are more characteristic of the Dobro company and bluegrass slide guitar. National resonator guitars first made their appearance around 1927, predating electric guitars, and were designed to allow guitarists to compete in volume with other musicians in an orchestra. Such an instrument isn't absolutely required for bottleneck playing, but it offers a quick way of getting that sultry, haunting slide sound.

PETE MADSEN

OPEN D AND SLIDE TECHNIQUE

The great practitioners have used a wide range of tunings over the years, some containing unusual intervals of their own choosing, but often simply the open chords that form the commonly used alternatives to standard tuning. Open D is one of the most popular of the latter, and is also good to use for getting to grips with slide playing because it offers an instant full barre chord – a D major with strings open or with a slide placed at the 12th fret, and others in different positions on the fretboard. It also provides plenty of open root notes to keep the bass going while you pick out melody lines with the slide on higher strings. To get into open D you need to alter four of the six strings from standard, tuning from low to high to DADF#AD.

In **exercise 1** you will simply be learning how to hold the slide, and where to place it on the strings in order to get a good sound with proper intonation. Put the slide on your left pinkie. As you place the slide on the string – in this case the high E-string (which is in fact a high D in this tuning) – use just enough pressure to make the string sound above the specified fret. Remember, the slide should be placed directly over the fret, rather than between the frets like you would normally do if you were fretting with your finger in non-slide playing. Use the slide to cover only the string you are playing – the E-string. Play the dominant seventh scale and try to make it sound as clean as possible.

In this **exercise 2** you will be sliding between the notes of the dominant seventh scale, during which we will also practice another important part of slide playing: string dampening. This can be achieved with both the left and right hand. In this case, try letting your left index finger gently touch the same string that your slide is playing. This is a real subtle manoeuver and takes a little time to get the hang of. When done properly, it should dampen a lot of the string noise associated with slide playing. Play the scale ascending and descending. The slide should be in constant contact with the string as it slides from note to note. The amount of pressure you use should be enough to make the note sound but not so much that you hear unwanted fret noise. Keeping consistent pressure is also very important; if you move the slide away from or towards the fretboard as you slide you will get some awkward inconsistencies in the tone of the note you are sliding from or to.

Sliding back and forth between notes can be a very exciting and evocative way of using the slide. In **exercise 3** you will pick the note once, then slide back and forth. Make sure that notes you are sliding from and to are pitch-perfect. You can check yourself by playing the same notes fretted with your finger to make sure you are hitting the note right – this is also a good ear training exercise.

BASIC RIFFS

Now let's start getting into the things that most of you are probably reading this for. **Exercise 4** displays a cool slide riff for the first four bars of a 12-bar blues. In open tunings, such as open D and G, you will hear a lot of riffs centered on the 12th fret. You can actually break this exercise up into two distinct two-bar sections. The first two bars are centered around the 12th fret, the second two-bar section goes down to the third and fifth frets and some open D-strings – remember, you have three open D-strings, so you can get a lot of mileage out of them. Finally, you do a multi-string slide back up to the 12th fret. This kind of playing evokes the natural qualities of speech, with higher registers and lower registers. Whenever you play a solo, slide or otherwise, try to think of having a conversation: using different cadences, pauses, exclamations, questions, statements... Avoid chatter and monotonous responses: people will tune you out.

Here's a nice slide phrase for the IV chord in a 12-bar sequence. **Exercise 5** is centered on the fifth fret, which, if you were to play all six strings, would give you the entire IV chord. **Exercise 6** takes you form the V chord to the IV chord. The V chord is found at the seventh fret and again, the IV chord at the fifth. Both this example and the one preceding it show how you can play 'around' the chord position to get some nice slide riffs going.

CD 1 TRACK **31**

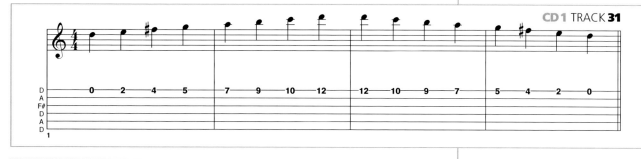

CD 1 TRACK **32**

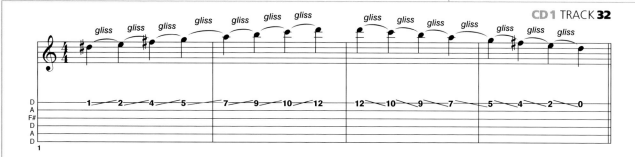

CD 1 TRACK **33**

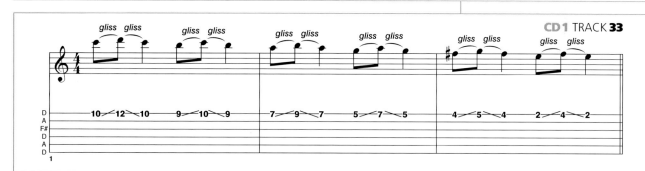

CD 1 TRACK **34**

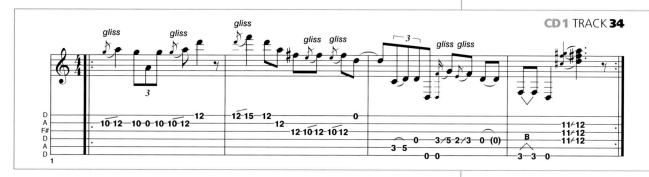

CD 1 TRACK **35**

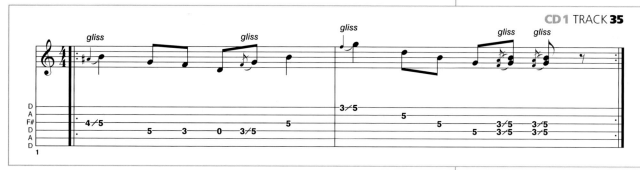

Exercise 7 is a Robert Johnson-style turnaround. Use your thumb on the right hand to play the descending bass line and any finger to play the accompanying melody notes on the high E-string (which, again, is actually tuned to D here).

12-BAR BLUES
Exercise 8 is simply the last four exercises you worked on above combined into one 12-bar blues sequence, but it's a lot more challenging playing them all together and keeping the rhythm going. Having another guitar play a shuffle rhythm behind you will help you get the feel for how these phrases work together. Otherwise record yourself playing a shuffle rhythm in D (with the appropriate chord changes, of course), and then practise these riffs over the rhythm.

ALTERNATING BASS
Here is a 16-bar fingerpicking piece for those of you who can play an alternating bass. In **exercise 9** you will find that all the slide notes happen on the high E-string, which helps simplify things. If you have never tried playing an alternating bass with an accompanying melody this will prove a bit of a challenge, but it's a lot of fun. Notice the nice A and G chords in this tuning. These chord voicings will give you more options for the IV and V chords beyond simply placing the slide over all six strings at the fifth and seventh frets.

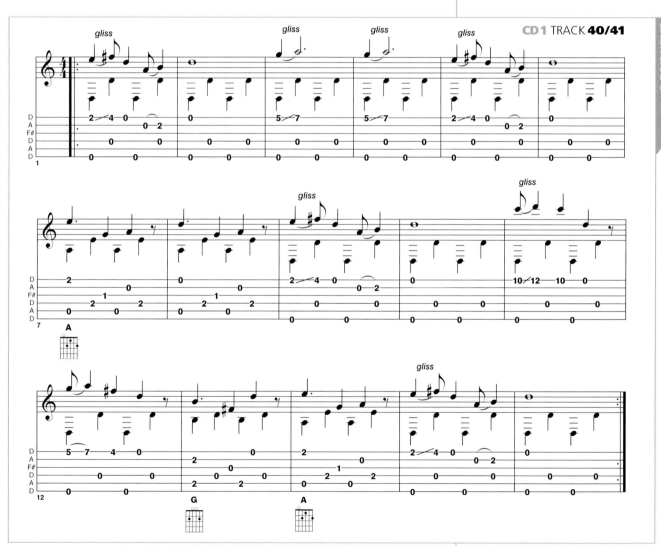

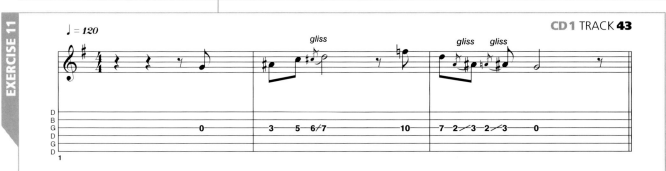

134

Here is another 12-bar blues. **Exercise 10** makes a good complement for a solo singer/performer. The opening riff, repeated in the third bar (measure) and throughout, is a way of breaking up the rhythm and giving a singer a break. Robert Johnson used this device very effectively in many of his tunes.

For the opening lick, your slide will cover three strings, GBE (tuned to G#AD), and you will play a triplet rhythm with a strumming action. In the 11th bar you have another turnaround (this time ascending instead of descending), which should give you a few options for repetition of the 12-bar sequence.

Now that you have a range of classic open D slide licks at your disposal, you can also try interchanging turnarounds and phrases from most of these exercises to begin working toward your own compositions in the style.

OPEN G TUNING

From here on out we move into open G, which is also popular with blues players, and is used by many bluegrass Dobro players as well. Open G runs D-G-D-G-B-D. To get there from open D, some players might find it easiest to first bring the G-string back up from F# to G (by fretting the D-string at the fifth fret), then bringing the B-string back up from A to B (G-string, fourth fret). Leave the high E at high D, then drop the A-string to an octave below the pitch you get when you pluck the open G-string. (Note that for ease of reference, we'll continue to refer to the strings using their pitches from standard tuning.)

In **exercise 11** you will be playing a simple riff on the G-string. Try to employ your string-dampening technique, using the left hand index finger to keep the B- and E-strings quiet while you play the riff. You can also play this riff in standard tuning – since the G-string remains G in both tunings. This is similar to a Billy Gibbons-style riff, of the type you hear in the song 'Tush' by ZZ Top.

Exercise 12 offers another good example, but of course this time in G tuning, of playing notes around the 12th fret to get some cool sounds. This is the 'call' in a call-and-response phrase. Try moving the slide over only the string you are playing as you move from E-string to B-string to G-string. **Exercise 13** is the 'response' to the 'call' in exercise 12. Notice the phrasing between these two examples: one is voiced high, with the notes at the 12th fret; the

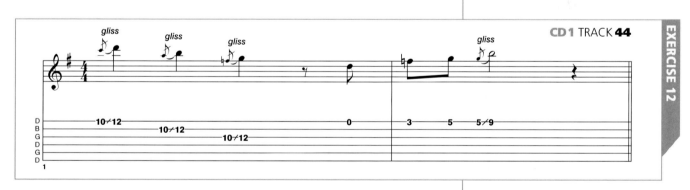

other, exercise 13, is lower. This is typical of the genre, and in these examples you can begin to hear how the sound of slide playing resembles the human voice. Following these, **exercise 14** puts the two licks together to show you how they flow as a single musical line – always more challenging than playing the phrases individually.

Exercise 15 is reminiscent of Son House, the great Delta bluesman. It's also a good place to start if you have never played a melody against a steady bass. The example starts out with an eighth-note bass riff, then backs off the bass to quarter-notes (the pulse) and a simple single note slide riff. Many Delta bluesmen used just the thumb and the index finger for fingerpicking. In this example you can play the melody notes on the high E-string with your index finger.

Exercise 16 offers a fun alternating bass slide tune in G tuning. G tuning allows you to play a bass rhythm with the thumb playing the root on the fifth string, then alternate playing the D (fifth) on the fourth and sixth strings; this gives the music a nice 'bounce'. The IV chord in this example (C7) looks like a C chord from standard tuning and has a mournful sound to it. In bar 13 there's a descending bass line played on the E- and D-strings that repeats at bar 15.

Exercise 17 has some of the feel of Blind Willie Johnson's 'In My Time Of Dying'. When you see a slur mark going from one note, passing over a second note and landing on a third note that means you pick the first note and slide to the second and land on the third without picking the string again, just like in Exercise 3 from the exercises in open D tuning. Play this exercise slow, and you can work it into a deep, soulful blues that really evokes the sound of the Delta.

CHAPTER 5

Country

Nashville, Tennessee, is one of the world's most respected centres of excellence when it comes to making records, and country music today has come along way from its roots as a form that was disparagingly called 'hillbilly' by its detractors. The teams of session players who work in the studios of 'Music City' are second to none, and the guitarists, especially, are considered by discerning fans and fellow musicians alike to be among the hottest pickers on the planet. Yet most good country guitar still contains a healthy dose of rootsy twang, and the current genre – for the player – combines feel, attitude and vibe with technical demands that can rival those of the highest forms of guitar music.

Country lead guitar playing has its roots in Hawaiian (steel) guitar music, which coexisted alongside equally influential early blues and, to an extent perhaps, jazz: the incredible Belgian Gypsy guitarist Django Reinhardt's work throughout the late 1930s and early 1940s was clearly an influence on players as diverse as Chet Atkins, Les Paul and John Jorgenson, an ex-member of the Desert Rose Band, current Hellecaster and one of today's hottest guitarists. The lap-steel evolved into pedal-steel, with its evocative bends, and this is one of the ingredients mimicked by classic country lead guitar playing. It is more difficult to execute on an acoustic than on an electric, of course, but it remains a building block of the genre nonetheless. Another significant element comes from players such as Chet Atkins and Jerry Reed who both favoured a thumbpick, and undoubtedly influenced modern day guitarists such as Steuart Smith and Brent Mason, whilst James Burton – who worked with, amongst others, Ricky Nelson, Elvis Presley, Merle Haggard and Emmylou Harris – was, along with country-jazzer Jimmy Bryant, a big influence on the phenomenal Albert Lee.

The development of country rhythm guitar, on the other hand, can be traced back to 1920s hillbilly music and, in particular, the acoustic guitar playing of Maybelle Carter, whose thumb-plucked bass lines and to-and-fro finger strumming style were somewhat akin to the frailing of banjo players – which, interestingly, would be adopted in essence some 40 or so years later by Beatle Paul McCartney (witness his technique on 'Blackbird'). Consider too, if you will, the blues players of Maybelle Carter's era, such as the legendary Robert Johnson, Charley Patton and Blind Lemon Jefferson, and you might well ask yourself the question: where does rhythm guitar end and lead guitar begin? Whatever, country guitar progressed when Kentucky guitarists Mose

Rager and Ike Everly pioneered that alternating bass and melody style, which Merle Travis continued and popularised so much in the 1950s: 'Travis picking'. And, of course, in the 1960s and beyond, the technique would be taken to unimagined heights by Chet Atkins.

Finally, it's important to realise the impact that the rock sounds of the 1970s and the pop sounds of the 1960s to the 1990s have jointly had on modern country music. Meanwhile, pure country is alive and well.

This chapter aims to demystify the idiosyncrasies of country guitar playing by looking at the various approaches to both lead and rhythm guitar. In terms of rhythm guitar, you'll be guided through some relatively easy strumming in classic country style – including bluegrass and ballads – before tackling the alternating-bass style of Merle Travis, as well as the amazing finger style techniques of Chet Atkins and Jerry Reed. But country lead guitar isn't just the territory of the electric, so for solo and fill ideas, you'll be shown various classic and modern examples in the styles of some of the greats, including James Burton, Albert Lee, Jerry Donahue, Brent Mason and Dann Huff.

In addition, after beginning with a few useful scale patterns (which will include the major pentatonic scale and the complete major scale – brief theory lesson on the Mixolydian mode included!), you'll progress through practical exercises which introduce double stops (thirds and sixths) and essential vocabulary in the form of licks and runs. Plus, there are some tasty chords to learn along the way. And to improve your playing ability there are various technical exercises involving hybrid picking patterns, cross-picking, finger style/fingerpicking and so-called chicken pickin'.

LEE HODGSON

COUNTRY LEAD SCALES

The A scale pentatonic pattern outlined in **diagram 1** below might look familiar. Indeed, the five 'shape boxes' (as labelled above and below the fingerboard diagram) are essentially similar, if not identical, to what rock and blues guitarists may know as minor pentatonic scale patterns. Briefly, the root note for the 'minor thing' would be a minor third – three frets – below that of the 'major thing.' Put another way, our A major pentatonic scale here has the same notes as F# minor pentatonic. Country tunes, however, often work in the major side of things, so emphasise and resolve on the root notes and major thirds (shaded).

After learning the five individual patterns you should ultimately try to see things in terms of the whole area of the fingerboard. Accordingly, practise weaving back and forth and across, through the complete pattern – which is essentially how Albert Lee works (many of his lines are based on major pentatonic scale patterns).

Next, against a slow, repeating A-D-A-D chord progression, practise shifting licks between the scale pattern boxes. Hint: D and A are a fourth (five semitones) apart so in order to match D major, simply shift any of the material seen here up five frets (or down seven frets). Even professionals often negotiate chord changes by merely regurgitating a pre-learned lick, phrase or pattern elsewhere on the fingerboard. Hey – if it works, use it!

MAJOR PENTATONIC SCALE LICKS AND RUNS

You might wish to learn the individual licks in **exercise 1** at your leisure before seeing how the various fragments fit together. Note that only the notes of the A major pentatonic scale are used throughout, despite there being chord changes. Analysis will reveal, for example, that what is the sixth of A is also the third of D. Remember though, country players often match the scale to the chord, eg, A major pentatonic scale for A, D major pentatonic scale for D, and maybe E Mixolydian mode for E – more on which later. The concluding bar will make for some tricky (maybe impossible) finger stretching on a guitar without a cutaway, but so many people own cutaway models these days that it is worth including some high lead figures here.

Notes in the A major pentatonic scale

A	B	C♯	E	F♯
1	2	3	5	6

Picking-wise, check out the picking suggestions shown in between the notation and tablature – it's pretty much strict alternate picking throughout, but notice that sometimes the up/off beat is a downstroke (in accordance with sixteenth-note picking) while occasionally it's an upstroke, which feels natural for eighth-note grooves. Also observe the liberal use of slides plus a few hammer-ons and pull-offs, which serve to keep it all flowing.

DIAGRAM 1 **THE A PENTATONIC MAJOR SCALE**

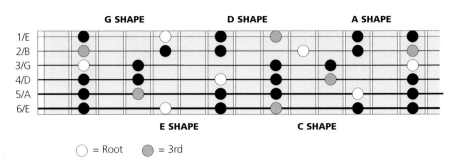

THE A MAJOR SCALE

There may seem to be a lot of dots on **diagram 2** below – and there are, because it offers the full A major scale, from open strings at the nut right up to the 14th fret.

Examine the area of the fingerboard where the scale steps are shown as arabic numbers (1-7), which correspond to the seven degrees of the major scale and hence, chords built from those degrees (I, II, III, IV, V, VI and VII). This is the basis of the so-called 'Nashville Numbers System'. So, in the key of A major you might expect to find some or all of the following chords: A (I), B minor (IIm), C# minor (IIIm), D (IV), E (V), F# minor (VI), while the VII chord, which is rarely heard in country music, would be diminished. Some or all of these chords may appear as seventh extensions: Imaj7, IIm7, IIIm7, IVmaj7, V7, VIm7 (and VIIm7♭5, also known as 'half diminished'). See if you can pick out some shapes of chords from within the overall scale pattern – they're all there!

Now take a look at the 'Dominant Chord Tones' chart (below). The line below the first

The Dominant Chord Tones Plus Extension

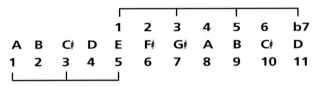

				1	2	3	4	5	6	b7
A	B	C#	D	E	F#	G#	A	B	C#	D
1	2	3	4	5	6	7	8	9	10	11

portion of the scale highlights the relationship between the 'one' (root), third and fifth of the scale as the dominant chord tones. As you will have learned elsewhere there's more within each major scale than simply that scale itself.

While the A major scale runs from A to A (and so-on from octave to octave right up the neck) on the neck diagram and as outlined in the explanatory chart, we can also construct other modes by playing the notes of A major but starting from different degrees of the scale. One mode that is occasionally useful in country playing is E Mixolydian, found by playing from E to E in the A major scale (highlighted by the roman numerals in diagram 2). E Mixolydian provides a useful alternative for soloing over the V – that is, the E chord – of songs in A major. **Exercise 2** offers some A major licks and phrases to further test your new skills.

DIAGRAM 2 **THE A MAJOR SCALE**

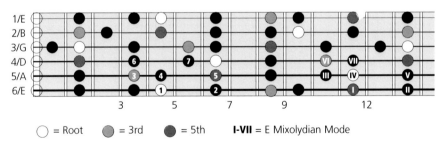

○ = Root ◐ = 3rd ● = 5th **I-VII** = E Mixolydian Mode

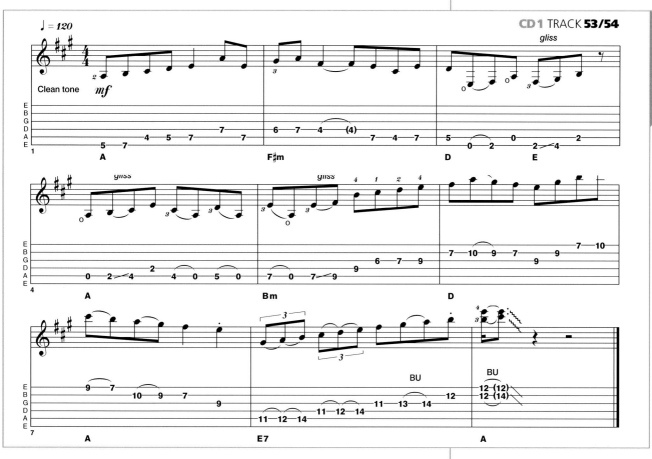

CD 1 TRACK **53/54**

CHORD VOCABULARY

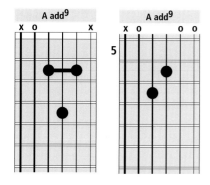

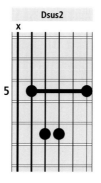

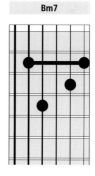

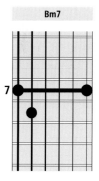

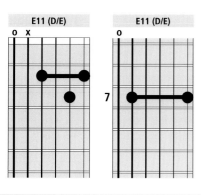

These chords would most likely be heard in a song in the key of A major: A add9 equals the I chord ('one'), Dsus2 is the IV, Bm7 is the IIm ('minor two'), E11 is the V11. Try playing them in various orders: I, IV, II, V; IV, II, V, I; II, V, I, IV... Keep rearranging them, sometimes omitting one or two chords, until you discover a progression that you like. Hey, you're a composer!

LICKS IN THIRDS AND SIXTHS

In addition to single-note soloing and some complex bending, a great deal of country lead playing is executed in double-stops, two notes played together. This is done primarily in scales made up of pairs of thirds or pairs of sixths ascending and descending the major scale – that is, one note ascending from root to octave, paired by a second ascending the same scale, but starting from a third or a sixth away.

The sound of this is likely to be instantly familiar to you: thirds have a slightly south-of-the-border flavour to them, while sixths ring of classic twang. Both are essential to your mastery of country lead playing.

The neck diagrams below give you these scales in thirds and sixths respectively, all in the A major scale. Before moving on to exercise 3 below, spend some time with these diagrams, playing them up and down the neck on all suggested string groupings (five groups of adjacent strings for thirds, four groups of next-but-one pairs for sixths). It takes some practice to

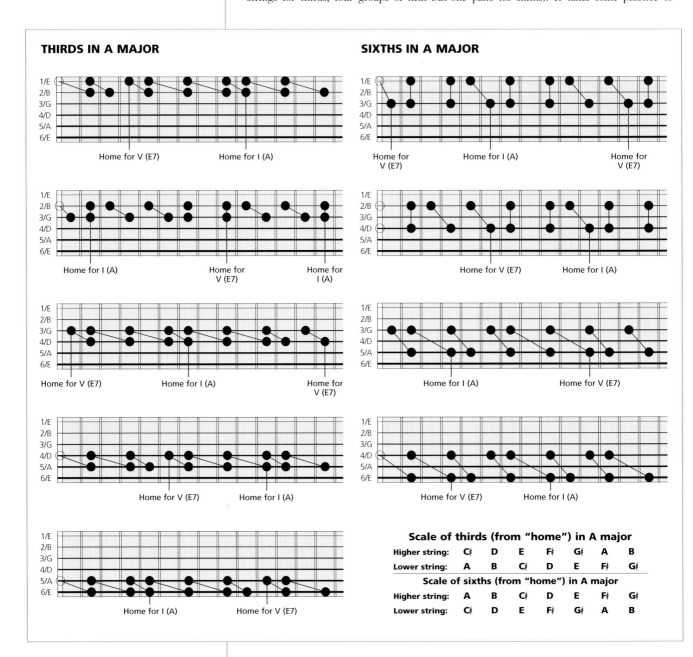

THIRDS IN A MAJOR

SIXTHS IN A MAJOR

Scale of thirds (from "home") in A major

Higher string:	C♯	D	E	F♯	G♯	A	B
Lower string:	A	B	C♯	D	E	F♯	G♯

Scale of sixths (from "home") in A major

Higher string:	A	B	C♯	D	E	F♯	G♯
Lower string:	C♯	D	E	F♯	G♯	A	B

memorise them on all string pairings (and, beyond that, in all keys), but familiarise yourself with a couple of different groupings now, and you'll soon learn to recognize their sound.

You should constantly monitor what sounds 'resolved' and what doesn't; try to remember – in physical and sonic terms – where you are at any given point relative to either the 'home base' for the root note or secondary points of resolution, as well as the 'homes' for the third and fifth chords of your scale. As for memorising the physical aspects of these scales, you'll soon note there are only three 'shapes' for your fingers to make as you move up and down the neck: 'straight' (both strings fingered at the same fret), 'diagonal' (the lower string fingered a fret higher), and 'stretch' (lower string fingered two frets higher. Simpler still, some pairings require only two shapes. In time, both sound and feel should become intuitive.

Exercise 3 lays out an extended run in thirds, keeping the double-stops to the highest two pairs of strings, with single-note licks linking them. Follow the recommended bends and glisses (slides) to start with, and use the chord accompaniment to check how the lead runs sound against the changes. Be aware of the two-string pre-bend toward the end of bar two, and notice the brief yet effective use of pull-offs to the open high E-string in bar seven.

Like all the exercises in this chapter, this sequence merely represents one particular permutation and the possibilities are almost endless. It might be a good idea, therefore, to noodle around further for a while, stretch out the raw material that this exercise and the neck diagrams provide, and take the opportunity to develop your improvising skills.

Taking us into a full-length run in sixths, **exercise 4** comprises chords that are not all from the key of A major. There are three non-diatonic chords – A7 (I7), D minor (IVm) and B7 (II7) – along with the more unusual Dm add9, A/C# and E7/G# (the diagrams for the latter three are given on the facing page to help ease the way). See if you can find ways of matching these chords using the sixths shapes already outlined.

Incidentally, you might find of particular interest the fact that all this A stuff sounds great for E7 (V7), too; as you play bars nine through 12 you'll be playing Mixolydian sixths, whether you know it or not!

Note that although two of the chords shown opposite appear to be 'slash chords,' they are in fact just first inversions (that is, the third is in the bass). A true slash chord would be a triad over a note that isn't a chord tone, such as a Bb/E (as used for the dramatic penultimate chord in Garth Brooks' live version of 'Friends In Low Places' – play such a chord only if you can afford to bribe the jazz police).

Once you've got the hang of exercise 4 as written, try improvising to the same chord changes using sixths in A major in different positions taken from the neck diagrams on the previous page. Your ear should guide you toward certain sounds and away from others. You'll hit some sticking points with the non-diatonic chords above, but try them out and see how you do.

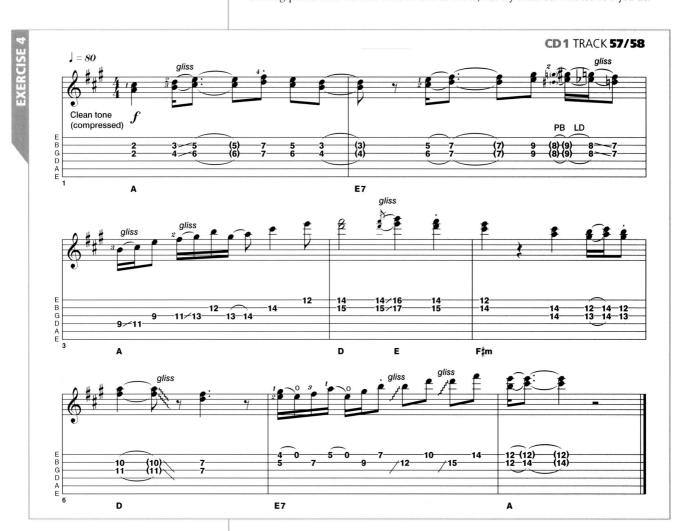

EXERCISE 4

CD 1 TRACK **57/58**

RHYTHM GUITAR

Turning our attention to rhythm guitar for a change, let's begin with the classic bluegrass-style strumming pattern in **exercise 5**. You could strum the full chord, but here it's a 'bass-chord' approach. Observe the occasional fills – which shouldn't be overdone.

Exercise 6 ditches the pick for a while; try fingerpicking throughout the piece, being aware of the few 'anticipated' moments where all or some of the upcoming chord appears early, adding momentum – which is effectively syncopation.

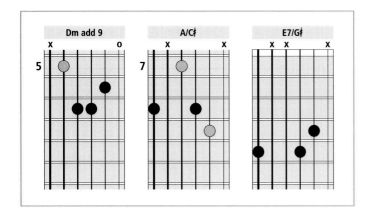

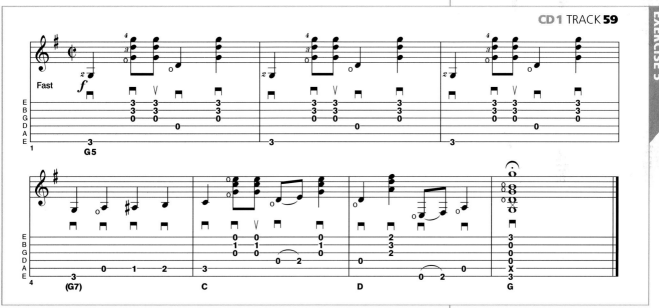

CD1 TRACK **59**

EXERCISE 5

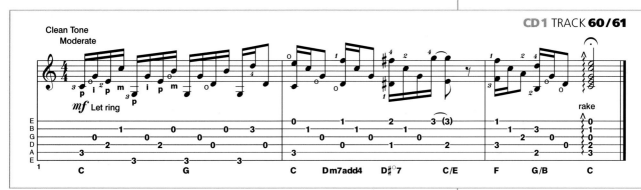

CD1 TRACK **60/61**

EXERCISE 6

For **exercise 7** use a pick again, and aim to cleanly articulate the notes of the chords. It's a slow ballad that will give you some cross-picking practice. This isn't quite arpeggiating per se. Notice the sophisticated sounds which are on offer. The 'rakes' aren't rock-style sweeping like hard rock styles; rather, they're controlled glide strokes (most often in a downward direction). Top session guitarist Dann Huff would probably add vibrato to certain chords (especially sus2 types).

Exercise 8 takes us to the key of D major. If you think the rakes are too gratuitous, stab at the chords more accurately. There's a real slash chord in bar four: G/A, which is a 'chord synonym' of A11 – they're similar or identical sounds but spelled differently. (Note: the root note often tends to be perceived as being the bass note, as shown to the right of the slash.)

SOLOING

Exercise 9 is a complete solo. Try to acknowledge the following ingredients: the A major pentatonic or A major scale (be especially on the lookout for E Mixolydian sounds over E7), stringbending, thirds and sixths, while checking out a little 'chicken picking' amd the odd pinched harmonic. If you're unfamiliar with the latter, skip ahead a page. This exercise is tougher on acoustic than on electric, but there's some hot country playing here.

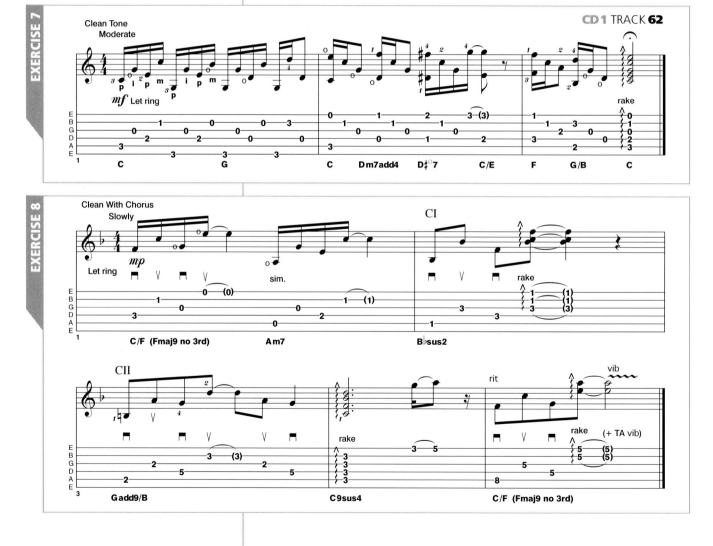

Exercise 10 gets us into 'Travis picking'. Merle Travis was highly influential in the 1950s – he even influenced Chet Atkins. Incredibly, he used a thumbpick plus index finger only. (Most thumbpickers, including Chet Atkins, Steuart Smith, Brent Mason, and Jerry Donahue, use at least the middle finger and commonly the third finger as well for plucking duties.)

If this style is totally new to you then take it slowly – and don't think about this kind of playing too much, just develop your motor skills while keeping that alternating bass pattern steady. Speaking of which, the bass notes should be palm damped (muted) for an authentic sound; just lean gently but firmly on the wound strings near the bridge/saddles. It can take some work to get into the swing of Travis picking, but once you've got it it's an effective and impressive tool, and can sound great in the right circumstances.

It's also important to get to grips with closed positions for your Travis picking – that is, barre chords. **Exercise 11** is in the key of E major but starts on the V chord of E, B7. Check out the rest of the chord shapes carefully because the fingerings and voicings may be unfamiliar to you, or at least unexpected. It should get your thumb and fingers working well together after a couple of passes.

Exercise 12 introduces 'hybrid picking', which involves using a pick plus fingers to grab chords or articulate patterns cleanly and relatively easily. Travis picking is itself a form of hybrid picking. Interestingly, Albert Lee and Danny Gatton have both featured the use of their pinky whilst plucking, which is very uncommon (see the explanation of right-hand finger use for Exercise 10, too).

Turning our attention to the fretting fingerings, these may be atypical as well. It's a good idea to take it slower than suggested at first, and break down the individual sections to work out any tougher licks before linking them all together. Once you've got it all together you'll be into some pretty accomplished country guitar playing. Some of these bends are going to take real work at first, especially with medium or heavier string sets, and with a wound G in general. Keep at it – the effort will pay off.

This workout should remind you of several great pickers: Chet, Albert, Danny Gatton, Brent Mason and maybe a hint of Dann Huff at the very end. Good luck – and remember: if you don't pick it, it won't get better!

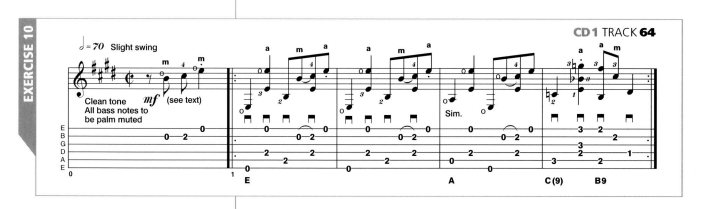

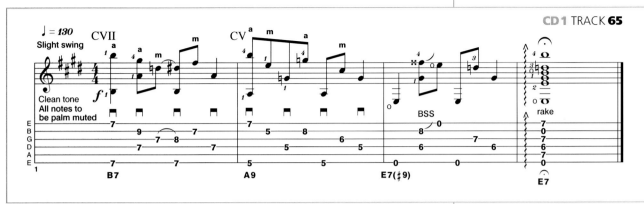

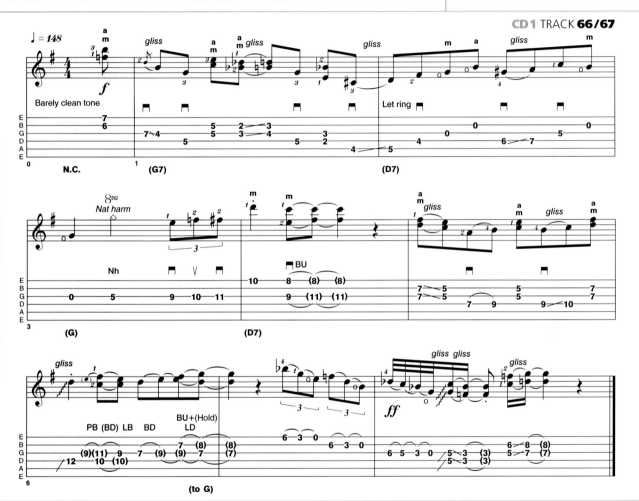

Exercise 13 is entitled 'Chetude', and is a piece by the author, respectfully dedicated to Chet Atkins. Chet always acknowledged the influence of the incredible Lenny Breau, especially when it comes to what Chet used to call 'false' harmonics. Technically speaking, an artificial harmonic is the result of fretting a note – so it's not 'natural', unlike a harmonic produced by damping a string lightly over the 12th, fifth or seventh frets, for example.

Here's how you play artificial harmonics: fret a note, then touch your index finger gently onto the point an octave (12 frets) beyond it, and pluck it using your thumbpick (many people, including the author, just use a flat pick) whilst possibly also plucking a normally fretted/plucked string – which is typically two or three strings away – using your third finger. This gentle damping of a note an octave away from where it is fretted will produce a soft harmonic, through the same process that gives you open-string harmonics at the 12th fret. The designations 'T' and 'Ah' in Ex.13 tell you where to perform these – with a number in parentheses telling you where to damp the string.

One of Chet's friends and collaborators, Tommy Emmanuel, can perform this technique at lightning speed, and it's amazing to hear. There's quite a lot of technically challenging stuff on offer here, so practise slowly and carefully, then work up to speed.

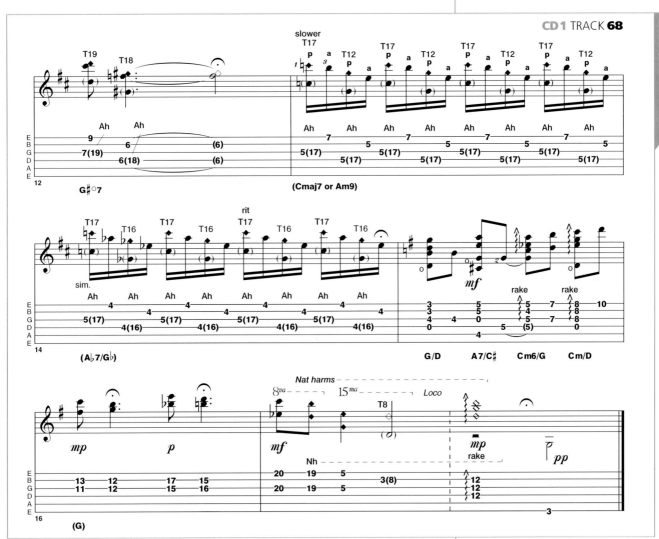

CHAPTER 6

Bluegrass

Bluegrass guitar, the exciting sound of fast, apparently effortless flatpicking on a flat-top steel strung guitar, is today one of the most popular styles in the world of acoustic guitar. Even so, the label 'bluegrass' deserves a bit of definition, because its meaning has evolved over the years. These days, a broad spectrum of acoustic country music, ranging from old-timey and traditional to modern and progressive, is described as 'bluegrass'. Its first usage, however, can be traced to the impact of Bill Monroe and his Bluegrass Boys. Using acoustic instruments – mandolin, fiddle, guitar, bass, and Earl Scrugg's innovative style on the five-string banjo – they forged a new, widely imitated style of country music at the end of World War II. The band's name came to identify the whole genre, which was distinct from the more modern, electrified bands with drums, the other post-war trend. As bluegrass evolved, the guitar became a prominent lead instrument, while still maintaining its strong rhythmic role.

Bluegrass guitar can be technically demanding, but the real power of the genre comes in its expressive style. Listening to recordings of the musicians who created the style will inspire your own playing. Perhaps the single most influential guitarist is Doc Watson, who first attracted national attention around 1960, performing at festivals and concerts during the 'folk revival' era, and is still doing shows today at over 80 years of age. Doc's repertoire featured spectacular arrangements of old-time fiddle tune melodies, as well as tasty breaks to country songs, creating a stylistic template that has been widely emulated. At such shows Doc sometimes teamed up as a duo with the 'Father of Bluegrass,' mandolinist Bill Monroe, and this pairing can now be seen, historically, as an important development in the evolution of the music, linking flatpicked guitar with bluegrass more strongly than it had been until then.

Doc and Bill's early 1960s shows included performances in Los Angeles, greatly inspiring a teen-aged guitar prodigy named Clarence White, who showed off his mastery and elaboration of Doc's style in The Kentucky Colonels, establishing lead guitar as a normal part of the bluegrass lineup. As it happens, southern California continued to be a fertile field for flatpicking; Tony Rice, the next major stylistic innovator, grew up there, hearing Clarence's playing from childhood.

The real roots of melodic country guitar picking predate the evolution of bluegrass by a couple of decades. Every flatpicker is indebted to the genius of Maybelle Carter, who began

recording in 1927 at the age of 17, with the extremely popular and influential Carter Family. Her elegant and efficient style, a seamless melding of melody and rhythm playing, is a perfect model for classics like 'Wildwood Flower' and 'Bury Me Beneath the Willow'.

The key to strong flatpicking is discipline in the wrist of your right hand. To develop a big tone that can compete with the other bluegrass instruments, you want to exploit the full mass of your hand, moving it straight up and down, hinging from the wrist, rather like hammering a nail. Throughout rhythm and lead playing, maintain a steady pulse in your right hand, placing your downstrokes on the downbeat and catching the upbeat with your upstroke.

The exercises that follow are designed to train both your fingers and your musical mind to execute the kinds of phrases that are the building blocks of the bluegrass flatpicking repertoire. Often repeating the same melodic idea through a series of chord changes, they'll give you a feel for the different fingering patterns you'll use to pick out tunes and songs. You'll notice that most of the exercises are in the keys of G and C. These keys are favoured by bluegrass flatpickers, because the melody notes lie conveniently beneath the chord shapes, and also because the open strings make a full, ringing sound that is 'right' for the style. For other keys, use a capo to transpose. This technique often makes a nice, bright tone that flatters the sound of the guitar.

ERIC THOMPSON

PICKING TECHNIQUE

Exercise 1 combines rhythm and single-note playing to train your wrist to execute the regular down-up movement of the right hand that is central to bluegrass flatpicking technique. Be sure to remember to use downstrokes on the downbeat and upstrokes on the upbeat. Try to get the same pulse in both the strumming and the picking. **Exercise 2** illustrates using 'hammer-ons' to accent the melodic eighth-notes, combined with rhythmic strums, in the seminal style of Maybelle Carter. Pick the open string and then bring your fretting finger down squarely to sound the higher pitched note.

We combine 'hammering-on' with 'pulling-off' in **exercise 3**. Pick the fretted bass note, then pluck that same string with the fretting finger of your left hand, sounding the lower note on the open string. Now let's get started with playing simple, measure-long melodic phrases, mostly on a single string. To jump-start your right hand, we warm up with **exercise 4**, which includes a measure of repeated notes to set a pulse preceding each melodic lick.

Exercise 5 continues with the single string idea, repeating a short chromatic phrase in G and D, and **exercise 6** (over page) works further toward building your right hand technique, with repeating melodic patterns focusing on one string. These will all seem simple enough after a few passes, but the repetition of such exercises – while working all the while on keeping a steady rhythm and an even pulse – is crucial for developing the stamina and consistency required of good flatpicking technique.

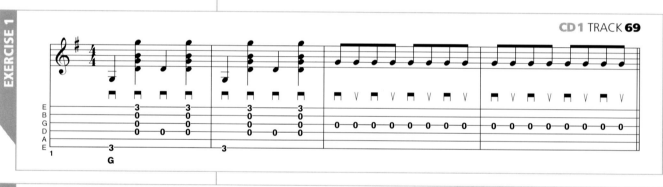

CD1 TRACK **71**

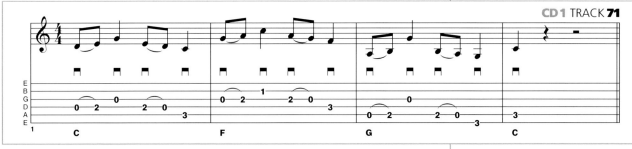

CD1 TRACK **72**

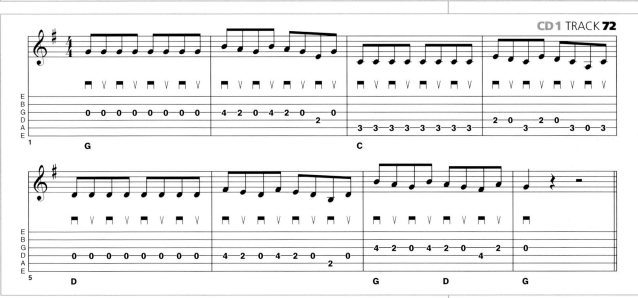

CD1 TRACK **73**

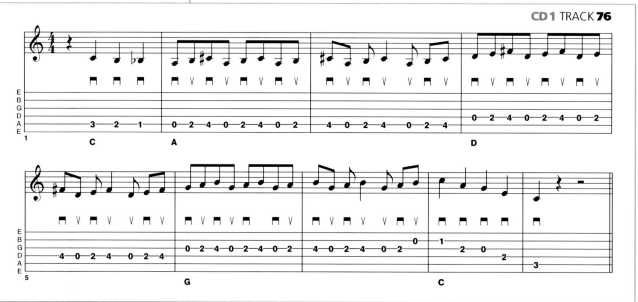

THE G-RUN

Of all the standard licks used in bluegrass, the 'G-run' is probably the most characteristic of the genre. **Exercise 7** takes this phrase through some chord changes. This lick is widely used both to punctuate the rhythm and as a melodic line in lead breaks. **Exercise 8** once again uses melodic phrases that centre around one particular string. You'll find that it is easier at first to focus your right-hand picking on a single string: combining adjacent strings is more challenging. This exercise follows a 'cycle of fifths' chord progression used in raggy songs like 'Don't Let Your Deal Go Down' and 'I Know What It Means To Be Lonesome'. **Exercise 9** moves in ladder-like steps, one at a time, up and down the scale, through a typical chord progression. Fiddle tunes are largely made up of long strings of eighth-notes like this. **Exercise 10** is a similar, step-wise melodic pattern, showing up in many songs and tunes.

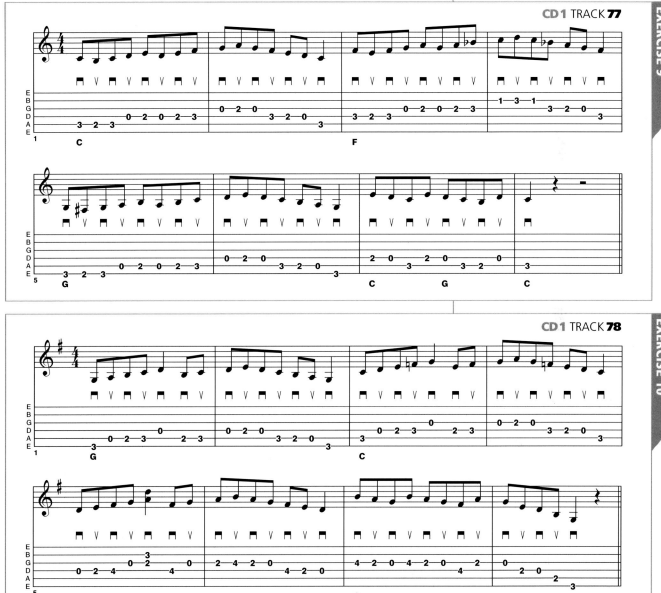

Exercise 11 explores more of these fiddlistic ideas, this time in the key of G, and includes a bluesy slur in the last line. Next, let's check out a cool 'filler' lick that I first heard used by Doc Watson, as demonstrated in **exercise 12**. Try using it in breaks to songs to dress up the space after the end of a melody line. Note that the same group of three notes is repeated twice in a row in each key. Check your right hand to make sure that it is continuing with a regular 'down-up' pattern through this passage. The first group of three should start with a downstroke, and the next group should begin with an upstroke.

    Exercise 13 expands the width of your melodic range, moving over a spread of four strings in a single phrase. You'll find this easier if you can develop a 'free' wrist, supported by your arm. Try to avoid using an 'anchor,' or 'pivot point,' tieing you to the bridge or top of the guitar in one spot.

    Exercise 14 uses a repeating 'cross-picking' pattern to make a ringing chord sound with a shuffle rhythm. It is demanding for the right hand, because each successive note is played on a different string. Again, pay close attention to your pick direction.

CD 1 TRACK **81**

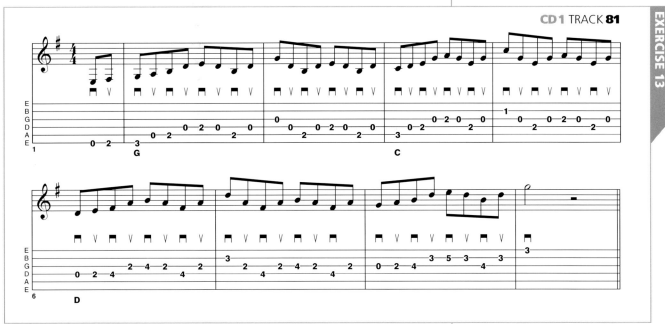

CD 1 TRACK **82**

CROSS-PICKING

Exercise 15 illustrates another kind of cross-picking. Here, we imitate the syncopated rolls of Scruggs-style banjo playing, perhaps the most recognized sound in bluegrass music. Each measure is subdivided in two groups of three notes, plus one group of two notes, each with a strong accent on the first note of the group. These can be ordered either (2-3-3) or (3-3-2). You'll notice from the pick direction notation that this type of cross-picking breaks the rules: here, we play either down-up-down/down-up-down/down-up, or down-down-up/down-down-up/down-up. This puts the strong and weak accents in unexpected places, for a very exciting (and demanding) technique. George Shuffler, Clarence White, and James Shelton are all excellent cross-pickers.

Bluegrass Blues

The blues is an important component of bluegrass guitar style. **Exercise 16** is a descending blues line, with a flatted seventh note and dissonant thirds, which can be used as an intro, in a break, or as an outro.

Bluegrass banjo pioneer Don Reno was also one of the first musicians to feature lead guitar in a bluegrass context. He was musical friends with Arthur 'Guitar Boogie' Smith, and often played 12-bar blues like **exercise 17**. A hot final line is a very common way to build excitement at the end of a guitar break. **Exercise 18** is a great example of this, also in the style of Don Reno.

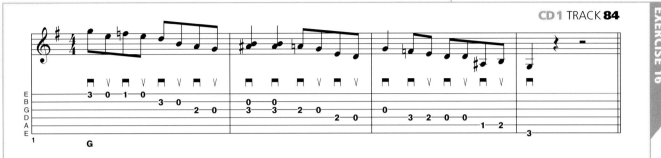

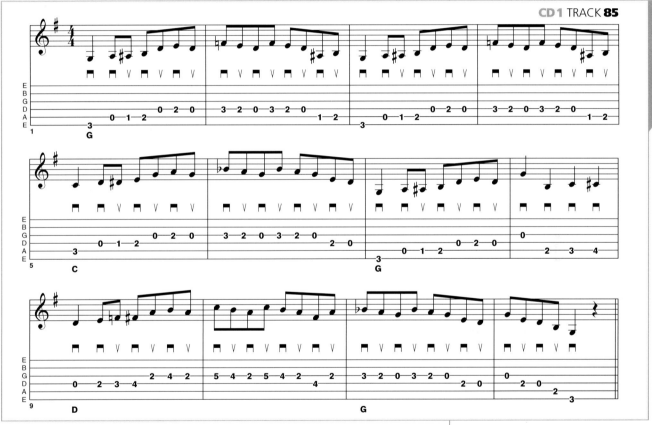

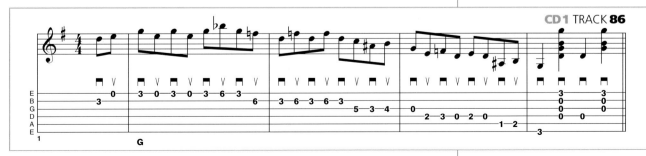

163

HOT ENDINGS

Although plenty of bluegrass guitar playing takes the rhythm role, there is also a tradition of virtuoso picking in the breaks, and ultra-hot ending lines are characteristic of the genre. **Exercise 19** gives another hot ending line in the style of Clarence White, for breaks in the key of C. Note the little bit of 'cross-picking' in the final measure.

Exercises 20 and 21 illustrate still more ending lines in various keys. Swing is another style, along with fiddle tunes and blues music, from which bluegrass has borrowed licks and ideas. **Exercise 22** is a chromatic 'clarinet' riff that is nearly universal in the language of flatpicking.

Time to put some of this learning to work in an extended piece. **Exercise 23** is a hypothetical bluegrass instrumental which I'll call 'Thompson's Ramble'. It repeats the same melodic idea through a long series of quick chord changes, giving you good practice at making position shifts with your left hand.

CD 1 TRACK **90**

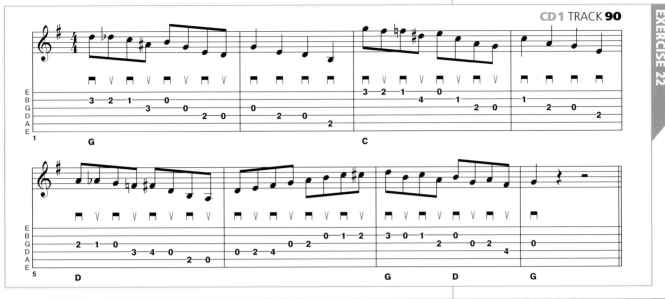

CD 1 TRACK **91**

To wrap things up, let's combine even more of the ideas we have covered. **Exercises 24** and **25** show how to put the different ideas taught in the earlier lessons together to make exciting, engaging guitar solos. Extended solos like these can weave their way through an eclectic brew of influences that together make up the bluegrass soloing style. It's a powerful, melodic, and engaging form of music that becomes extremely addictive once you latch onto it.

Far from being a musical form from 'the old days', contemporary bluegrass features some of the hottest guitarists who have ever worked in the genre. New players are coming up all the time, while new listeners are simultaneously learning to appreciate this stirring music. For further inspiration check out such contemporary players as Bryan Sutton from the Nashville scene (with Ricky Skaggs and others), Norman Blake, David Grier, Russ Barenberg, Jim Nunally and Scott Nygaard.

Jazz

From the early days of jazz to the present, guitarists have constantly challenged the limitations of their instrument – not only with their sound but with their technique. In the 1930s, the electric guitar allowed the jazz player to break free from the bounds of the rhythm section and become a soloist. But today many players are once again appreciating the sweetness and subtlety of unamplified jazz guitar, and that has brought a renaissance in both the playing and making of acoustic archtops.

Today's jazz players enjoy a legacy that includes the entirety of jazz history. Rather than being limited to the pre-electric styles that formed the first wave of acoustic jazz guitar, they can bring into the unplugged approach all of the electric playing that has followed. They also benefit from the many fusion and 'crossover' styles that have influenced the genre. From Charlie Christian's fluid, swing-influenced lines, executed using all-down strokes, to Pat Metheny's post-bop lines, with heavy use of left-hand hammer-ons and pull-offs, there is a lot of ground to cover in this music that we broadly refer to as 'jazz'. In between – and way out on the fringes as well – there is a whole lot more to bring into the stew.

As rock'n'roll and the blues attained popular status in the 1950s and 1960s, many jazz guitarists were influenced by these sounds. At the same time, the central core of the 'jazz guitar sound' was continually evolving, too. Wes Montgomery came into prominence in the late 1960s and many consider him to be the father of modern jazz guitar. Wes was a modern bop player who displayed a sophisticated melodic and harmonic sense. The keys to his style were the use of his thumb, which produced a very warm sound, and his ability to play octaves faster than most guitarists could play single lines. At that time this made him instantly recognisable and created a new standard in modern jazz guitar.

Carrying on in the tradition of Wes were two incredible guitarists, George Benson and Pat Martino. Each man had amazing technique and used a pick for most of his single note lines.

These two virtuosos elevated the sound of jazz guitar once again. Just check out their solos on *The George Benson Cookbook* and Pat Martino's *Footprints* and you'll see what I mean.

Jim Hall, an incredible guitarist, has probably influenced the sound of contemporary jazz guitar more than anyone else. He was one of the early guitarists to employ hammer-ons and pull-offs to achieve a more fluid sound. This was quite a departure from the percussive technique of picking every note. He helped inspire the next generation of great players, including Mick Goodrick, Pat Metheny, John Scofield, Mike Stern, Bill Frisell and John Abercrombie. Jim Hall is the bridge that connects the traditional elements of jazz and points them to the future.

It now becomes easier to hear how contemporary guitarists fit into all this, their styles arising from the infinite possibilities of combining jazz with the elements of rock and beyond. Contemporary guitar is capable of incredible sounds, and has come a long way musically since the early days of Charlie Christian. Guitarists now are more harmonically advanced and technically proficient and have a higher profile in the jazz world than ever before. On top of that, modern tastes tend not to limit players nearly as much as did the standards and expectations of old. Whether your instrument is a high-end Benedetto acoustic archtop, an old Yamaha flat-top or a nylon-strung La Patrie classical, no holds are barred for the jazz player of today. You can make an amazing amount of beautiful music on a hollow wooden box with six thin strings attached.

CARL FILIPIAK

SEVEN BASIC SOUNDS

Now that we've seen the direction jazz guitar is headed, let's take a look at some of the things you have to learn in order to get there. Knowing how to recognize the seven basic sounds in all keys is very important. They are the major, minor, dominant, diminished, minor seventh with a flattened fifth (also known as half-diminished), augmented and suspended sounds. The first three (major, minor and dominant) sounds are especially important. Use the sixth and the fifth string to locate the nearest root, match the appropriate sound and you will be able to play just about any chord progression (we'll get to them soon). For now, try these examples in the keys of G (sixth string root) and C (fifth string root), then see if you can transpose them elsewhere.

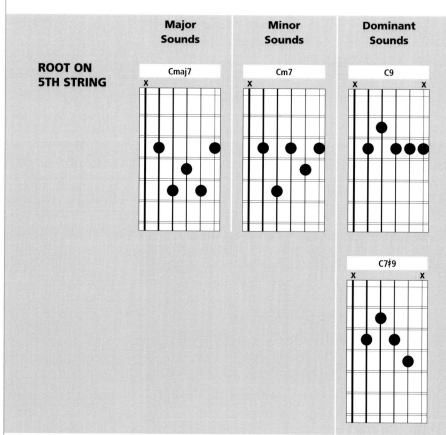

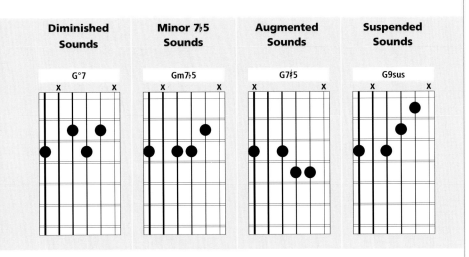

Diminished Sounds — G°7

Minor 7♭5 Sounds — Gm7♭5

Augmented Sounds — G7♯5

Suspended Sounds — G9sus

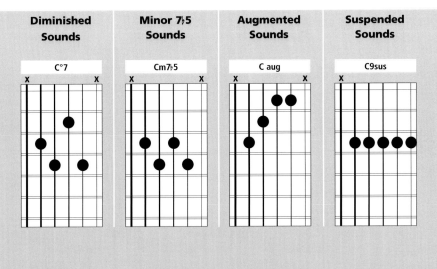

Diminished Sounds — C°7

Minor 7♭5 Sounds — Cm7♭5

Augmented Sounds — C aug

Suspended Sounds — C9sus

171

TWO NOTE DIADS

Don't be deceived by the simplicity of these 'diads' (two-note chords). In many musical settings they sound great. They are the guide tones of chords, the thirds and sevenths, which imply the quality of the chord (major, minor or dominant). They work great played alongside a bass player who fills in the root of the chord.

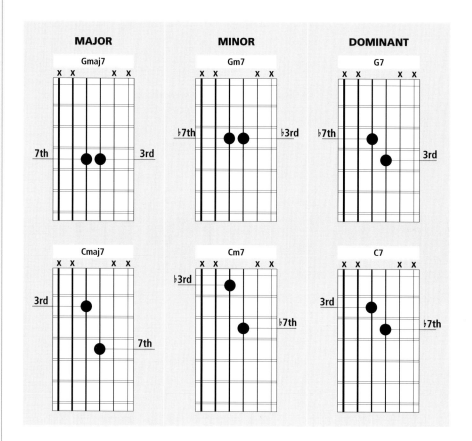

II-V-I PROGRESSIONS

The II-V-I (2–5–1) progression is one of the most widely used in jazz. When you take a C major scale and build chords in thirds on each note of that scale, the seven chords will be:

Cmaj7,
Dm7,
Em7,
Fmaj7,
G7,
Am7,
Bm7♭5

The second (II) chord is Dm7, the chord that starts on the fifth (V) degree of the scale is G7 and the 'one' (I) chord is Cmaj7. A II-V-I in the key of C is: Dm7, G7, and Cmaj7. Here is a page of assorted II-V-I patterns. I would suggest starting out by mastering the two examples on the top line, then proceed to each of the remaining progressions. One of the examples uses a substitute chord for the V, and another uses substitutes for both V and I chords. Chord substitution will be discussed later in this chapter.

II-V-I progressions with root on fifth and sixth strings

II
Dm7
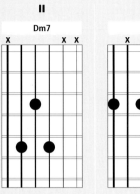

V
G7

I
Cmaj7
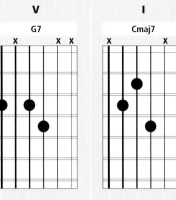

II
Dm9
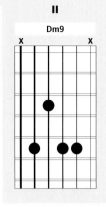

V
G13
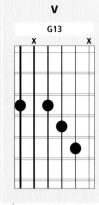

I
Cmaj9

II-V-I progression with root on fifth string and substitutes for V and I chords

II
Dm11
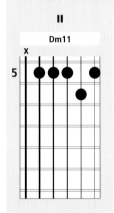

V
E♭m11

I
Em11
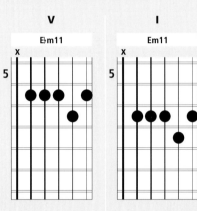

II-V-I progression with root on sixth string

II
Dm9

V
D♭9

I
Cmaj9
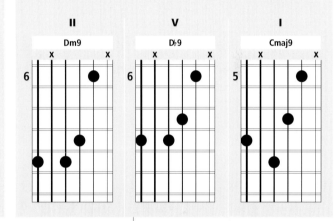

II-V-I progressions with root omitted

II
Dm9

V
G13

I
Cmaj13
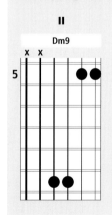
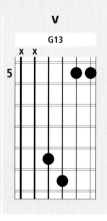
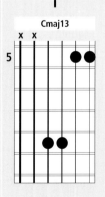
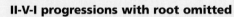

II
Dm9

V
G13

I
C6/9
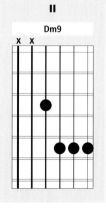
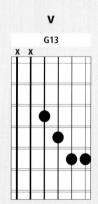
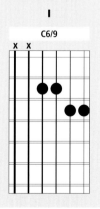

173

MINOR II-V-I PROGRESSIONS

The II-V-I in a minor key is a m7♭5 chord, followed by a 7♭9 chord, then a minor seventh or minor ninth chord. In Cm the sequence would be Dm7♭5, G7, and Cm7. The first two examples are extremely useful but try all of them for different settings (which we will explore later).

Minor II-V-I progessions with roots on fifth and sixth strings.

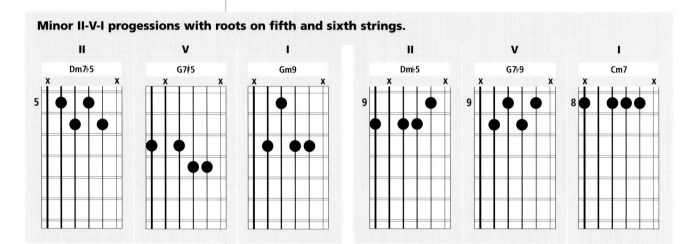

Minor II-V-I progressions on the upper four strings, no roots

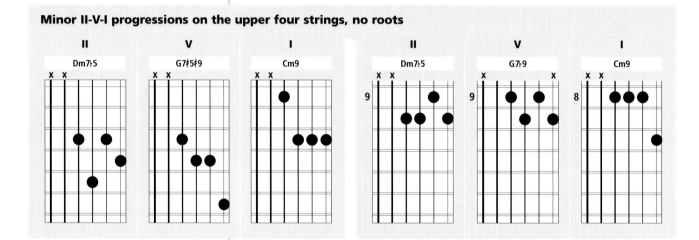

UPPER VOICINGS

Master the shapes on the opposite page and you will see how you can move chords around and resolve to the next sound with great voice leading. Practise by transposing to different keys and work out some 2–5–1 sequences. Resolve to the nearest form when the sounds change from minor to dominant to major.

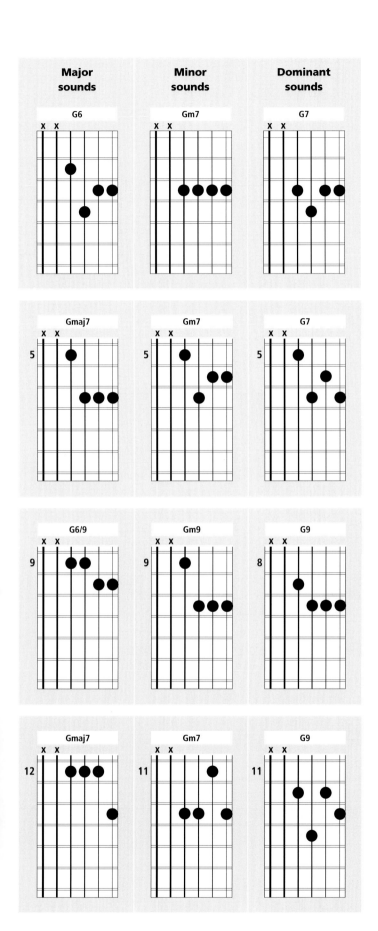

I-VI-II-V PROGRESSIONS

This is another pattern of equal importance. A quick look at the seven chords in the key of C (diatonic harmony) shows that the chord that occupies the sixth scale degree is an Am7 chord. A I-VI-II-V in the key of C major would be: Cmaj7, Am7, Dm7, G7. You may notice there is only one dominant chord in a key, built on the fifth scale degree. This chord, the G7 in the key of C, creates tension that resolves to the I chord, Cmaj7. You can do the same thing with any chord in the key by creating a dominant chord to resolve to it. This is called a secondary dominant and that's how the A7 chord will be explained in the following sequence:

1	6	2	5
Cmaj7	**A7**	**Dmin7**	**G7**

The secondary dominant A7 is the dominant of II, or the 'V' of II. Many tunes feature this sequence so try to learn it in as many keys as possible. Some 'standards' employing the I-VI-II-V include 'Oleo', 'Rhythm-a-ning', 'The Theme', 'Moose The Mooch', 'Ready And Able' and 'Tipping' (all in the rhythm changes 'A' section) and 'Have You Met Miss Jones', 'Turnaround In Blue' (last two bars) and 'St. Thomas'. Try these three four-chord I-VI-II-V patterns (right) to hear the sound of A7 resolving to Dm7, as well as G7 resolving to Cmaj7. The first sequence is made up of roots and guide tones, the second features added tensions, and the third uses upper-four-string voicings.

MOVING FURTHER

Understanding just a few concepts like diatonic harmony, related seconds and fifths, subflat fifths and chord families can help you produce some harmonically complex chord sequences. This may take a while to understand thoroughly, but don't let this discourage you from trying out some new and interesting patterns.

Diatonic harmony is based on the tonic, subdominant and dominant chords built on the root (I), fourth (IV) and fifth (V) degrees of the major scale respectively. 'Diatonic' means they are based entirely on the notes of the major scale: and all three have several notes in common. The second degree (II) chord has subdominant harmony, meaning it shares most of its notes with the IV chord, and the seventh degree (VII) chord has dominant harmony. A II-V pattern is important because it implies a key. A dominant chord can be preceded by its related II chord, a fifth above its root. Since the third of one dominant chord is the same as the seventh of another dominant chord a tritone (three whole notes) away, and vice versa, they are considered substitutes for one another: G7=Db7. Chords with upper tensions 9, 11 and 13 don't affect the basic quality of sound. Cm7, Cm9 and Cm11 are all minor family chords and are interchangeable. The major family includes C6, Cmaj7, Cmaj9, C6/9. The dominant family includes C7, C9 and C13.

I-VI-II-V progressions with root and guide tones

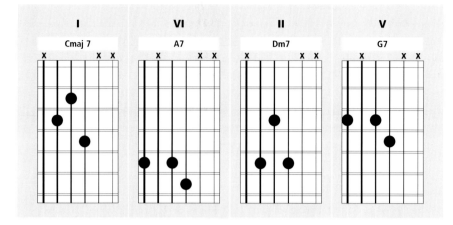

I-VI-II-V progressions with added tensions

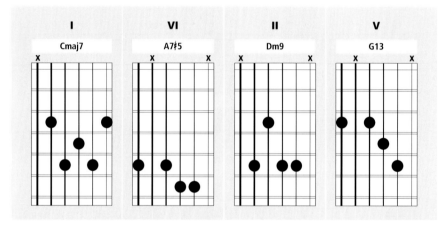

I-VI-II-V progressions on the upper 4 strings

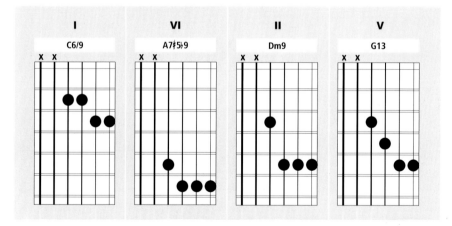

SONG FORMS

Finally, let's play some tunes! There are three basic forms you should master: jazz blues, minor blues and rhythm changes – illustrated in turn in **exercises 1–3**. These will help you learn tunes from *The Real Book* (a 'fake book' owned by every jazz player, containing hundreds of popular jazz standards). For example, the jazz blues form is used in many tunes by Charlie Parker, Wes Montgomery, Sonny Rollins, Thelonius Monk and many others. Learn these in a few more keys and you'll get a lot of mileage out of this section with a little practice and perseverance. Notice that no rhythms are given here. For now, use basic chord forms or chords you've just learned and strum through each of these exercises in your own style. Next, we'll put some rhythms to them to start playing some more familiar songs.

EXERCISE 1

CD 2 TRACK **1**

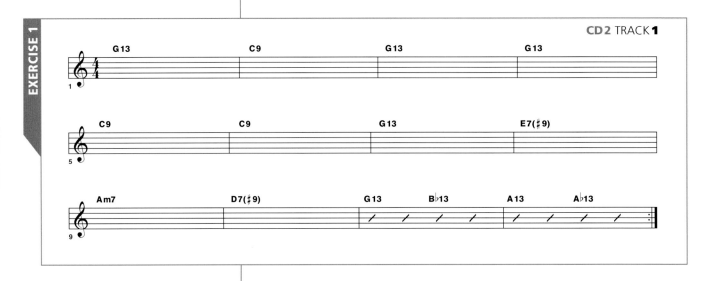

CD2 TRACK **2**

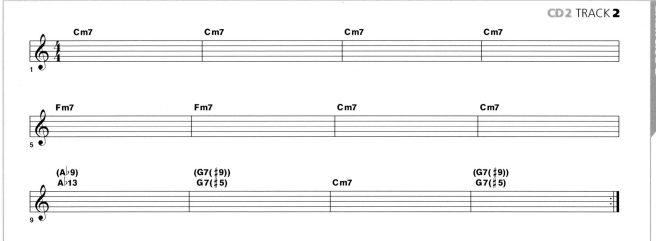

CD2 TRACK **3**

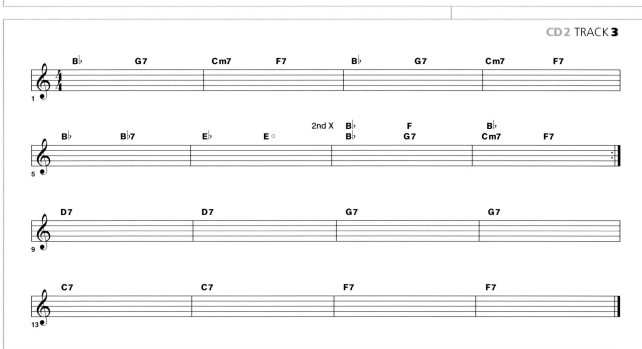

179

ESSENTIAL RHYTHMS

Let's talk about how to play the five essential rhythms that will not only help you with the three basic forms, but with many others as well. These will allow you to function in a variety of musical styles.

Exercise 4 is a rhythm called 'four to the bar'. This perfectly exemplifies the 4/4 time signature, and is a rhythm you'll hear in plenty of classic jazz. Four to the bar is traditionally played with all downstrokes on the quarter-notes, sometimes with the occasional upstroke on an eighth-note for emphasis, to suggest a solid rhythm, with chord changes according to the tune. It often works best when you are supplying the time (no bass player or drummer) or for playing rhythm guitar charts in a big band – think Freddie Green. Sometimes chords change as fast as one per beat, which takes some fancy finger work, but here we'll strum two bars against muted strings to get the rhythm down, then play two bars with a chord change every two beats. As in the previous exercise, use basic chord forms or those you have already learned elsewhere. After you've got the feel of it, try playing four to the bar against the jazz blues in exercise 1.

Exercise 5 is a 'jazz waltz'. As you might guess it's in 3/4, but a jazz waltz also works great in 6/8, just double it up. Also, note the importance of the rests for the feel of the rhythm. Repeat the two bars until you get a feel for it. After you've got this down, try it on the standard tunes 'Alice In Wonderland', 'Bluesette', 'Someday My Prince Will Come' and 'Windows'.

The 'bossa nova' rhythm in **exercise 6** works great for sambas as well as bossas – a samba being faster. While there are many variations of Latin and Brazilian rhythms used in jazz, this is a great one to start out with, and it is multi-functional. Listen out for these rhythms in the standard tunes 'Blue Bossa', 'One Note Samba', 'Wave' and 'Triste', all of which you can learn yourself. (Get deeper into these rhythms in the 'Latin' chapter.)

The easy way to approach a 'ballad' is to play the root on beats one and three. On beats two and four play the notes of the chord that are left on the D, G and B strings, as exemplified in **exercise 7**. Simple, but effective.

Exercise 8 gives an example in 'odd time', in this case 5/4, probably the most-used odd time signature in jazz. Think of it as a jazz waltz in 3/4 plus two extra quarter-notes: 3+2=5. Many odd time signatures can be played using this concept. Pianist Bill Brubeck's 'Take Five' is a classic jazz tune in 5/4 that most of you will recognise, and a good one to learn on your own once you get this rhythm down. Again, note the major contribution the rests make to the rhythmic feel of this exercise.

IMPROVISATION

Finally it's time to move on to what many guitarists think of as the essence of jazz: soloing and improvisation. We'll start by talking about soloing 'over' and 'through' the chord changes.

Learn the C major scale in all positions and you've also learned the location of its related modes. They are: D Dorian, E Phrygian, F Lydian, G Mixolydian, A Aeolian, B Locrian. We'll learn more about modes a little later in the chapter, but for now let's use it as a C major scale. Since a II-V-I in C major is built from the notes of the second, fifth and root of the scale, simply play notes of the C Major scale over all three changes. The scale generates the harmony and the chords imply the scale. Chords are scales and scales are chords – simple.

While playing a C major scale may not make you sound like Joe Pass, it will be a fairly easy and melodic way to start playing 'through' changes – improvising in the scale of the key of the tune, while the changes go on behind your solo.

Another way that jazz players solo to chords is to use a different scale for each chord. Chord-scale relationships is a way to start playing 'over' the changes instead of through them. One is not better than the other, just different.

Playing over the changes reflects the sound of each chord in a II-V-I progression. For the II chord, Dm7, play in the D Dorian scale – simply a C major scale starting on the second scale degree: D-E-F-G-A-B-C-D. Over the V chord, G7, play G Mixolydian, which starts on the fifth degree of the C major scale. Its scale spelling is: G-A-B-C-D-E-F-G. Over the I chord, Cmaj7, you're back to the notes of the C major scale. That's a basic look at modes as applied to the theory of improvisation used in jazz guitar soloing. We'll explore some ways to use each mode a little better in the next section.

Right now, however, let's break down some more elements essential in jazz soloing. We have already talked about guide tones – the thirds and sevenths that define the quality of the chord – and chord scales, which reveal the melodic relationships between scale, chord and harmony. Let's move on to arpeggios and how to use melodic embellishments.

MELODIC EMBELLISHMENT

Arpeggios outline the targeted chord tones (root, third, fifth, seventh and above) and melodic embellishment approaches the chord tones chromatically, scale-wise, from above and below. In the following exercises I've used a Dm7 arpeggio and have shown several ways to approach each chord tone to produce a more melodic effect. By combining notes that are chromatically above and below the targeted chord tones, our playing becomes more melodic and still defines the harmonic sound of the chord, in this case Dm7. **Exercise 9** takes a 'chromatic below' approach to the chord tone (guide tones are indicated by arrows in the exercise). **Exercise 10** uses a scale tone above approach, while **exercise 11** combines the two in one approach and **exercise 12** combines them in another. **Exercise 13** uses a double chromatic below and **exercise 14** a double chromatic above.

Now do the same for G7 and Cmaj7 and you'll hear what we're getting at. When combined with other concepts (guide tones, chords, scales and arpeggios) melodic embellishments will get us closer to some of the ways jazz lines are created.

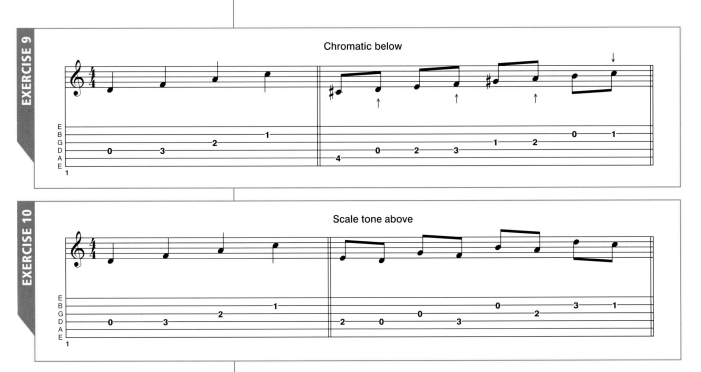

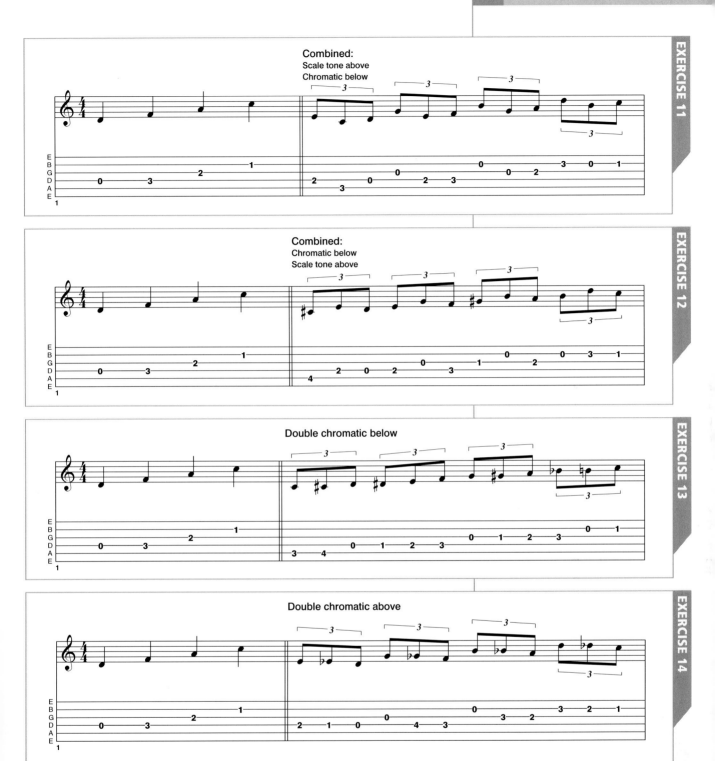

DEVELOPING A JAZZ LINE

You now have a handle on many of the essential building blocks of jazz soloing, so let's examine a series of different ways of combining these melodic approaches to chords and scales in order to develop a variety of solo lines with different moods and feels, starting with the extremely simple and building to some more complex approaches. Still in our familiar key of C major, we'll use our four-bar II-V-I progression of Dmin7, G7 and Cmaj7 over 11 great ways of building your solo lines.

Play them individually to hear how each approach works, then try stringing selected examples together – or even all of them – for a long solo that shifts between techniques. When you get the hang of it, record the chord progression for as many bars as you like and try playing along.

There isn't a whole lot to say about each exercise; you just need to play through them to hear and feel how each approach works. **Exercise 15** starts us off simply hitting the guide tones; **exercise 16** takes it a step further, linking thirds and sevenths. **Exercise 17** uses 'octave displacement' to run down from the II toward the V, then jumps to the octave and runs down to the I, while **exercise 18** uses an example of 'altered tension' in the flatted ninth.

Exercise 19 picks up the pace with eighth-notes (squeezing three into a triplet for starters, to boot), while **exercise 20** keeps it breezy to outline minor seventh arpeggios over the changes. **Exercise 21** gets your fingers stretching a little further with 'interval leaps,' and **exercise 22** outlines some short hops in lines made up of jumps between fifths.

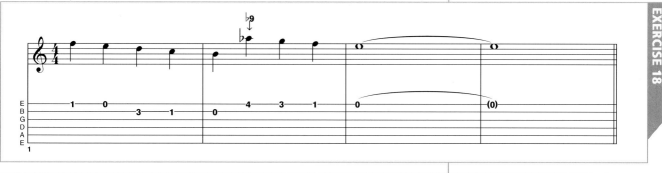

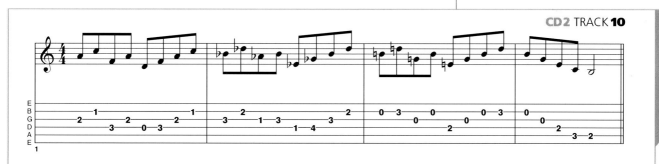

CD2 TRACK **9**

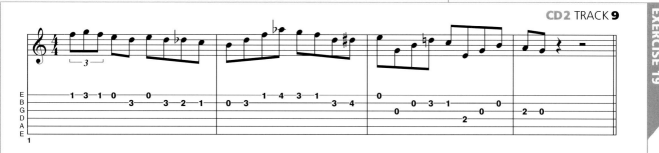

CD2 TRACK **10**

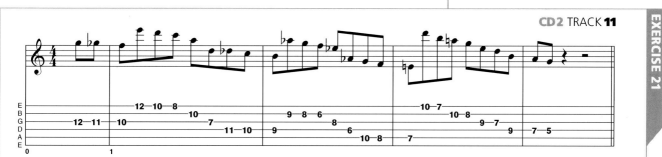

CD2 TRACK **11**

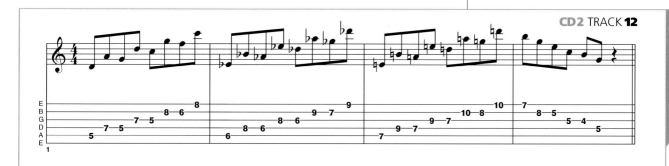

CD2 TRACK **12**

We'll wrap up our 11 techniques for developing jazz lines with three more effective approaches, still using our II-V-I progression in C major (Dm7, G7, Cmaj7). **Exercise 23** shows you a 'chord over chord' technique, which layers chords on top of each other. **Exercise 24** uses 'motifs', melodic riffs similar to each other in shape and feel, that move with the changes.

Finally, **exercise 25** uses 'chromatic' lines – runs that move short intervals for a tight, occasionally off-key sound that still falls in at all the right reference points and makes a great change from sweet, strictly melodic runs.

Although these are 'only' eighth-notes, these lines move pretty swiftly at faster tempos, especially with some of the unfamiliar tonal leaps required, so take your time and go at them slowly at first, building speed with practice.

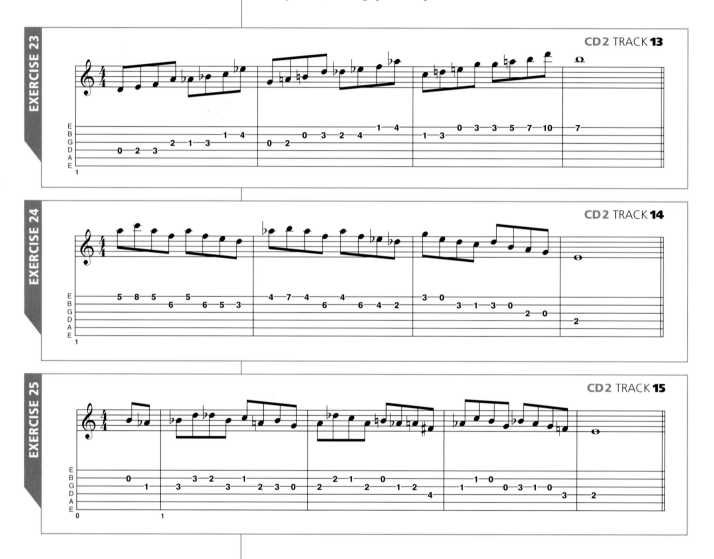

ESSENTIAL SCALES AND MODES

Before concluding our exploration of jazz guitar with a bebop exercise, let's look briefly at a few techniques that will help you extend your playing beyond the obvious clichés and simple melody lines. If this chapter has whetted your appetite to explore jazz guitar further, you can expand on these concepts on your own, or seek out more in-depth instruction.

The four essential scales to know are the major scale, melodic minor, diminished scale and the whole-tone (or whole-note) scale. Knowing their spelling and scale formulae will aid you greatly in knowing how to use them. We'll look at them in our old friend C major, but once learned they can be transposed to any key to give you a full arsenal of improvisational tools.

Here are the chords built from a C major (Ionian) scale and its corresponding modes. As we briefly discussed earlier in this section, you find these modes in any key by playing the major scale in that key but starting on each subsequent note rather than on the root (I). Thus:

Cmaj7	**C Ionian**
Dm7	**D Dorian**
Em7	**E Phrygian**
Fmaj7	**F Lydian**
G7	**G Mixolydian**
Am7	**A Aeolian**
Bm7♭5	**B Locrian**

So the following relationship would give you a modal approach to soloing over our familiar II-V-I changes in C major.

	Dm7	**G7**	**Cmaj7**
use:	**D Dorian**	**G Mixolydian**	**C Major Scale**

C melodic minor is an easy variation of C major, simply: C-D-E♭-F-G-A-B-C. Two modes that are extremely useful are built from the fourth and seventh degrees of the C melodic minor scale. They are: F Lydian ♭7 and B altered dominant. Play F Lydian ♭7 over F9#4 chord types; play B altered dominant over B7#9, B7♭9, B7♭5, B7#5.

Diminished scales come in two types: 'whole-step half-step' and 'half-step whole-step'. They have the same notes in the same order: only the starting note is different. A whole-step half-step diminished scale like C-D-E♭-F-Gb-Ab-A-B-C goes well over a C diminished chord. A half-step whole-step diminished scale starting on B works over these chord types: B7♭9, B7#9, B7♭5, B13.

The C whole-tone scale is: C-D-E-F#-G#-B♭-C. Play it over C aug, C7#5, C9#11 and chords of that type. Remember chords are scales and scales are chords. One implies the other. For example, look at D Dorian – the notes of the scale reveal the chord qualities:

D	**E**	**F**	**G**	**A**	**B**	**C**	**D**	**E**	**F**	**G**	**A**	**B**	**C**	**D**
R		**♭3**	**5**		**♭7**		**9**			**11**			**13**	

D Dorian sounds great over a Dm7, Dm9, Dm11 and even Dm13 chords (sometimes the 13th will appear an octave lower as the sixth). Now look at a G altered dominant scale over a G7 chord:

G	**A♭**	**B♭**	**C♭**	**D♭**	**E♭**	**F**
Root	**♭9**	**#9**	**M3**	**♭5**	**#5**	**♭7**

Play this scale over G7, G7♭9, G7#9, G7♭5, G7#5, or any combination of these.

II-V-I-VI BOP LINES

Exercise 26 offers eight bop lines over a new progression, II-V-I-VI, in a new key, D major. (The chords from the first four bars repeat throughout each four-bar line, though you can try your own variations.) Have someone play the chords or tape them to hear the sound of the line and its various degrees of tension.

Not only are they eight useful lines to study, but they can also be played in one continuous etude. As always, start off slowly at first then build speed as you get the hang of it. Speed in itself isn't the objective; we're looking to build melodic and harmonic awareness and compile a handy bag of lines (derived from scales and modes) to use as improvisational building blocks to apply to your other playing.

Try to work out appropriate chord voicings for yourself to use in your own backing track. As an added challenge, refer back to the Essential Scales And Modes page to help you analyse some of these licks. I hope you have fun with this exercise and it helps you to master some of those great lines that you've heard your favourite artists play.

CD2 TRACK **16**

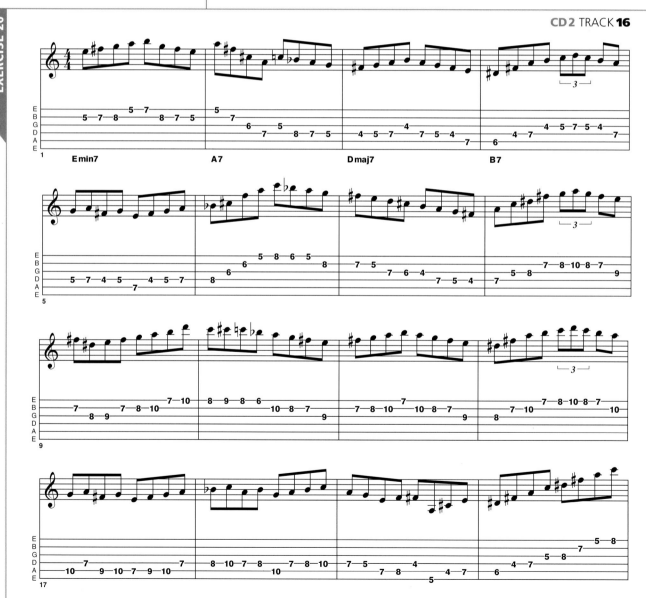

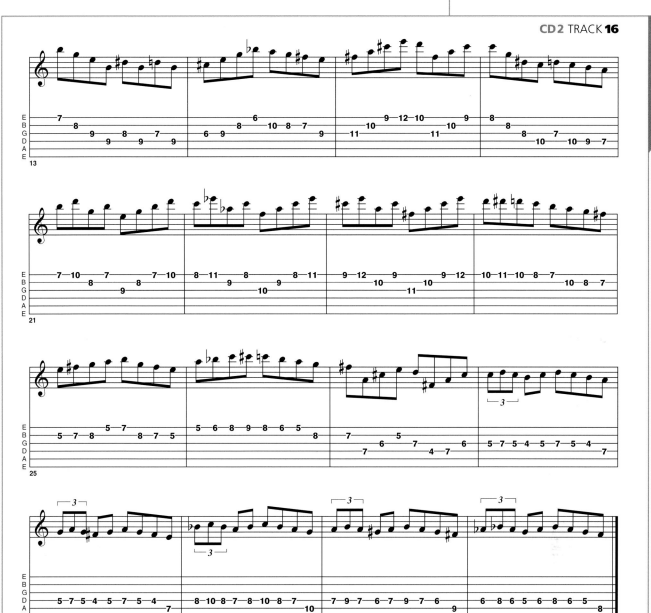

Gypsy Jazz

Every so often a musician comes along who is so original, so technically adept and so influential that he spawns an entire musical genre based solely on his own style. The virtuosic Gypsy guitarist Django Reinhardt was such a figure. Django's brilliant recordings with the Quintette of the Hot Club of France forged a uniquely European style of jazz, with influences ranging from Louis Armstrong and Duke Ellington to French musette and Hungarian Gypsy music. This music, and Django's playing in particular, has inspired generations of players ever since.

Throughout his teens, Django paid his dues accompanying musette accordionists in the dance halls of Paris. His promising career in music was nearly ended when his left hand was severely damaged in a fire. Fortunately, the pull of music was too strong for Django, and against all odds he retrained himself to play guitar by using mainly the two uninjured fingers of his left hand. During this period of convalescence Django discovered jazz, which subsequently became his life long passion and set him on course to changing the very music that possessed him.

Although Django's music influenced nearly every other jazz guitarist after him (including Charlie Christian, Barney Kessel, Kenny Burrell, and many others), the only musicians to maintain the pure Django style were the Sinti Gypsies of France, Germany, and the Benelux countries. Hence the name, 'Gypsy jazz'. From Django's death until the 1990s, performances of Gypsy jazz outside the Gypsy community were relatively rare. The immense talent of contemporary Gypsy guitarists such as Boulou Ferré, Stochelo Rosenberg, and Biréli Lagrène was mostly unrecognised until a recent revival which has brought increased awareness of this wonderful style. Gypsy jazz is now flourishing not only in Europe, but also in North America, Japan, Australia, and diverse other parts of the globe.

To give you a sense of this style, I have compiled a number of exercises that are characteristic of the types of idea Django used in his solos. Before we continue, readers should be aware that Gypsy jazz has a much more systematic approach to technique than most contemporary jazz guitar styles. Because Gypsy jazz was mostly transmitted via oral tradition to successive generations of Gypsies, approaches to picking, improvising, accompaniment, and so forth have become highly standardised. Most of these techniques were originally used by Django and have remained part of the genre because of their effectiveness and musicality.

The musical exercises I will be using in this lesson will reflect the 'traditional' way of playing this genre. Because of this, you'll often see fingerings and picking techniques which directly contradict contemporary jazz guitar wisdom. Although much of Django's music can be executed using more conventional techniques, there is usually a distinct difference in tone, phrasing, and articulation between these and the pure Gypsy technique. These differences are especially distinct when playing on an acoustic instrument.

Django, and nearly all other Gypsy guitarists, use the 'rest stroke' system of picking. This style of picking is ideally suited to the acoustic guitar because it allows the player to achieve volume, tone, and speed without uncomfortable tension or pain. In a nutshell, Django's right-hand technique is a plectrum version of the commonly used classical guitar fingerstroke known as 'apoyando' or rest stroke. When applied with a plectrum, this technique has all the benefits of the fingerstyle stroke – reduced fret buzz; a secure feeling of placement; reduced muscle tension; and a loud, full tone. In addition, the plectrum rest stroke takes advantage of basic principles of physics by using the weight of the hand, instead of the muscles, to propel the pick in much the same manner as a hammer falls on a nail.

Unlike the more commonly used 'free stroke', which activates the string by pushing the pick through the string, the rest stroke activates the string by letting the pick hand fall, primarily using gravity rather than your muscles to provide the necessary force. A rest stroke is completed by letting the pick rest on the next adjacent string, hence the name. The result is volume, tone and speed without the discomfort of tense muscles in your wrist and forearm. (For more detailed instruction on the rest stroke technique see my book *Gypsy Picking*, from DjangoBooks.com.)

MICHAEL HOROWITZ

ARPEGGIOS

One of the defining characteristics of Django's style was his heavy reliance on arpeggios. **Exercise 1** demonstrates a Cmaj13 arpeggio (with no ninth) that Django often used. Notice that it can be fingered mostly – or entirely – with two fingers. **Exercise 2** is a Cmaj13 arpeggio, this time including the ninth. **Exercise 3** is a minor 6/9 arpeggio played as triplets.

Django had a strong tendency to place emphasis on the sixth and ninth chord tones (in the key of C, the sixth/13th is A and the ninth is D). The sixth and ninth tones are only mildly dissonant, but since they are outside of the basic triad (root, third, and fifth) they help to create some harmonic interest. The 6/9 sound (both major and minor) is extremely pervasive in the playing of Django and his Gypsy contemporaries. Major seventh and minor seventh chords became more common in the bebop that followed. Django's later recordings incorporate some of these more modern sounds.

DORIAN MODE

When Django did play minor scale passages, he often used the Dorian mode (seen in **exercise 4**) to achieve the minor 6/9 sound. The Dorian scale differs from the natural minor scale in that its sixth scale degree is a semitone higher, a major interval rather than a minor. The major sixth (the note B in the key of D), used in the minor sixth chord, creates the 'minor sixth sound' that Django preferred. Notice that since the Dorian scale is built on the 2nd degree of the major scale, the D Dorian scale has the same key signature as the C major scale. So C major and D Dorian are made up of the same pitches; the only difference is usage. **Exercise 5** demonstrates a Dorian-based pattern that Django used. **Exercise 6** demonstrates how Django used a combination of Dorian scalar and minor 6/9 arpeggio ideas to link a Cm6 chord to a Gm9 chord.

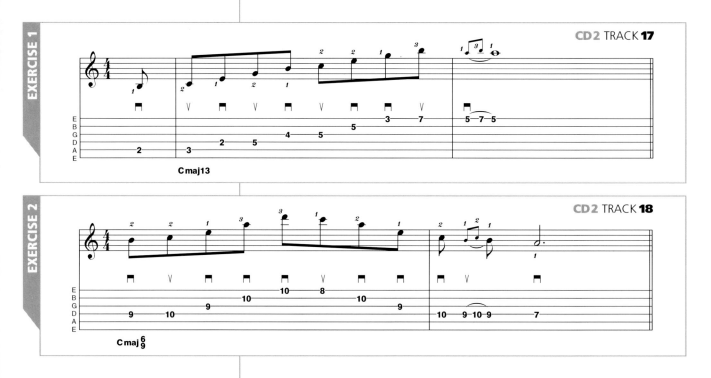

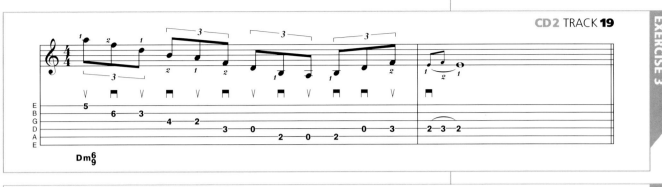

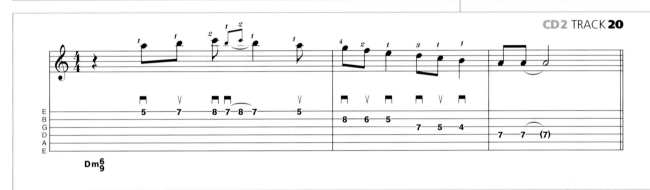

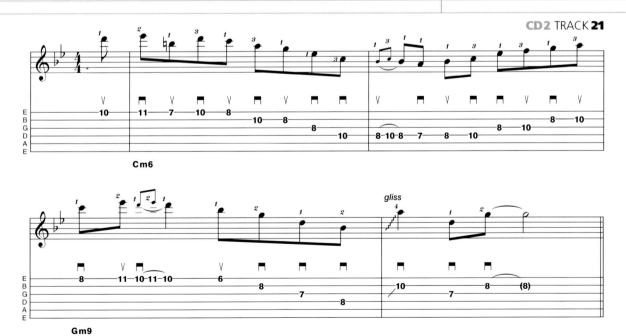

MIXOLYDIAN MODE

When playing over dominant chords, Django relied heavily on the Mixolydian mode, seen in **exercise 7**. The Mixolydian mode differs from the major scale in that its seventh scale degree is a semitone lower. The flattened seventh (the note F in the key of G) creates the 'dominant sound' that is desirable for dominant chords.

Notice that since the Mixolydian mode is built on the fifth degree of the major scale, a G Mixolydian mode has the same key signature as a C major scale. So C major and G Mixolydian are made up of the same pitches: again, the only difference is their usage. **Exercise 8** demonstrates a G Mixolydian run that links to a C major arpeggio.

Django also frequently employed the 'bebop Mixolydian' scale when playing over dominant chords. This scale developed in the bebop era of the 1940s. However, its existence can be traced as far back as Louis Armstrong's 1927 solo on 'Hotter Than That'. Django, who was heavily influenced by Armstrong, also made extensive use of the various 'bebop scales'.

The bebop Mixolydian scale adds an extra passing tone to the normal Mixolydian mode so that chord tones will fall on the beat. The passing tone falls in between the seventh scale degree and the root, as demonstrated in **exercise 9**. In the Mixolydian bebop scale you get the root, third, fifth, and flattened seventh chord tones all falling on the beat. These chord tones make up the basic structure of a dominant chord and therefore are the strongest target notes. **Exercise 10** shows how Django used the A Mixolydian bebop scale over an A7 chord resolving to a D6 chord.

Django used numerous arpeggios that target the flattened seventh, ninth, and 13th chord tones. **Exercise 11** demonstrates a Django-style G13 arpeggio.

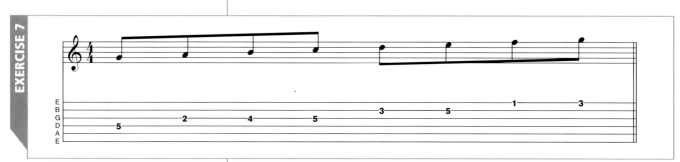

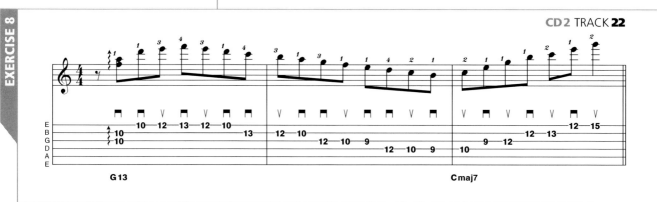

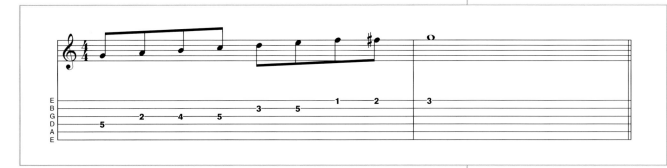

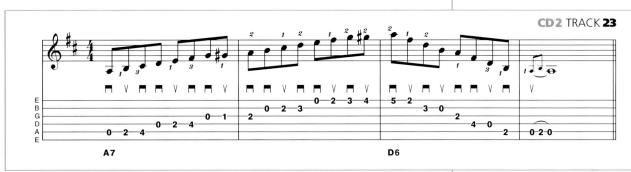

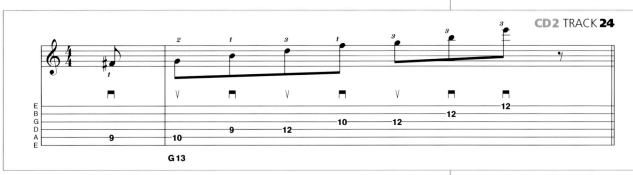

HARMONIC MINOR

The harmonic minor scale was an integral part of Django's sound. The harmonic minor scale is identical to the natural minor, with the exception of a raised seventh scale degree, demonstrated in **exercise 12**.

The raised seventh scale degree allows for strong resolution to the tonic chord. So, in the key of D minor harmonic, the seventh scale degree is C#, which is the third chord tone of A7 (the dominant chord in D minor harmonic). The D minor harmonic scale also has the note B♭, which is the flattened ninth of an A7 chord. Although Django would occasionally use the harmonic minor over a minor chord, he mostly used it to achieve the 'dominant seventh' and 'flattened ninth' sounds over dominant chords. **Exercise 13** demonstrates how Django used the harmonic minor scale to go from A7♭9 to D minor.

DIMINISHED ARPEGGIOS

Django also made extensive use of the diminished arpeggios, as demonstrated in **exercise 14**. Diminished and dominant flattened ninth arpeggios have nearly the same pitches (the diminished arpeggio lacks the root of the chord). Django used these devices to take advantage of the flattened ninth chord tone. If you ascend a diminished arpeggio a semitone away from the root of any dominant chord, you will automatically get the desirable third, fifth, flattened seventh and flattened ninth chord tones. **Exercise 15** uses a diminished arpeggio to link an A7 chord to a Dm6/9 chord.

Exercise 16 uses a diminished arpeggio with some chromatic embellishment to link a D7(♭9) chord to a Gm7 chord. In a similar manor, but using a different approach, **exercise 17** uses a diminished based arpeggio to link an A7(♭9) chord to a D6 chord.

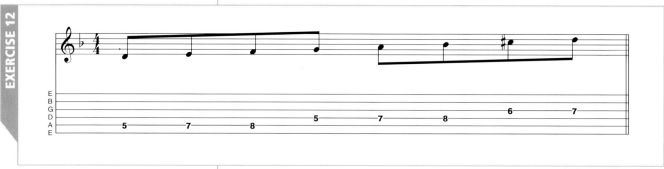

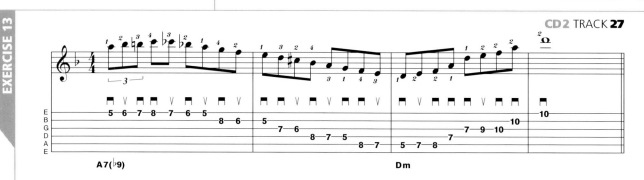

CD2 TRACK **27**

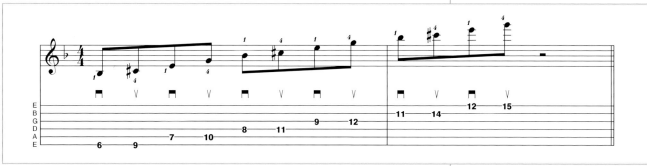

CD2 TRACK **26**

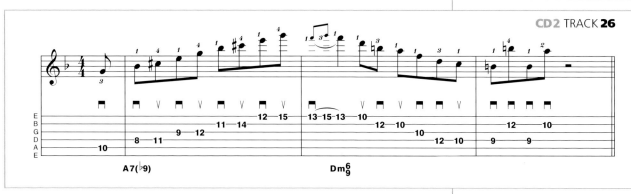

CD2 TRACK **27**

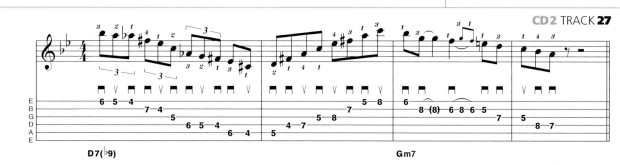

CD2 TRACK **28**

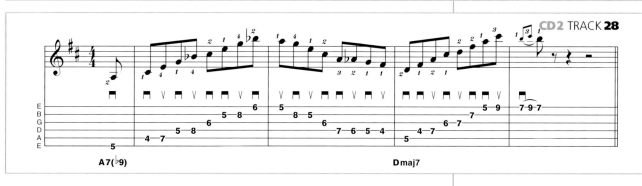

EXERCISE 18

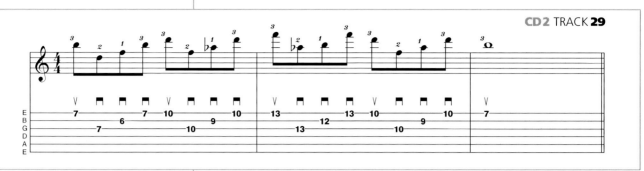

EXERCISE 19

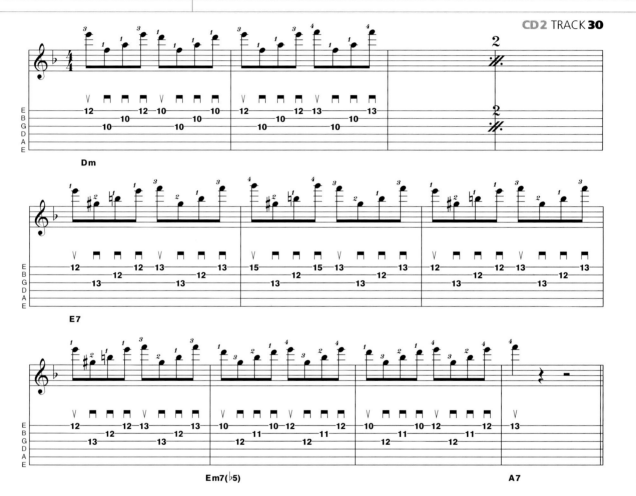

PICKING TECHNIQUES

Exercise 18 demonstrates a sweeping diminished arpeggio that keeps repeating the third, fifth, flattened seventh, and flattened ninth of a G dominant chord. The same exact pattern can be used over a D minor chord to get the root, flattened third, flattened fifth, and sixth chord tones. The flattened fifth offers an effective dissonance that Django also used extensively.

Notice the sweeping right-hand picking pattern used in Exercise 18 (up-down-down-down). Django used this pattern to achieve a number of virtuosic effects. **Exercise 19** demonstrates this same picking pattern applied to the chord changes of the contemporary Gypsy Latin standard 'Bossa Dorado'. This pattern is commonly used by Dutch Gypsy guitar virtuoso Stochelo Rosenberg.

Exercise 20 demonstrates another picking pattern Django used extensively. It repeats the strokes down-down-up to create a syncopated effect. When used in conjunction with chord tones, one achieves a pleasing virtuosic effect. Exercise 20 also uses chord tones that outline the chord progression for the last eight measures of Django's classic composition 'Minor Swing.'

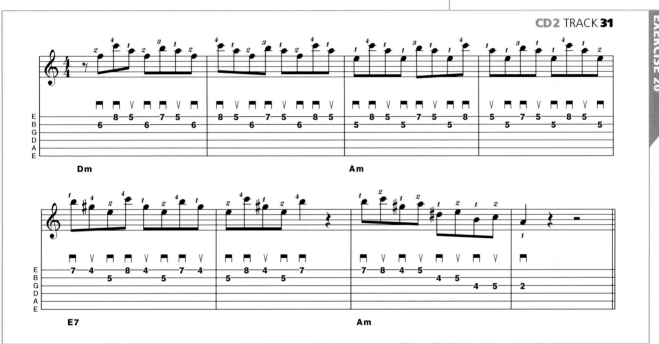

CD2 TRACK **31**

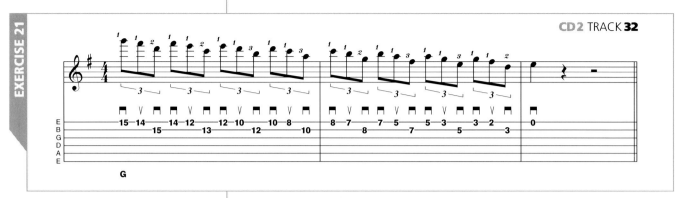

G

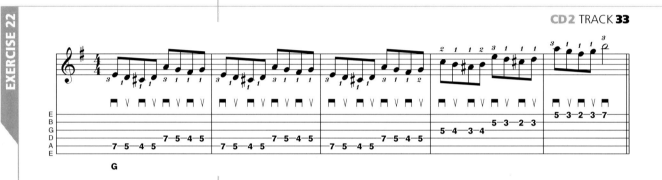

G

Exercise 21 uses the down-down-up pattern to play a G major scale in descending triplets. (Note that the first down stroke is absent.)

VIRTUOSO TECHNIQUES

Exercise 22 demonstrates a G major enclosure pattern that Django made frequent use of. An enclosure is when you embellish a chord tone by playing a note above and below. Django often used the pattern to achieve a lightning fast double-time effect.

   Exercise 23 demonstrates a series of ascending arpeggios. Django used this type of idea often. This particular version works well over 'rhythm changes' chord progressions. The chord symbols above the music are the most literal interpretation. They are only a suggestion. You'll find that this idea works well over numerous other chord progressions as well. Play through these exercises as often as you can to become familiar with the style and feel of Gypsy jazz, then try putting some rhythmic and melodic ideas together for yourself.

CHAPTER 9

Celtic

From its banshee-crazed jigs and reels to its heart-rending ballads, the Celtic genre possesses some of the most moving, emotive music known to mankind. Contemporary Celtic music evolved primarily from the dance music traditions of Ireland and Scotland. Historically this music was played on the fiddle, flute, pennywhistle and various types of bagpipes, without accompaniment of any kind. The characteristic rhythmic drive of Celtic melodies allows them to sound complete on their own, which makes it possible for a single fiddler to be a one-man dance band. But the energy and vitality of this music have driven countless guitarists to seek out the style, and to perform it both as solo artists themselves, or as accompanists to the more traditional Celtic solo instruments.

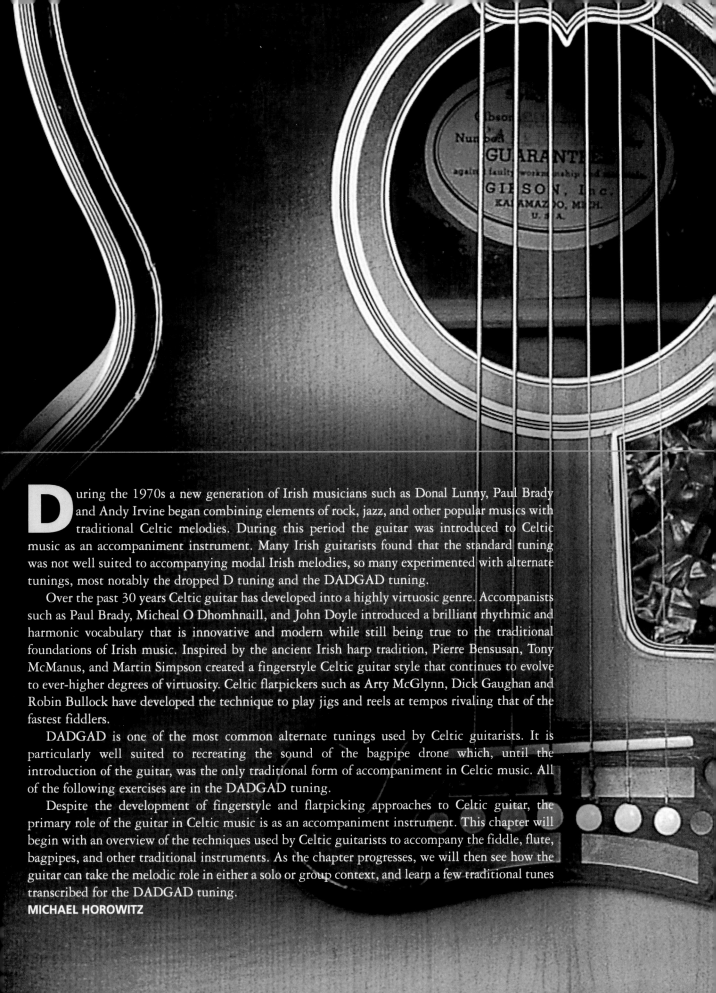

During the 1970s a new generation of Irish musicians such as Donal Lunny, Paul Brady and Andy Irvine began combining elements of rock, jazz, and other popular musics with traditional Celtic melodies. During this period the guitar was introduced to Celtic music as an accompaniment instrument. Many Irish guitarists found that the standard tuning was not well suited to accompanying modal Irish melodies, so many experimented with alternate tunings, most notably the dropped D tuning and the DADGAD tuning.

Over the past 30 years Celtic guitar has developed into a highly virtuosic genre. Accompanists such as Paul Brady, Micheal O Dhomhnaill, and John Doyle introduced a brilliant rhythmic and harmonic vocabulary that is innovative and modern while still being true to the traditional foundations of Irish music. Inspired by the ancient Irish harp tradition, Pierre Bensusan, Tony McManus, and Martin Simpson created a fingerstyle Celtic guitar style that continues to evolve to ever-higher degrees of virtuosity. Celtic flatpickers such as Arty McGlynn, Dick Gaughan and Robin Bullock have developed the technique to play jigs and reels at tempos rivaling that of the fastest fiddlers.

DADGAD is one of the most common alternate tunings used by Celtic guitarists. It is particularly well suited to recreating the sound of the bagpipe drone which, until the introduction of the guitar, was the only traditional form of accompaniment in Celtic music. All of the following exercises are in the DADGAD tuning.

Despite the development of fingerstyle and flatpicking approaches to Celtic guitar, the primary role of the guitar in Celtic music is as an accompaniment instrument. This chapter will begin with an overview of the techniques used by Celtic guitarists to accompany the fiddle, flute, bagpipes, and other traditional instruments. As the chapter progresses, we will then see how the guitar can take the melodic role in either a solo or group context, and learn a few traditional tunes transcribed for the DADGAD tuning.

MICHAEL HOROWITZ

CHORD SCALES

Exercise 1 demonstrates a D major chord scale. Notice that regardless of the chord, the two top strings (A and D) ring out. The drone pitches are notated with the stems up, the actual chord tones are notated with the stems down. This is one of the many drone-like effects that are easy to achieve in DADGAD tuning. Also take note of the ergonomic left-hand fingerings. These will allow you to switch chords quickly at fast tempos. (Note: in this and all other exercises, the chord nomenclature does not take into account the drone pitches.) **Exercise 2** demonstrates the D minor chord scale.

Another advantage of the DADGAD tuning is the number of easily fingered 'neutral' chords. A neutral chord lacks the third chord tone, so it is neither major nor minor. Many Celtic melodies have a very ambiguous third scale degree. It can suddenly switch back and forth between major and minor, actually be a non-standard pitch between major and minor, or be absent altogether. Bagpipe drones are also neutral, so these chords strongly imply the sound of the bagpipes. **Exercise 3** demonstrates a number of neutral chords.

DADGAD also allows one to easily finger 'unisons' on the second and third strings. A unison is the same exact pitch played on two strings simultaneously. The timbrel and intonation differences between the two strings produces a pleasing 'chorus' effect reminiscent of instruments such as the 12-string guitar, mandolin, and the Greek bouzouki (which, surprisingly, has also become a very popular instrument in Irish music.) **Exercise 4** demonstrates the D Mixolydian scale played as unisons on the second and third strings. The unison pitches are notated with their stems up, the other drone strings are notated with their stems down. The combination of the unisons and the drone strings produces a sound reminiscent of the Appalachian dulcimer.

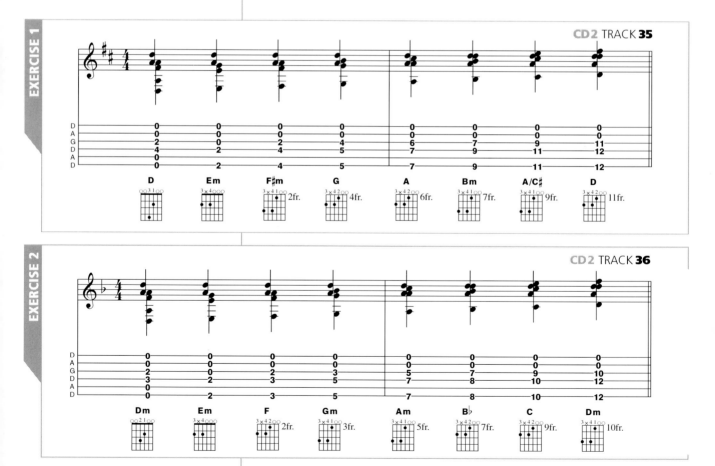

The Mixolydian scale (in the key of D: D-E-F#-G-A-B-C) is one of the most common scales used in Irish melodies. The flattened seventh scale degree gives it a distinctive sound. Three other scales are common in Irish music:

Natural minor (Aeolean): D-E-F-G-A-B♭, C

Dorian: D E F G A B C

Major: D E F# G A B C#

The natural minor scale is common in popular music and should be very familiar. The Dorian scale differs from the natural minor in that its sixth scale degree is a semitone higher. The raised sixth scale degree produces a distinctive sound, which is extremely pervasive in Celtic music. And the major scale is of course the most common scale in Western music. Try adapting exercise 4 to the pitches of the major, natural minor, and Dorian scales.

DADGAD guitarists also frequently make use of thirds fingered on the second and third strings. **Exercise 5** demonstrates a major scale in thirds. Try adapting this exercise to the pitches of the minor, Dorian, and Mixolydian scales.

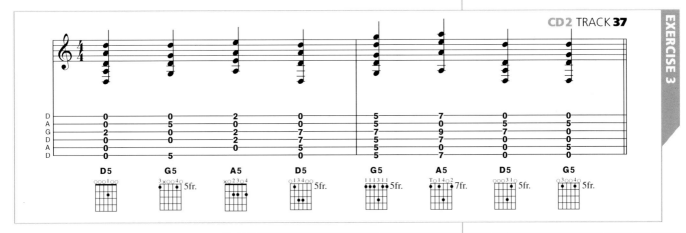

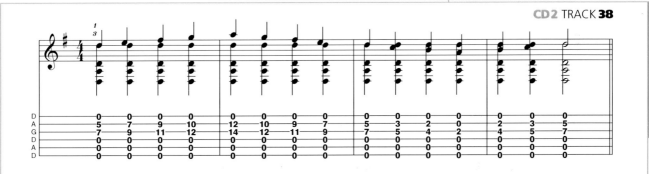

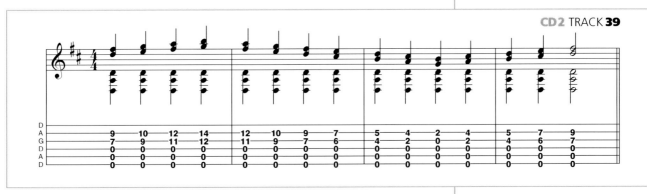

THE REEL

The most common Celtic dance rhythm is the reel in 4/4 time. Celtic accompanists generally avoid a 'two-beat' feel which tends to sound like American 'Old Time' and bluegrass music. Instead, Celtic guitarists base their accompaniment on an eighth-note pulse. **Exercise 6** demonstrates the basic rhythm for reels, straight eighth-notes played with alternating down and up strokes. The entire chord is only struck on the first beat of the bar. The remaining beats are played on the drone strings only (first and second strings), keeping the accompaniment from being too loud and obtrusive. Celtic guitarists prefer thin picks (around .5mm). The rhythmic 'click' they produce is part of the aesthetic of Celtic music.

Exercise 7 demonstrates another way to play an eighth-note rhythm. Instead of strumming only the top strings, you strum only the bass notes on most beats. Paul Brady and John Doyle are particularly adept at playing long sections like this. They mute the other strings, and occasionally hit an entire chord as an accent, staying out of the way of the melody.

Exercise 8 gives you the melody and chords for a popular Irish tune called 'The Congress Reel', in the key of A Dorian. Most of the accompaniment revolves around A minor and G major chords (I and ♭VII), a common pattern in Celtic music. The second section can also be played with the same two chords. However, in A Dorian tunes Celtic musicians will frequently replace an A minor chord with a D major chord, and a G major chord with a C major chord. This suggests that the tune has modulated to D Mixolydian (which has the same key signature as A Dorian). Also note that the F major chords throughout the arrangement are not natural to A Dorian (which has an F# in the key signature). They are 'borrowed' from the natural minor, but are commonly used this way and sound good nevertheless.

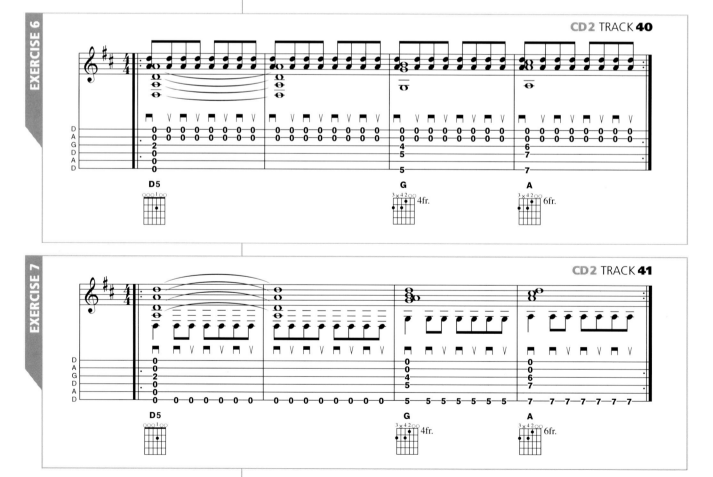

THE JIG

Another common Celtic dance rhythm is the jig, demonstrated in **exercise 9**. Jigs are in 6/8 time, which gives them a bouncy triplet feel. To get the correct rhythmic accents when playing jigs, you must use a down-up-down/down-up-down strumming pattern. This pattern puts a strong accent every three beats, which is essential when playing in 6/8 time. Also try playing this exercise using the bass strumming technique used in Exercise 7.

Exercise 10 demonstrates the melody and chords for a popular Irish jig called 'East at Glendart'. This tune is in the key of D major. Most of the accompaniment revolves around the D major, G major and A major chords (I, IV, V), a common chord pattern in Celtic music. The B minor chord is a common substitution for D major. The second section of the tune uses the thirds demonstrated in exercise 5. The C major chord does not normally occur in the key of D major. It is borrowed from the D Mixolydian mode and is used to create some harmonic interest.

The melody on the recording is played on the penny whistle. The standard notation reflects what the pennywhistle is playing. The tablature is a guitar version that has been slightly altered to make it more idiomatic for the guitar. If you attempt to learn the melody on guitar, try to use the jig picking pattern as much as possible: down-up-down/down-up-down. This well help you obtain the correct accents for 6/8 time.

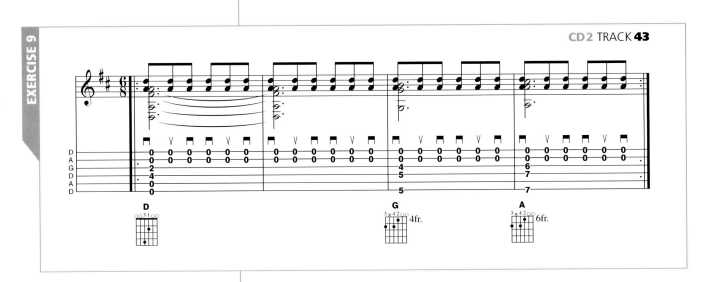

EXERCISE 11

Exercise 11 is a fingerstyle arrangement of the popular jig 'Banish Misfortune'. This arrangement is based on techniques used by Celtic fingerstylists such as Pierre Bensusan, Tony McManus and Martin Simpson. Use of the DADGAD tuning allows one to create a rich, full sound that is sometimes called 'harp style' guitar playing. To maximize the harp effect, let all notes ring out as much as possible. The octave technique, which is easy to execute in DADGAD tuning, is used in the third section of the arrangement (above).

Irish musicians frequently embellish melodies with an ornament called a 'roll'. A roll is played by adding a grace note above and below the primary pitch to create a triplet. However, this technique doesn't work on the guitar as well as it does on the fiddle, flute and other traditional melodic instruments. Celtic guitarists have devised numerous ways to imitate the sound of a roll, one of which appears in the second half of bar four. A combination of hammer-ons, pull-offs and picked notes creates the triplet sound of a roll.

CHAPTER 10

World Music

The term 'World Music' has become a catch-all in recent years for anything outside the broad range of popular American and European music styles. It has certainly become a genre that is too large to encompass easily. With the greater availability of recorded music from Africa, Latin America, Asia, the Balkans and the Middle East, guitarists normally treading the rock, blues, jazz and country paths are bringing fresh new chops and rhythms to their playing and spicing up the musical brew in the process. Out of the wealth of World Music styles pervasive today, Latin, African and Klezmer make excellent starting points in any quest to broaden your technique.

Latin music has long had a following on fringes of pop and rock, and has occasionally found its way to superstardom, for instance in the hands of a Carlos Santana. The recent proliferation of Latin rhythms in pop and dance hits, however – along with the close focus on Latin styles in Ry Cooder's popular and influential Buena Vista Social Club – has breathed new life into the genre, and turned new listeners on to the infectious rhythms and melodies of this compelling music.

To avoid some common misconceptions and misuses of the Latin style, we will start by learning the original patterns so you can identify the source of these traditional tunes; then you can transform them, if you like, into something more original, or blend them into the other styles you play. We're going to look at some basic riffs from the Afro-Cuban tradition: 'son montuno', 'mambo' and 'cha-cha-cha'. These are three of the most common styles in a 'descarga' – a Latin jam session – and we're going to examine some of the basic ingredients to help you cook up some hot salsa. This music is all about rhythm, but even a whole heap of rhythm is useless without feel. Latin music is designed to make you move your hips, so if they're stationary you haven't quite got it yet!

NESTOR GARCIA

Infectiously rhythmic, explosively joyous, delightfully melodic, **African** guitar is a style that works its way quickly into your blood and stays there for good. It's as much fun to play as it is irresistible to listen to, and the fundamentals aren't particularly difficult to tackle, given a little practice and close attention to the rhythmic essentials. Once mastered, it can be pursued as a style in itself or blended into countless other genres of music to give your usual playing some extra life and sparkle. In this brief look at African guitar styles we're going to explore two 'Palm Wine' guitar grooves, the Sikyi (pronounced see-chi) and the Amponsah (arm-pawn-sa), then move on to explore the broader 'highlife' style of music. As well as supporting traditional

musicians, these sounds influence a growing list of stars who have enjoyed collaborations with African musicians. Take Ry Cooder's work with Ali Farka Toure, Taj Mahal and Fouday Musa, or Paul Simon's work with Ladysmith Black Mambazo. Africa possesses the largest menu of both traditional and urban grooves in the world, a potential source of inspiration for anyone needing to resuscitate their creative energy.

KARI BANNERMAN

Klezmer music evolved from a mixture of Jewish, Romanian, Greek, Gypsy, Turkish and other folk musics of south east Europe. Its driving rhythm, exotic melodies, and virtuoso technique have much in common with those of other Balkan musics. Klezmer is distinguished, however, by its Jewish character, much of which is due to the influence of Hasidic vocal music and the ancient Jewish cantoral tradition.

In the first half of the 20th century a sophisticated, urban form of klezmer flourished in New York. During this 'golden era', virtuoso clarinettists such as Dave Tarras and Naftule Brandwein performed and recorded constantly for immigrant Jewish audiences. Unfortunately, their success was only fleeting. As the next generation began to assert its assimilated musical tastes (jazz, rock, etc), klezmer fell by the wayside and became almost obsolete by the 1970s. A revival began to take shape in the early 1980s, bringing these sounds back to the attention of a flock of young Jewish musicians in search of their 'roots'. In the hands of a new generation of players, klezmer became 'hip' again, and the music itself quickly began to evolve, with bands such as the Klezmatics, Hasidic New Wave, and Masada incorporating influences from rock, jazz and other ethnic genres. If you have never experienced this music, its compelling melodies and driving rhythms can really take you by surprise, and it offers some scales and modes that can broaden any playing style.

MICHAEL HOROWITZ

LATIN
by Nestor Garcia

In Latin music, the guitar, like the piano, is used as a percussion instrument; think drums, cowbells, anything. The way to take control of the groove is to use repetitive patterns, just like a percussionist would. In this context, most of the guitar patterns are based on patterns from piano and the Cuban 'tres', a fretted instrument with three courses of double strings tuned G, C and E.

Rhythm patterns are centred around the 'clave'. A clave is one of a pair of short wooden sticks used as a percussion instrument in Latin music. They usually play the clave rhythm, a two-bar pattern that is considered to be the centrepoint of Afro-Cuban music. Sometimes they are referred to as 3:2 or 2:3. This merely refers to the number of rhythmic hits in each bar.

Exercise 1 shows the two basic types of clave: son clave and rumba clave. Away from your guitar and in any possible situation, tap a clave rhythm with your right hand while keeping time, in quarter-notes, with your left hand. Then reverse hands. (I've written the son clave in 2:3 as this is the most common form used for cha-cha-cha and mambo, though you find them in 3:2 as well – just reverse the bars.) In 2:3 clave the guitar starts on a downbeat; the upbeats are in the 3 side of the clave.

Exercise 2 is the pattern played by the timbale player on the side of the timbales, here combined with a 2:3 son clave. It is called 'cáscara'. Use this as a warm-up exercise, playing it purely as a rhythm pattern, and then try to use it in the scale in **exercise 3** and play it with your own scales and arpeggios, just to get the idea firmly seated in your body.

Exercise 4 is a line based on the pattern played by the 'tres cubano', outlining a second inversion C major triad. Sometimes you can find it in D. This is used primarily to play 'son montuno', the oldest form of what we know today as salsa. This line is played in the 2:3 son clave. All the salsa and mambo patterns are based on son montuno patterns.

Hundreds of tunes and styles are based on the I-IV-V chord progression: faster, slower, in major or minor flavour. Three chords, three inversions and twelve keys equal 108 possible varieties of finger entertainment for a Sunday morning, and you can transpose the line in **exercise 5** over many variations of them. Then add some of these rhythms and you are done. What about a bit of tapping at the same time? Perhaps a 2:3 son clave? Sunday afternoon is starting to look busy too? It's easy to change into a minor feel, if you ignore the trickier fingering. Just take the thirds of the I and IV chords and flatten them, taking them from major thirds to minor thirds, as in **exercise 6**. Try transposing the major riff from Exercise 5 to other keys, then transpose it into the minor as has been done here for you. If you also slow the tempo down to something around 70-100 bpm, it becomes a 'guajira' tempo. Pronounced 'gwa-hear-ah', this is a traditional music of the peasants of Cuba, usually accompanied by tres cubano.

EXERCISE 1

Son Clave

CD2 TRACK **46**

Rumba Clave

CD2 TRACK **47**

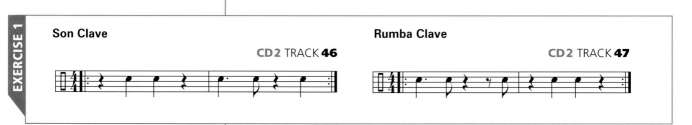

EXERCISE 2

CD 2 TRACK **48**

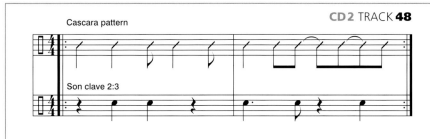

EXERCISE 3

CD 2 TRACK **49**

EXERCISE 4

CD 2 TRACK **50**

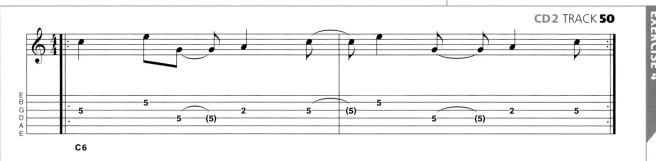

EXERCISE 5

CD 2 TRACK **51**

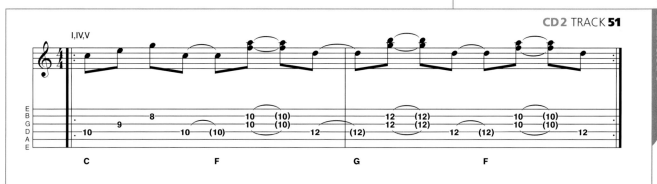

EXERCISE 6

CD 2 TRACK **52**

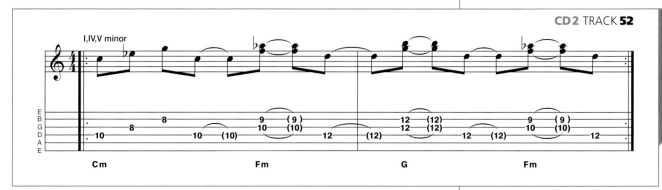

Exercise 7 is another typical chord progression, similar to those found on the *Buena Vista Social Club* CD (check it out for some pure Afro-Cuban grooves). It outlines the I-V-V-I in the key of A minor in 2:3 clave. Transpose it to different keys.

Exercise 8 is a montuno line. This is one of the most common patterns found in salsa and Latin jazz. You may find you'll get a better feel if you follow the pulse in 'cut time'. It outlines a Dm7 type of vamp but you can use it also over a Dm7-G9 progression.

Exercise 9 is a typical son montuno line in 2:3 clave. Notice that the downbeat of the montuno falls on the 'two side' of the clave (the bar with two notes in it), and the syncopated bar of the montuno falls on the 'three side' of the clave. How you use the clave direction depends on whether the melody of the tune is in either direction (2:3 or 3:2). For the moment just try to get this line together. Concentrate on tempo and the ability to hold it for a long time. Record the clave and then play the line over it.

Exercise 10 is a pattern in the 3:2 clave. This is a very basic pattern to describe the concept of playing with the clave, but remember that there are many variations to this pattern. It is just a starting point. It maintains the same chord progression as the previous example in 2:3 and begins with an eighth-note rest.

The basic rhythm for the cha-cha-cha is found in **exercise 11**. We all know this pattern from the organ riff in Santana's version of 'Oye Como Va'. Try to play this line while tapping the 2:3 son clave with your foot. Concentrate on the note lengths and don't rush!

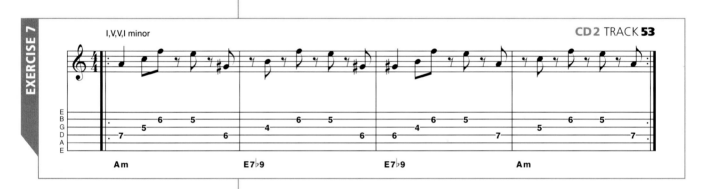

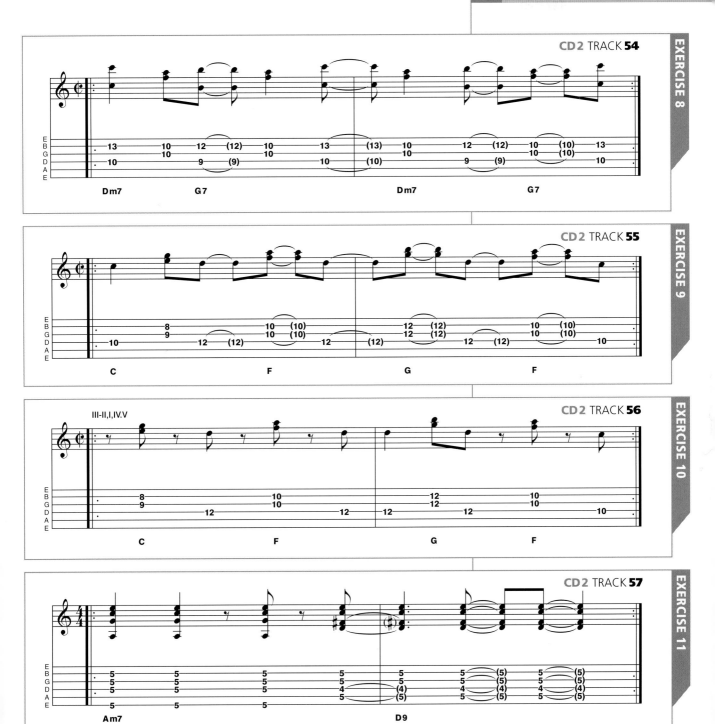

Exercise 12 is going to add some variation to the cha-cha-cha. It would originally have been played on a piano; here it has been adapted for guitar. It is important to have some co-ordination between thumb and fingers here, so don't worry if it takes a bit of time to get going. Remember, this is only a variation, so don't overdo it unless you want a really busy feel. Hold it tight.

Playing during a percussion solo, like congas or timbale, requires lots of concentration and a good sense of rhythm. Close your eyes if necessary to improve your concentration and be relaxed at the same time. **Exercise 13** is a common montuno line, often used over a percussion solo. This is just another exercise to reinforce your rhythm. This time it outlines a C7 mambo in 2:3 clave (remember?). Transpose it. You would use the same pattern over, for example, D7 to C7, for two bars each. Try taking it through the A blues progression.

CD**2** TRACK **58**

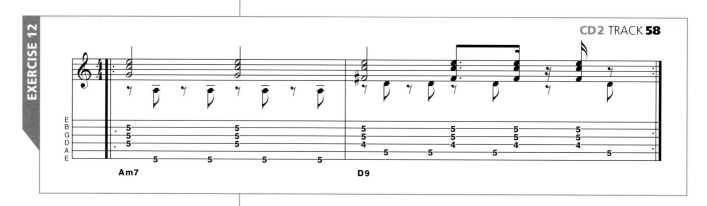

Exercise 14 is the sort of thing you might find in a Mongo Santamaria tune. It's just two triads with a nicely syncopated rhythm. If you're playing this over a conga solo, be prepared to play this groove, and only this groove, for five to ten minutes – and maybe even longer. You think it sounds easy, but you'll need to really focus on your playing, because the soloist will be playing patterns and fills that will throw you off in no time.

Exercise 15 and **16** are examples of lines used in mambo and cha-cha-cha. Take note of the use of octaves, with fingers one and four of your left hand, and double stops. Start playing them slowly (90 bpm, cut time) and work up to 120 bpm. The first example can be played over Am7-D7 or over just a D7. Hips starting to move?

CD2 TRACK **59**

EXERCISE 13

CD2 TRACK **60**

EXERCISE 14

CD2 TRACK **61**

EXERCISE 15

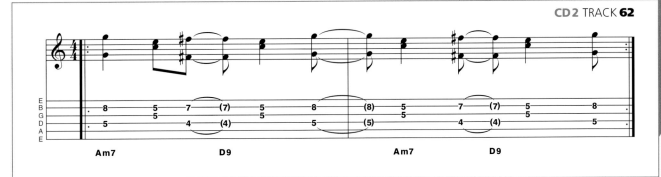

CD2 TRACK **62**

EXERCISE 16

AFRICAN
by Kari Bannerman

Like the other styles in our World Music chapter, African music has its roots far from the guitar as we know it. For this reason, it's important to be aware that much of this style of playing has been adapted for the guitar down the years, and would originally have been played on a more traditional stringed instrument, such as a 'kora'.

The kora is a traditional Senegambian instrument which resembles a balalaika in shape, using a large gourd as a body. It does, however, have considerably more strings, which are played in a harp-like fashion, without fretting them at all. Some of the exercises to following will contain suggestions for approximating this sound and feel on the guitar.

SIKYI RHYTHMS

The heartbeat of Sikyi and most African music is to be found in the drum section. For practical reasons, we will use a drum machine to recreate that feel.

Exercise 1 is a simple, three-part rhythm you can set up to accompany yourself with. Otherwise, if you don't have a drum machine, you could play the bell rhythm with a coin on an empty bottle, as is done in west Africa. Once you have programmed it in (a 'cabasa' is a shaker, incidentally) try to feel the rhythm so that you hear the pattern of the bell, and not the four-beat pulse of the time signature. It's a pattern that is similar to the 'chop' rhythm of reggae but without the first beat of the eighth-note.

Rhythmical independence is crucial to all African music. Some forms have no time signature at all, being made up of a polyrhythmic structure whereby, for example, signatures of 2/4, 4/4 and 6/8 will coexist in a staggered bar system. This makes them completely unintelligible to the uninitiated. You have to develop a feel for this music to play it right.

Traditional Tunes

The most direct translation that I can manage of the folk tune 'Mumunde' (pronounced 'Mom-moo-dey') that we're going to look at now is 'Happy Magical Dwarf'. **Exercise 2** gives us the melody, the chorus repeating three times from bar four onwards. Play it with a happy feeling and record it, along with the drum pattern you have programmed, four or five times. We'll use this as the backing to practise our other exercises to. Listen to it over and over again until you really feel it.

Exercise 3 is a simple rhythmic strum. Even though it is based on two chords, the note and inversion choice is important to retain the flavor of Sikyi. Play the A minor with a crisp and tight plectrum action, and the G7 a little looser. If you're using a 4-track, record this onto your tape as well.

You may find that when you play **exercise 4**, you will start to feel the African vibe coming through; what Osibisa used to call 'criss-cross rhythms that explode with happiness.' Practise it with your ever-expanding backing track. Whether you are playing this with a plectrum or fingerstyle, practise it until there's a flow, or dance, to your right-hand action. Left-hand fingerings are suggestions only (*p*: thumb, *i*: index, *m*: middle), so check them out and then make up your mind.

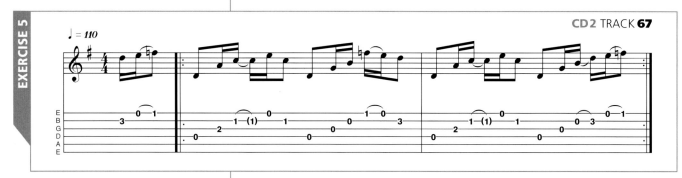

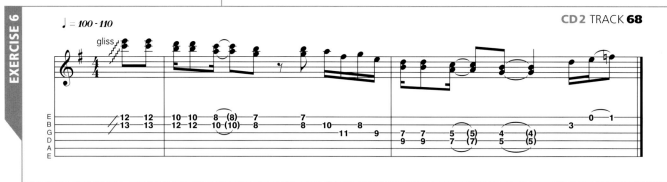

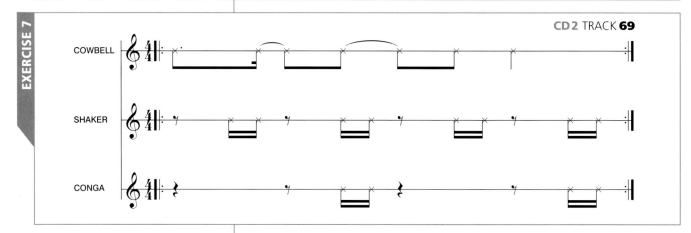

Play the groove in **exercise 5** smoothly and in time to the backing tape and you will be merrily adopted by every Ghanian family in town, for you are now playing Sikyi music. If you add a 'head' with a slur starting on the fourth beat of the intro, and a pulled-off tail on the next fourth beat, you will be playing the style as an Ashanti would really play it. We are using the Mixolydian mode here, as the F is natural, and this can be used as a tool for soloing.

Try playing Exercise 5 an octave higher than written to get an ethnic Kora feel. Use your index finger as a capo at the 12th fret – or even try it in open position on a Nashville-tuned guitar (a standard six-string guitar strung with the high-octave strings from a 12-string, or similar gauges).

Exercise 6 is a typical Palm Wine guitar solo intro, which you could join up to Exercise 5 (as the start of Exercise 5 and end of Exercise 6 imply). The phrase is in thirds from 12th position and moves down to third position. This downward movement is characteristic of most African melodies (see exercise 1). Note also how breaking away from the thirds on the fourth beat adds more character to the line you're playing. The line also echoes the cyclical, non-resolving nature of Sikyi, which is typical of the vast majority of African music forms. Clever use of your whammy bar to slide into the notes will give you a Sunny Ade 'Juju' feel. Again, a happy feel is vital before you can join it up with Exercise 5.

HIGHLIFE RHYTHMS

Our basic rhythm for this style is found in **exercise 7**. It cannot be overemphasized just how crucial rhythm is to this kind of music, so make sure you get it under your skin: dance to it. Make sure the tempo is comfortable; anything from 100bpm to 120bpm will be fine.

Exercise 8 is the melody from the song 'Yaa Amponsah', which is a story about a young, newly married bride. As before, record the melody and rhythm track to play along to.

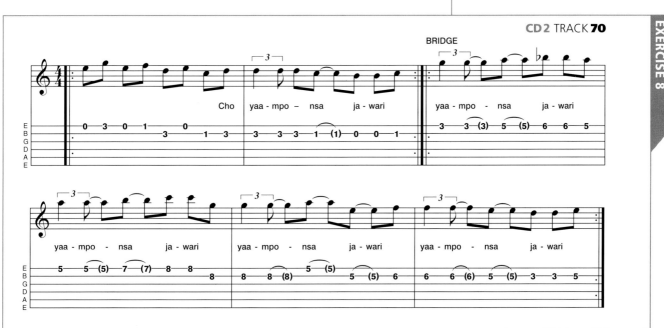

Exercise 9 is a typical Amponsah guitar groove. Practise it with your rhythm section, slowly at first, gradually building up the tempo until you can reach 120bpm comfortably. Essentially, it is a fingerstyle or two-fingers-and-plectrum groove, because some of the voicings are unplayable with a plectrum alone. In Africa, because of the dominant influence of the kora and the 'nyatiti' (another lute-style instrument), the right-hand two-finger picking style is predominant, but use whatever is comfortable.

The chord symbols are just a guide; to get the flavour use my exact inversions. Numerous variations of this progression have spawned songs all over west Africa and beyond – just ask Brian Eno or Mick Fleetwood. It is related to calypso and plays a crucial part in the ongoing cross-fertilisation of grooves between Africa, Europe and the Caribbean.

Highlife Jazz

Exercise 10 is a rhythm lick using the 7sus (a dominant seventh chord with a fourth but no third) and dominant seventh chords. Here we are moving into the area of highlife big bands and highlife jazz. Try the more complex chords written underneath as a jazzier variation. This is more big band highlife, as it uses these crossover chords. The essence of Amponsah is retained in the melody lines, rhythm and bassline. Use a semi-muted, snappy plectrum style to make the rhythms come alive. When you have mastered it, practise it alternately with Exercise 3.

Exercise 11 is a typical Amponsah phrase used by local guitarists – the sound of the diminished chord is very reminiscent of the tonality of several indigenous harmonies and that's why it's used. This exercise is really quite simple. Start with the diminished triad and just move the shape down the fretboard, retaining the fingering until you hit the F6 chord and C. The following phrases are played in sixths, much like those played by Steve Cropper at the beginning of 'Soul Man' by Sam and Dave.

Finally, **exercise 12** gives you an impression of an Amponsah bassline. Note the syncopation and polyrhythms against the guitar. Practise until you really feel it, when you don't need to think of notes, bars or phrases. This is called 'adakamu' style, as it is traditionally adapted from the phrasing of the square box bass drum: adakamu means 'box'.

CD2 TRACK **71**

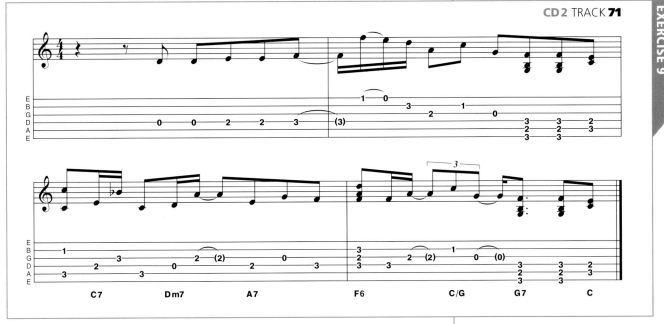

CD2 TRACK **72**

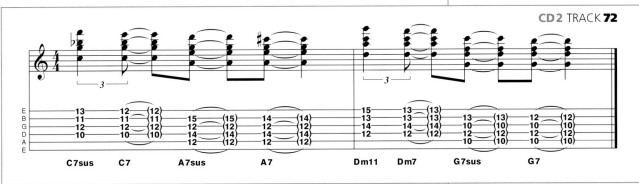

CD2 TRACK **73**

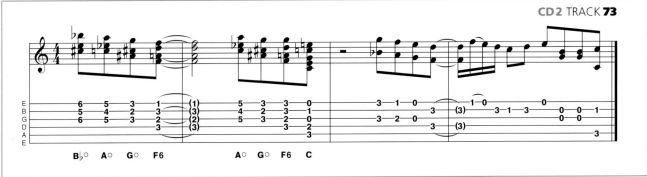

CD2 TRACK **74**

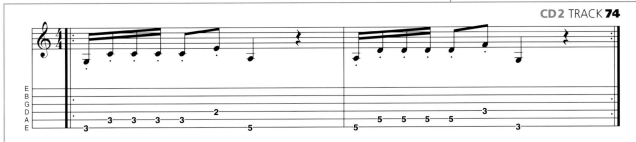

KLEZMER
by Michael Horowitz

In the Old World, klezmer was performed primarily on the violin. A 'cymbalom', an instrument similar to the hammered dulcimer, was used for accompaniment. Later the clarinet and brass instruments were added. The 'klezmorim' in New York adopted elements of jazz instrumentation, most notably a piano, bass, and drums rhythm section. The guitar is a very new addition to klezmer music which wasn't really used before the 1980s.

In most cases, the guitar will imitate what the cymbalom, and later the piano would traditionally play. However, the role of the guitar in klezmer music is being explored and expanded by numerous talented guitarists. Jeff Warschauer's CD *The Singing Waltz* features fingerstyle guitar arrangements of klezmer tunes. David Fiuczynski's electric guitar work with Hasidic New Wave combines elements of avant garde jazz, rock and even heavy metal.

RHYTHMS

Exercise 1 demonstrates the most basic klezmer accompaniment pattern, the two-beat oom-pah rhythm. Use alternating down and up strokes. To get the correct accents, mute on the down beat and let the chord sound on the off beat. Another rhythmic pattern that is often played along with the more basic oom-pah rhythm is displayed in **exercise 2**. This pattern produces a syncopated effect by placing an accent every three sixteenth-notes. The pattern 'resets' every measure. The accented beats are played with a downstroke and the chord is sounded. The unaccented beats are played with upstrokes and the chord is muted. Traditionally, the piano would play a straight oom-pah rhythm, while the drums played this syncopated rhythm. It works well, however, to play either of these rhythms on the guitar, individually or simultaneously.

THE FREYGISH AND MISHEBERAK SCALES

Exercise 3 demonstrates the D freygish, or altered Phrygian scale. It is the fifth mode of the G harmonic scale. So if you take any harmonic minor scale and start from the fifth scale degree, you'll have the pitches for the freygish scale. The augmented second interval (E♭ to F#) produces a very distinctive sound. Notice the unusual key signature, which has two flats and a sharp. This exotic-sounding scale is used in a great many klezmer melodies, the most famous of which is 'Hava Nagila'. The freygish scale is also found in Greek, Turkish, Arab, and Flamenco music.

The D Misheberak, or altered Dorian scale, is shown in **exercise 4**. It is the fourth mode of the A harmonic scale, so if you take any harmonic scale and start from the fourth scale degree, you'll have the pitches for the Misheberak scale. The sharp fourth scale degree (G#) and the natural sixth scale degree (B) produce a very distinctive sound. Notice the unusual key signature, which has only one sharp – but a G# instead of the customary F#. Misheberak is most common among Jewish musicians, but is also used in some forms of Romanian music.

EXERCISE 1

CD2 TRACK **75**

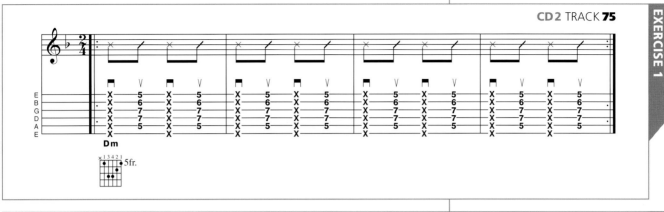

EXERCISE 2

CD2 TRACK **76**

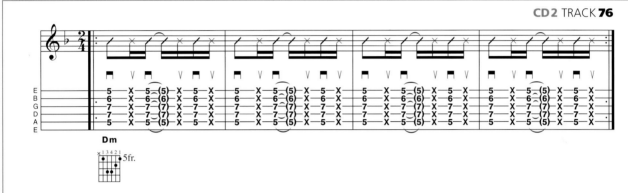

EXERCISE 3

CD2 TRACK **77**

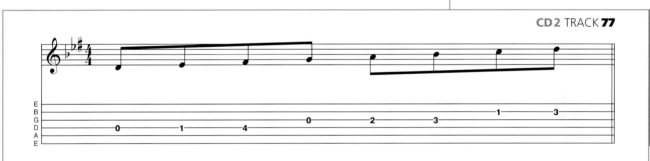

EXERCISE 4

CD2 TRACK **78**

ODESSA BULGAR

Now we're going to put it all together to play a complete tune. **Exercise 5** demonstrates the melody and accompaniment for the classic klezmer tune 'Odessa Bulgar'. A 'bulgar' is one of the most common types of klezmer tunes. It is in 2/4 time and is usually played at a quick tempo. The entire melody is derived from the Misheberak scale. 'Odessa Bulgar' has three sections, and the last section is played in 'stop time', which means you only hit a chord at the beginning of the measure and then lay out. Notice that on the recording the rhythm switches back and forth between the rhythms demonstrated in exercise 1 and exercise 2. Enjoy!

CD2 TRACK 79

CD2 TRACK 79

229

CHAPTER 11

Advanced Fingerstyle

Alternate tunings have been an essential part of the development of modern fingerstyle guitar. Their use is not a necessity in achieving an advanced level within the genre – players like Duck Baker or Tim Sparks rarely, if ever, use them – but it can't be denied that they have become a major aspect of expanding the instrument's tonal palette. Combine these tunings with the agile virtuosity and advanced technique of many players today, and the acoustic guitar becomes an instrument with possibilities that few could have imagined in the early days of the guitar's popularity.

Although a variety of guitar tunings must have played a role in the instrument's music prior to the evolutionary establishment of what we now call 'standard' tuning (EADGBE), the most easily documented history of using alternate tunings leads us back to the blues players of the early 20th Century. Folks such as Robert Johnson, Big Bill Broonzy and Tampa Red often tuned the guitar based on the sounds they liked, rather than on established rules of how it was 'supposed' to be done. In most cases, these players ended up with straight 'open' tunings, which actually sound like a chord when the open strings are strummed. Open G (DGDGBD), open D (DADF#AD), and open E (EBEGBE) were and still are probably the most frequently used tunings for various styles of blues, as well as other fingerpicking styles.

Hundreds of stunning recordings are a testament to the fact that there is nothing wrong with playing in these very logical tunings based on major chords. However, the fact that the guitar sounds great when its open strings are strummed or picked is perhaps also the biggest trap these tunings hide: all too often a tune played in, say, open G, will sound like, well, a tune played in open G. It's difficult to resist the temptation of letting the sound of the tuning dictate a composition, and the result is that many inexperienced players end up sounding alike. If you feel like you fall into this category, let me add that I'm as guilty as anyone. But to break out of the box, you ought to try a handful of less common or harmonically more complex tunings.

One of the easiest ways of adding to your repertoire of alternative tunings is to explore those that spell out minor chords. While it is true that these have the same inherent pitfalls as major tunings, they are used far less frequently, and you might be surprised by their possibilities. In this chapter, we'll take a look at D minor and G minor tunings. If you're familiar with their major counterparts, these should only require a short adjustment, as only one string is retuned.

The other family of tunings to look into are those that spell out neither a major nor a minor chord. Probably the most well known of these is Dsus4 tuning, which is generally referred to as DADGAD. This is probably the single most popular alternative tuning used by modern

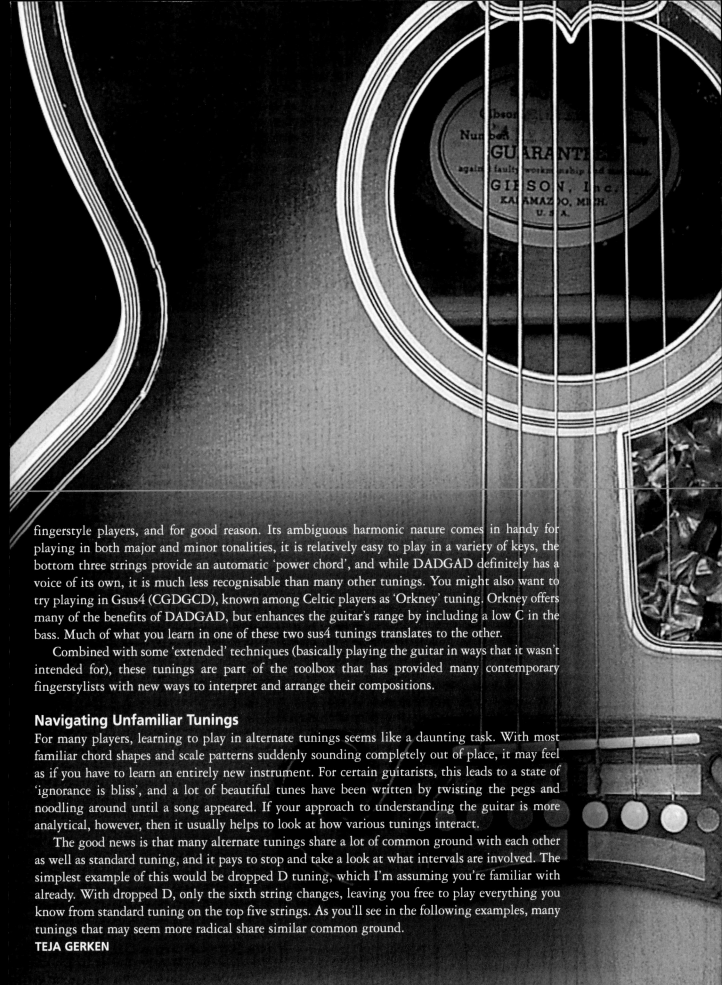

fingerstyle players, and for good reason. Its ambiguous harmonic nature comes in handy for playing in both major and minor tonalities, it is relatively easy to play in a variety of keys, the bottom three strings provide an automatic 'power chord', and while DADGAD definitely has a voice of its own, it is much less recognisable than many other tunings. You might also want to try playing in Gsus4 (CGDGCD), known among Celtic players as 'Orkney' tuning. Orkney offers many of the benefits of DADGAD, but enhances the guitar's range by including a low C in the bass. Much of what you learn in one of these two sus4 tunings translates to the other.

Combined with some 'extended' techniques (basically playing the guitar in ways that it wasn't intended for), these tunings are part of the toolbox that has provided many contemporary fingerstylists with new ways to interpret and arrange their compositions.

Navigating Unfamiliar Tunings

For many players, learning to play in alternate tunings seems like a daunting task. With most familiar chord shapes and scale patterns suddenly sounding completely out of place, it may feel as if you have to learn an entirely new instrument. For certain guitarists, this leads to a state of 'ignorance is bliss', and a lot of beautiful tunes have been written by twisting the pegs and noodling around until a song appeared. If your approach to understanding the guitar is more analytical, however, then it usually helps to look at how various tunings interact.

The good news is that many alternate tunings share a lot of common ground with each other as well as standard tuning, and it pays to stop and take a look at what intervals are involved. The simplest example of this would be dropped D tuning, which I'm assuming you're familiar with already. With dropped D, only the sixth string changes, leaving you free to play everything you know from standard tuning on the top five strings. As you'll see in the following examples, many tunings that may seem more radical share similar common ground.

TEJA GERKEN

DADGAD TUNING

Let's start with a look at DADGAD. Since you've only retuned the first, second, and sixth strings, everything you know from standard tuning can still be applied to strings three, four, and five. If you play the C major scale in **exercise 1**, you will recognise that it is played exactly the same as if the guitar was never retuned. You could move this scale pattern up and down the fingerboard to play in every key, and you'd never know that you were in an alternate tuning.

Similarly, let's have a look at the C-G-D5 (D5 is a D chord with no third) progression in **exercise 2**. Once again, the fact that you're in DADGAD doesn't change where the notes for these triads come on the strings in question, allowing you to play everything you already know. Of course, simply playing closed-position scales and chords is hardly the point of using an alternate tuning, so let's check out the next two exercises.

Exercise 3 shows the same exact C major scale as Exercise 1, but fingered with the use of open strings, which instantly lends a bigger sound as it allows you to keep strings ringing longer. **Exercise 4** adds open strings to the G and D chords of our previous example, giving the resulting sound a much bigger and more resonating quality than can be achieved using standard tuning.

This same concept can be applied to other tunings. A closer look at D minor tuning reveals that strings four and five are unchanged. More importantly, however, strings one, two, and three are all changed by the same interval – a whole tone down. This means that everything you know how to play on the top three strings in standard tuning can be applied, as long as you keep in mind that it will sound a whole-step lower. **Exercise 5** shows a C major scale that follows an identical fingering pattern to a major scale played on the top three strings in standard tuning. **Exercise 6** shows a D G D A chord progression, and you'll notice that the shapes are familiar friends from standard tuning. **Exercise 7** adds bass notes to the progression.

Exercise 8 is very similar to our previous DADGAD example (Exercise 2), but played in Orkney tuning, CGDGCD. Note that it uses the same exact fingering and intervals, only moved over one string. This illustrates how, even though the grouping of strings used for the exercise is tuned to different notes, it features the same intervals (fourths), resulting in the same relative chords, which are now F, C, and G. **Exercise 9** shows the progression with added open strings. Because we're still dealing with familiar intervals, it's also easy to play scales on strings two, three and four. **Exercise 10** shows another C major scale using the same fingering as previous examples. It's interesting to compare this scale with exercise 5, as it illustrates how the very same notes may fall into completely different positions on the fingerboard once the tuning is changed.

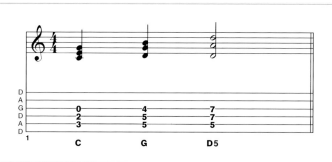

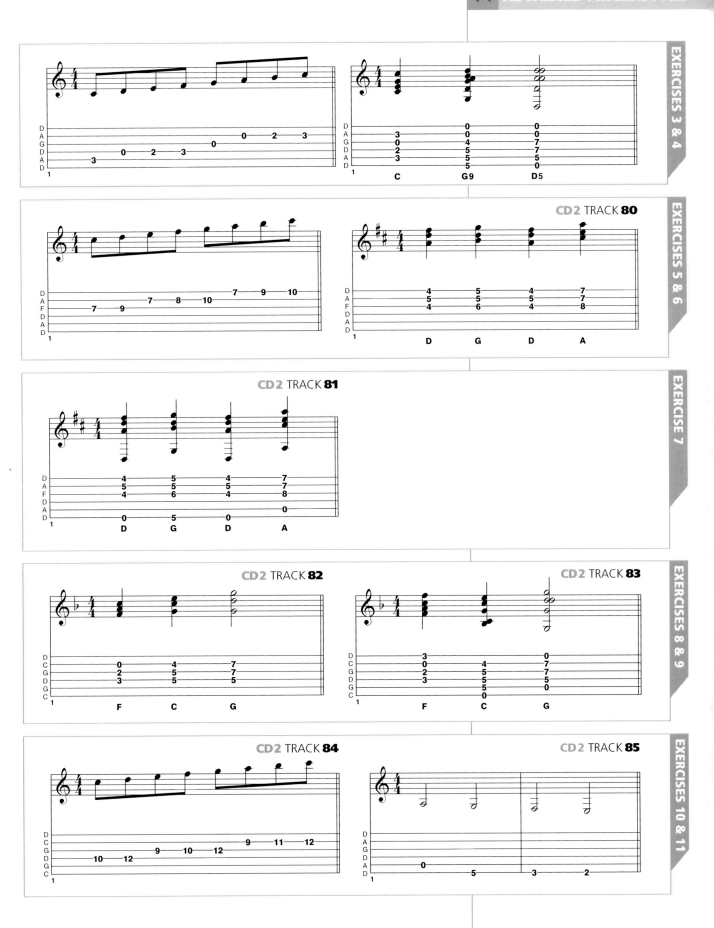

CD2 TRACK **80**

CD2 TRACK **81**

CD2 TRACK **82**

CD2 TRACK **83**

CD2 TRACK **84**

CD2 TRACK **85**

Obviously, there are limits to how much common ground you're going to find between various tunings. G minor tuning (DGDGB♭D) only has one pair of strings (third and fourth) that are identical to standard. The fifth and sixth strings, however, are both lowered by a whole tone, which allows you to use the same principle mentioned in relation to the first and second strings in DADGAD. You'll also notice that G minor and CGDGCD (Orkney) only differ by two strings, creating lots of familiarity from one to the other.

As you see, it's worth the effort of looking into similarities between tunings. By all means, keep the freshness of playing in an 'innocent' and unfamiliar tuning, but you might also want to analyse what's at hand and see how much of what you already know is applicable.

MOVING BASSLINES

One of the elements that separates many contemporary fingerstyle compositions or arrangements from earlier, more blues-based approaches is the use of a moving bass line. More traditional styles such as Travis picking are virtually defined by repetitive alternating bass notes. While this technique offers the opportunity for a driving rhythm, it can have a tendency to get static if applied to other styles of music. Influenced by classical music as well as jazz, folk-baroque guitarists such as John Renbourn began using more flowing bass lines, often adding rhythmic as well has harmonic variety. **Exercise 11** shows a simple descending bass line made up of half notes in DADGAD tuning.

Exercise 12 adds a melody and simple harmony, and, even though we haven't altered the basic two-bar bass line of Exercise 11, we now have a simple eight-bar tune, which is a section of my composition 'First Smile'. Notice how even though 'First Smile' is played in DADGAD, the tune is in the key of A minor, demonstrating how alternate tunings can be used in keys other than their obvious, open-string tonality.

MOVING AROUND THE FINGERBOARD

Regardless of tunings and styles, one of the challenges in keeping a composition interesting on the guitar is finding different ways of playing the same theme. One good way to accomplish this goal is to use different strings and positions on the fingerboard to play the same melody.

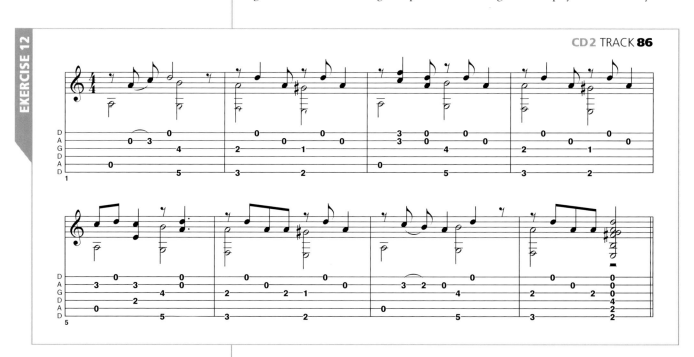

Let's have a look at the excerpts of my composition 'Her Red Hair' in **exercises 13** and **14**. Taking advantage of the open strings available in G minor tuning, I begin by playing the theme on the first string, while arpeggiating on the open second, third and fourth strings. In the variation (exercise 14), which differs from anything found in the full composition itself, I start the melody on the open third string, and choose a more syncopated rhythm instead of the arpeggios as an accompaniment. I also decided to vary the turnaround on bars seven and eight, which is now moved up the neck and involves open-string harmonics.

In the context of the entire composition (which follows on the four pages after the next), these examples could provide the basis for two variations of an 'A section', and while distinctively different, both undeniably feature the same structure and melody.

CD2 TRACK **87**

EXERCISE 13

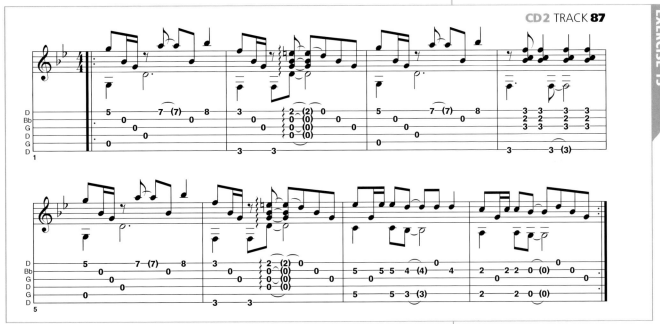

CD2 TRACK **88**

EXERCISE 14

NATURAL HARMONICS

Let's talk a little more about the harmonic notes introduced in the second variation of 'Her Red Hair'. If you're not familiar with playing harmonics, then start out by experimenting with their most accessible position on the guitar, right above the 12th fret. Just touch any string directly above the fret (rather than behind the fret, as you would if wanted to push down and fret the note), and pluck the string as you would normally. It may take a few tries, but what you will hear is a ringing, overtone-rich note that's an octave above the sound of the fretted note.

These harmonic notes are easily available at the fifth, seventh, 12th, 17th, and 19th frets, and with a little finesse you'll find that you can also coax them out of the instrument in other positions. Many contemporary fingerstyle players will often strum all six strings while fingering a harmonic position instead of playing an open string chord in an alternate tuning, adding complexity to their composition or arrangement. This technique works for single notes as well as open chords, and as these examples show, can often be integrated into more involved sections. The complete transcription of the composition **'Her Red Hair'** in G minor tuning follows.

237

CD 2 TRACK 89

HER RED HAIR

SLAPPED HARMONICS

What if you want the effect of harmonic notes, but your fretting hand is busy elsewhere on the neck? Even though there are limits to how it can be effectively used, you may try to use your picking hand to slap the strings directly above the harmonic position that you wish to access. If you've listened to Michael Hedges or Preston Reed, then you have heard slapped harmonics, as these players defined the technique. With a little bit of practice, slapped harmonics can add a great sense of rhythm and drama to a tune, making their use a favourite among contemporary fingerstylists.

As a technique that's not part of the 'Segovia-approved' set of rules, it helps greatly to have the advantage of seeing someone use harmonic slaps before attempting to apply them yourself. However, a little experimentation should allow you to achieve the desired results in any case. The general idea of slapped harmonics is to whack very quickly the desired strings at one of the harmonic positions of the fingerboard, using the fleshy part of the first digit of a finger. I tend to use either my index or middle finger, often alternating between the two. Once again, the fact that tunings such as DADGAD (which we return to now) offer a quick power chord on the bottom three strings turns out to be an advantage in slapping harmonics.

In **exercise 15**, I slap the open bottom three strings with my right-hand index finger exactly above the 12th fret. I then use my left hand to hammer on the chord at the second fret, followed by a 12th fret slap of the open second and third strings with my right-hand middle finger. Continuing to hold the chord, I now slap the bottom three strings again with my right-hand index finger, but this time I do so above the 14th fret, an octave above the fretted notes. You may want to listen to the recorded example to get an idea of what this should sound like if you're new to this technique.

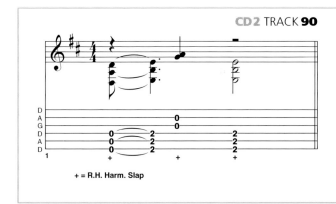

CD2 TRACK **90**

+ = R.H. Harm. Slap

Slapped harmonics are used further in my tune 'The Groomsmen' (which finds us back in DADGAD). **Exercise 16** starts out with a four-bar phrase of straightforward fingerpicking, then uses right-hand slaps to add drama to the following turnaround. Hammering on the chords on the three bottom strings at the eighth or seventh frets, I again use the technique of slapping with my right-hand index finger an octave above the fretted notes, that is, at the 20th and 19th fret. I use my right-hand middle finger to slap the open treble strings above the 12th fret, necessitating a swift movement between the two positions as I slap.

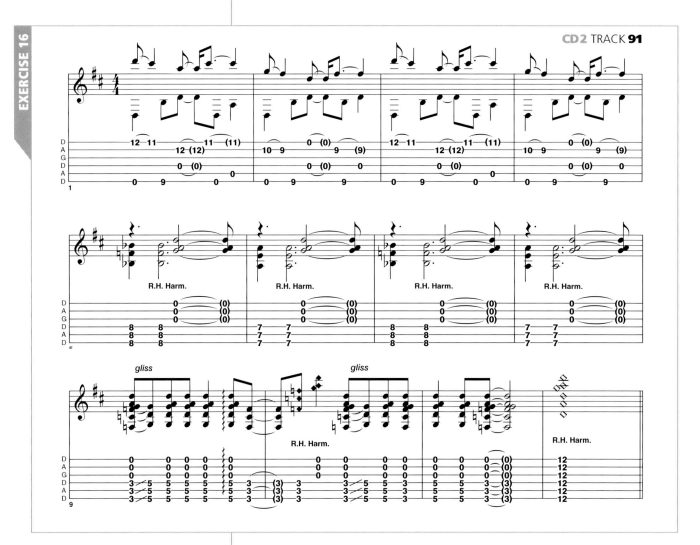

CD2 TRACK **91**

RIGHT-HAND FRETTING

When you first learned to play the guitar, you were probably told that one hand is for fretting and the other for strumming or picking. In modern fingerstyle playing, this may be only partially true, as it's not unusual occasionally to fret notes with what would ordinarily be your 'picking' hand.

Let's have a look at **exercise 17**, which consists of another short excerpt from my composition 'The Groomsmen'. In this case, I'm using my right index finger to form a barre chord over strings five and six. Similar to a standard hammer-on with the left hand, this has to happen with a little bit of force, in order to coax out the sound of the fretted notes.

While playing these basic root/fifth power chords by tapping with my right hand, I'm hammering on and releasing the third and fourth strings at the second fret with my left hand during the first two bars, then switching to hammer-ons and pull-offs for the short melodic phrase in the third bar. The entire section is played without any 'normal' picking or strumming. Due to the spread of notes, it would be difficult, if not impossible, to play using normal playing techniques.

A complete transcription of **'The Groomsmen'** follows on the next four pages.

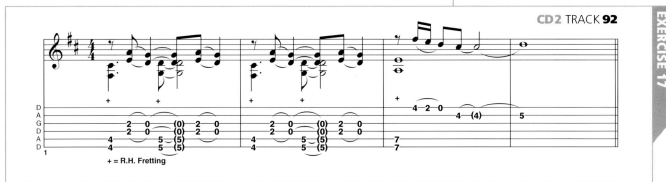

THE GROOMSMEN

245

THE GROOMSMEN

D MINOR TUNING

Now let's venture into D minor tuning (DADFAD), with some excerpts from my tune '7 Years'. It uses a similar right-hand fretting technique, so we can explore that idea further along the way. **Exercises 18** to **20** show three different approaches to playing the same section. **Exercise 18** combines right-hand fretting with harmonic slaps, while **exercise 19** shows the phrase played conventionally. **Exercise 20** features a descending bass line on the sixth string, for which I finger the notes at the seventh and third frets with the right-hand index finger. In this case, the same notes could easily be played with just the left hand, but the addition of right-hand tappings gives the passage a stronger rhythmic feel.

BEHIND-THE-NUT BENDS

You will notice that exercise 19 also introduces a new way to 'bend' a note. By pushing sideways on the second string behind the nut, between the posts of the first and second string tuning pegs, it's possible to achieve an effect that sounds similar to a string being bent on a pedal-steel guitar. This technique can be used in any tuning, but the lower string tension in tunings where the second string is dropped makes this application a lot easier.

Make sure you don't poke yourself on the loose string-ends (it's a good idea to bend them over into a loop and tuck them out of the way to avoid injury). It will take a little practice to avoid accidentally twisting the tuning pegs, and if your guitar's nut isn't cut properly for the gauge of strings you're using, then you might find that your guitar doesn't stay in tune after the bend. Once you mastered this technique, however, you'll find yourself with a simple new lick that is applicable in many musical situations.

CLASSICAL-STYLE TREMOLO

Although flashy techniques such as harmonic slaps or two-handed tapping often get all the attention, there are some other stylistic elements that can give your playing a unique edge. One of them is to adapt classical tremolo technique. This involves playing a melody or section of a melody on a single string, using a picking pattern of *a* (ring finger), *m* (middle finger), *i* (index finger), and back to *m*, which allows for a very smooth, repetitive motion.

You can play **exercise 21** in any tuning, since it's on a single string, but for the sake of moving on to the next examples, tune your guitar to Orkney tuning (CGDGCD). In this example, I also use hammer-ons and pull-offs, creating a repeatable phrase. If your fingers are used to each being 'assigned' to a different string, then it might take a little practice to get them to all strike the same string, and I recommend using a metronome to play the exercise until it is completely smooth.

CD2 TRACK **94**

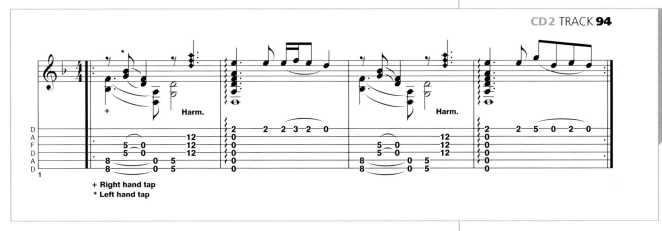

+ **Right hand tap**
* **Left hand tap**

CD2 TRACK **95**

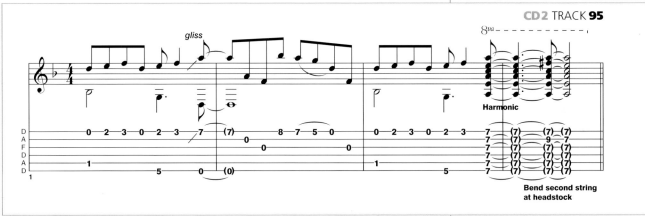

Bend second string
at headstock

CD2 TRACK **96**

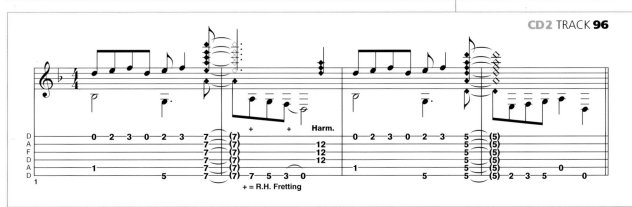

+ = R.H. Fretting

CD2 TRACK **97**

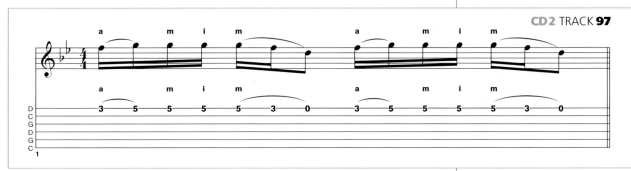

MIDDLE FINGER SNAP

The middle finger snap is a simple yet highly effective technique for providing texture and rhythmic accentuation. Similar to the 'frailing' used by banjo players, the middle finger snap is put to great use on the guitar by players such as Martin Simpson and Steve Baughman. In order to get the force necessary for successful execution of the middle finger snap, curl the finger up into the palm of your hand, and then release it as if you were trying to flick something off your hand. You'll be surprised how much volume you get if you use this flicking motion to hit one of the strings with the back of the middle finger's nail in this way.

Try playing **exercise 22** by alternating between using a regular thumb-stroke (*p*) to play the fourth string, and the middle finger snap to hit the third string. If you really want to be slick, you can try hitting the string at the harmonic spot available above where a 24th fret would be, or even between this location and the saddle. Finding the exact locations will take some experimenting, but getting the effect of hitting a harmonic note with the force of a middle finger snap is worth the effort.

Exercise 23 puts the tremolo and middle finger snap techniques into context. In addition, the big chord at the end of bar two demonstrates how having the bottom string tuned to a low C allows for a great, huge IV chord when using this tuning for playing in the key of G or G minor.

Play through this chapter as often as necessary and in your own time, and listen to as many of the guitarists mentioned as you can to hear how these techniques are used. With a little work, you will soon have a whole new arsenal of stylistic tools at your disposal.

CD2 TRACK **98**

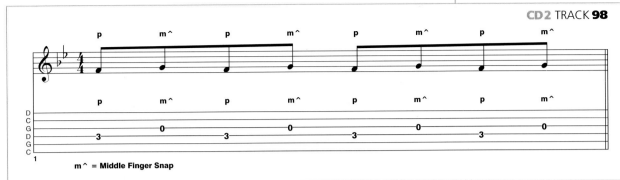

m^ = Middle Finger Snap

CD2 TRACK **99**

m^ = Middle Finger Snap

CD TRACK LISTS & NOTES

The exercises on the two CDs packaged with this book are all played and recorded by the authors themselves, except for the Latin and African sections of the 'World Music' chapter, which were performed and recorded by Rod Fogg. In all cases, the musical examples are the copyright of the authors of the respective chapters (except of course for the occasional non-copyrighted 'traditional' tunes used, where the authors have copyright in the arrangements). Click tracks, count-ins and rhythm tracks were not used except where noted. To make the best use of the space on the CD, we have chosen to supply music tracks mainly for the exercises that you really need to hear played to understand fully. Each listing begins with the track number, followed by the section and exercise number that the music relates to. Additional notes for some tracks come after that, in italic type.

CD 1

1 Getting Started, Ex4
2 Getting Started, Ex5
3 Getting Started, Ex7
4 Getting Started, Ex9
5 Getting Started, Ex10
6 Getting Started, Ex11
7 Getting Started, Ex12
8 Getting Started, Ex14
9 Getting Started, Ex15
10 Getting Started, Ex16

11 Rock & Pop, Ex2
12 Rock & Pop, Ex5
13 Rock & Pop, Ex11
14 Rock & Pop, Ex24
15 Rock & Pop, Ex25
16 Rock & Pop, Ex40
17 Rock & Pop, Ex49
18 Rock & Pop, Ex60
19 Rock & Pop, Ex61
20 Rock & Pop, Ex62

21 Blues, Ex1
22 Blues, Ex3
23 Blues, Ex4
24 Blues, Ex6
25 Blues, Ex8-11
A series of blues turnarounds played in succession.
26 Blues, Ex15
27 Blues, Ex16
28 Blues, Ex18
29 Blues, Ex20
30 Blues, Ex29

31 Bottleneck, Ex1
32 Bottleneck, Ex2
33 Bottleneck, Ex3
34 Bottleneck, Ex4
35 Bottleneck, Ex5
36 Bottleneck, Ex6
37 Bottleneck, Ex7
38 Bottleneck, Ex8
39 Bottleneck, Ex8 & backing
The riff from Ex8 played with rhythm guitar backing.
40 Bottleneck, Ex9
41 Bottleneck, Ex9 slower
Exercise 9 played slower.
42 Bottleneck, Ex10
43 Bottleneck, Ex11
44 Bottleneck, Ex12

45 Bottleneck, Ex13
46 Bottleneck, Ex14
47 Bottleneck, Ex15
48 Bottleneck, Ex16
49 Bottleneck, Ex16 slower
Exercise 16 played more slowly.
50 Bottleneck, Ex17

51 Country, Ex1 *Melody and rhythm guitar backing.*
52 Country, Ex1 rhythm gtr
A rhythm guitar accompaniment to the Ex1 melody, with four-beat lead-in.
53 Country, Ex2
Melody and rhythm guitar backing
54 Country, Ex2 rhythm gtr
A rhythm guitar accompaniment to the Ex2 melody, with four-beat lead-in.
55 Country, Ex3
Melody and rhythm guitar backing.
56 Country, Ex3 rhythm gtr
A rhythm guitar accompaniment to the Ex3 melody, with four-beat lead-in.
57 Country, Ex4
Melody and rhythm guitar backing.
58 Country, Ex4 rhythm gtr
A rhythm guitar accompaniment to the Ex1 melody, with four-beat lead-in.
59 Country, Ex5
60 Country, Ex6
61 Country, Ex6 slower
Exercise 6 played slower.
62 Country, Ex7
63 Country, Ex9
64 Country, Ex10
65 Country, Ex11
66 Country, Ex12
67 Country, Ex12
A rhythm guitar accompaniment to the Ex1 melody, with four-beat lead-in.

68 Country, Ex13
The author's tune 'Chetude', played 'rubato' with improvisation around bars 11-14.

69 Bluegrass, Ex1
70 Bluegrass, Ex2
71 Bluegrass, Ex3
72 Bluegrass, Ex4
73 Bluegrass, Ex5
74 Bluegrass, Ex6
75 Bluegrass, Ex7
76 Bluegrass, Ex8
77 Bluegrass, Ex9
78 Bluegrass, Ex10
79 Bluegrass, Ex11
80 Bluegrass, Ex12
81 Bluegrass, Ex13
82 Bluegrass, Ex14
83 Bluegrass, Ex15
84 Bluegrass, Ex16
85 Bluegrass, Ex17
86 Bluegrass, Ex18
87 Bluegrass, Ex19
88 Bluegrass, Ex20
89 Bluegrass, Ex21
90 Bluegrass, Ex22
91 Bluegrass, Ex23
92 Bluegrass, Ex24
93 Bluegrass, Ex25

CD 2

1 Jazz, Jazz Blues pattern
2 Jazz, Minor Blues pattern
3 Jazz, Rhythm Changes
4 Jazz, Ex4
5 Jazz, Ex5
6 Jazz, Ex6
7 Jazz, Ex7
8 Jazz, Ex8
9 Jazz, Ex19
10 Jazz, Ex20
11 Jazz, Ex21
12 Jazz, Ex22
13 Jazz, Ex23
14 Jazz, Ex24
15 Jazz, Ex25
16 Jazz, Ex26

17 Gypsy Jazz, Ex1
18 Gypsy Jazz, Ex2
19 Gypsy Jazz, Ex3
20 Gypsy Jazz, Ex5
21 Gypsy Jazz, Ex6
22 Gypsy Jazz, Ex8
23 Gypsy Jazz, Ex10
24 Gypsy Jazz, Ex11
25 Gypsy Jazz, Ex13
26 Gypsy Jazz, Ex15
27 Gypsy Jazz, Ex16
28 Gypsy Jazz, Ex17
29 Gypsy Jazz, Ex18
30 Gypsy Jazz, Ex19
31 Gypsy Jazz, Ex20
32 Gypsy Jazz, Ex21
33 Gypsy Jazz, Ex22
34 Gypsy Jazz, Ex23

35 Celtic, Ex1
36 Celtic, Ex2
37 Celtic, Ex3
38 Celtic, Ex4
39 Celtic, Ex5
40 Celtic, Ex6
41 Celtic, Ex7
42 Celtic, Ex8
43 Celtic, Ex9
44 Celtic, Ex10
Pennywhistle melody with guitar accompaniment.
45 Celtic, Ex11
Arrangement for solo guitar.

46 Latin, Ex1a
Son clave rhythm.
47 Latin, Ex1b
Rumba clave rhythm.
48 Latin, Ex2
2:3 son clave rhythm with 'cáscara' timbale pattern.
49 Latin, Ex3
Scale played to appropriate backing rhythm. (Note that, because of the importance of the specific rhythm in the Latin genre, all following Latin exercises are played against the appropriate backing rhythm.)
50 Latin, Ex4
51 Latin, Ex5
52 Latin, Ex6

53 Latin, Ex7
54 Latin, Ex8
55 Latin, Ex9
56 Latin, Ex10
57 Latin, Ex11
58 Latin, Ex12
59 Latin, Ex13
60 Latin, Ex14
61 Latin, Ex15
62 Latin, Ex16

63 African, Ex1
Sikyi rhythm on bell, cabasa and conga.
64 African, Ex2
Played to sikyi rhythm. (Note that, because of the importance of the specific rhythm in the African genre, all following African exercises are played against the appropriate backing rhythm.)
65 African, Ex3
66 African, Ex4
67 African, Ex5
68 African, Ex6
69 African, Ex7
Highlife rhythm played on bell, cabasa and conga.
70 African, Ex8
Played to highlife rhythm (as are all following...).
71 African, Ex9
72 African, Ex10
73 African, Ex11
74 African, Ex12

75 Klezmer, Ex1
76 Klezmer, Ex2
77 Klezmer, Ex3
78 Klezmer, Ex4
79 Klezmer, Ex5

80 Adv Fingerstyle, Ex6
81 Adv Fingerstyle, Ex7
82 Adv Fingerstyle, Ex8
83 Adv Fingerstyle, Ex9
84 Adv Fingerstyle, Ex10
85 Adv Fingerstyle, Ex11
86 Adv Fingerstyle, Ex12
87 Adv Fingerstyle, Ex13
88 Adv Fingerstyle, Ex14
89 Adv Fingerstyle
Complete tune: 'Her Red Hair.'
90 Adv Fingerstyle, Ex15
91 Adv Fingerstyle, Ex16
92 Adv Fingerstyle, Ex17
93 Adv Fingerstyle
Complete tune: 'The Groomsmen.'
94 Adv Fingerstyle, Ex18
95 Adv Fingerstyle, Ex19
96 Adv Fingerstyle, Ex20
97 Adv Fingerstyle, Ex21
98 Adv Fingerstyle, Ex22
99 Adv Fingerstyle, Ex23